W9-BSJ-654

great cooking
every day

250 Delicious Recipes
PLUS TECHNIQUES AND TIPS FROM
The Culinary Institute of America

WILEY

Wiley Publishing, Inc.

A Word About Weight Watchers

Since 1963, Weight Watchers has grown from a handful of people to millions of enrollments annually. Today, Weight Watchers is recognized as the leading name in safe and sensible weight control. Weight Watchers members form diverse groups, from youths to senior citizens, attending meetings virtually around the globe. Weight loss and weight management results vary by individual, but we recommend that you attend Weight Watchers meetings, follow the Weight Watchers food plan, and participate in regular physical activity. For the Weight Watchers meeting nearest you, call 800-651-6000. Also, visit us at our Web site: **www.weightwatchers.com**

For general information on our other products and services or to obtain technical support please contact our Customer Care Department within the U.S. at 800-762-2974, outside the U.S. at 317-572-3993 or fax 317-572-4002.

Weight Watchers Publishing Group

Creative and Editorial Director: **NANCY GAGLIARDI**

Editorial Assistant: **JENNY LABOY-BRACE**

Photography: **RITA MAAS**

Food Styling: **MARIANN SAUVION**

Prop Styling: **CATHY COOK**

Wiley Publishing, Inc.

Senior Editor: **LINDA INGROIA**

Senior Production Editor: **MARK STEVEN LONG**

Cover Designer: **EDWIN KUO**

Interior Designers: **EDWIN KUO and HOLLY WITTENBERG**

Manufacturing Buyer: **BOB CHERRY**

The Culinary Institute of America

Editor/Writer: **JENNIFER ARMENTROUT**

Photo Editor: **JESSICA BARD**

Director, Food and Beverage Institute: **MARY COWELL**

Certified Master Chef, Dean of Culinary, Baking, and Pastry Studies: **VICTOR GIELISSE**

Photo Studio Manager: **ELIZABETH CORBETT JOHNSON**

Photographer (how-to): **LORNA SMITH**

Library of Congress Cataloging-in-Publication Data
Weight Watchers great cooking every day : 250 delicious recipes plus techniques and tips from the Culinary Institute of America.
     p. cm.
    Includes index.
    ISBN: 0-7645-4479-9 (paperback)
    1. Reducing diets—Recipes.   I. Weight Watchers International.   II. Culinary Institute of America.
    RM222.2 . W3137   2000
    613.2'5—dc21   00-059671

Manufactured in the United States of America

10 9 8 7 6 5 4 3 2 1

table of contents

acknowledgments

Weight Watchers and The Culinary Institute of America would like to acknowledge the following individuals for their assistance in preparing this book: Rebecca Adams, Joyce Hendley, M.S., Carol Praeger, Deri Reed, and Christopher Thumann for recipe editing; Barbara Dunn, Kendra Glanbocky, Carol Hanscom, Deborah Hartman, Dena Peterson, and Gina Tori for their help with photography; and Diane Buscaglia, Sophie Cowell, Mary Donovan, Gypsy Gifford, Kendra Glanbocky, Wendy Karn, Fran Kearney, Laura Pensiero, R.D., Thomas Schroeder, and Belinda Treu for testing recipes.

introduction

When we at Weight Watchers set out to write a cookbook on expert cooking, we knew that creating great-tasting recipes that use high-quality ingredients wasn't the whole story. Proper preparation of those ingredients and correct cooking techniques, as well as smart and simple cooking hints and tips, also had to be included.

To include these important elements in the book, we decided to go straight to the foremost culinary school in the United States: The Culinary Institute of America (CIA). The faculty's commitment to educating the public on proper technique and creating recipes that stress fresh, natural ingredients was impressive and worth sharing.

Nutrition has always been an integral part of the curriculum at the CIA. (In fact, when the Institute first opened its doors in 1946, one of its first full-time faculty members was a dietitian.) In 1985, the CIA's commitment to teaching good nutrition was fully realized with the opening of the General Foods Nutrition Center at the Institute's Hyde Park, N.Y., campus. The Nutrition Center houses lecture rooms and a state-of-the-art computer laboratory where students develop skills in computer-aided nutrition analysis and the principles of healthy menu and recipe development. The centerpiece of the complex is St. Andrew's Café, a student-run restaurant open to the public where the principles of good nutrition and good cooking merge. It is in the St. Andrew's kitchen that students are given hands-on instruction in healthy cooking techniques.

Since we at Weight Watchers are committed to the creation of high-quality, easy, and delicious recipes, we feel that our recipe expertise coupled with the CIA's technique know-how results in the ultimate how-to guide for beginner and seasoned cooks alike. In fact, techniques, more than specific recipes, are at the heart of the CIA's educational mission. They feel that understanding the basic techniques that lie at the heart of good cooking allows a cook to use recipes as a starting—not ending—point when creating healthy, delicious dishes. Weight Watchers and the CIA adapted the school's tried-and-true techniques for you, the home cook.

In the first chapter of this book, we have outlined the principles that guide and shape healthy cooking techniques. Consider the step-by-step photo sequences used in this book as mini-lessons in culinary technique; each sequence clearly illustrates a valuable preparation or cooking method. And, so you can reap the benefit of their many years of experience, the CIA chefs have also added ingredient and technique tips and notes to many of the recipes. *Great Cooking Every Day* is an exciting, yet practical, cookbook that you can use again and again for years to come. We consider it the definitive cookbook for all cooks interested in cooking delicious, healthy dishes with expertise.

Nancy Gagliardi
Creative and Editorial Director

chapter 1

healthy eating in the twenty-first century

There is this great mystery surrounding what a chef learns in cooking school. There are countless lessons to be learned, particularly when it comes to techniques. Yet when it comes to creating delicious, healthy recipes, the lessons really aren't that mysterious at all.

The Culinary Institute of America has developed a set of principles for healthy cooking with the goal of creating nutritious food with great flavor. These principles will guide you to think in new ways about the foods you choose and the cooking techniques you use. They are not strict rules; rather, they should be regarded as ways to explore the possibilities of flavor and nutritious cooking.

choosing ingredients Select ingredients with care. Choose fresh, seasonal produce whenever you can and plan meals that include a variety of these foods. If you have a chance to buy directly from a farmer or at a farmer's market, take the opportunity; the flavor difference is usually impressive. Freshness is always the key factor. If an ingredient you need is out of season, frozen, dried, and canned products may be perfectly acceptable as long as you read the labels and choose brands of good quality.

Opt for whole grains with meals. Highly refined grain products lose much of their nutritional value during milling. Some lost vitamins and minerals may be added back during processing, but the fiber that "whole foods" provide is not.

storing ingredients Handle foods carefully to preserve the best possible flavor, texture, color, and nutritional value. Wrap dry goods tightly and store them in a cool, dry place away from direct sunlight. Refrigerate perishable foods as soon as possible after purchase. Set your refrigerator below 38°F to prevent bacterial growth and keep foods fresh. A refrigerator thermometer is an inexpensive and widely available tool that will help ensure that the proper temperature is being maintained. Prevent cross-contamination by storing raw meats, poultry, and seafood on the bottom refrigerator shelf so juices (which can contain harmful bacteria) don't drip onto other foods.

Do not peel, trim, or wash most produce until just before cooking—this maximizes nutrient retention. However, you should trim root vegetables with leafy tops—such as beets, turnips, carrots, and radishes—before refrigerating them. Otherwise, the leaves continue to absorb nutrients and moisture from the root.

expanding food choices: grains, fruits, and vegetables Include a great variety of plant-based foods in your daily diet. In addition, grains, breads, and pastas form the foundation of a healthy diet. They offer high levels of complex carbohydrates (the body's preferred energy source), vitamins, minerals, and dietary fiber. Grains can be eaten at every meal. For breakfast, they are a natural, appearing in cereals and muffins (see ours) among other things. At other meals, grains can be added to everything: breads (yes, try making your own with our easy-to-follow recipes), salads, stuffings, and desserts. Grains, such as rice and amaranth, can even be used for thickening soups and sauces.

Cuisines worldwide combine legumes with grains to round out the nutritional balance. Legumes are generally higher in protein than grains and are also a good source of soluble fiber. Pureed or stewed legumes can be served as rich sauces. Salads and stews based on legumes can also make a terrific backdrop for smaller portions of other more highly flavored foods.

Vegetables and fruits are nutrition powerhouses, providing impressive quantities of carbohydrates, fiber, water, vitamins, and minerals. With relatively few exceptions, they offer this nutritional banquet without adding much, if any, dietary fat and no cholesterol. And the array of flavors, bright colors, and textures is tantalizing.

choosing cooking techniques: braising, grilling, and roasting

Select cooking techniques that bring out the best in ingredients. With the exception of frying, most cooking techniques are suited to a menu built around healthy eating goals. Roasting, sautéing, grilling, broiling, and steaming will retain more water-soluble nutrients than simmering or boiling foods. Stewing and braising are also nutrient-preserving methods because the cooking liquid, which is normally served as a sauce, captures those vitamins and minerals that are not destroyed by heat.

Whenever foods are cut or cooked, they may be exposed to light, air, high heat, liquids, alkalis (baking soda), or acids (lemon juice, vinegar)—all of which can impact their nutrition content. Preparing foods as close to cooking time as possible is one of the best ways to minimize nutrient loss. Cook foods only until just done; foods will remain juicy and moist. Overcooked foods, on the other hand, become dry and unappealing, or soggy and insipid.

considering fat   Manage the amount of fat used both as an ingredient and as part of a cooking technique. Reducing fat provides one of the most intriguing challenges in healthy cooking because, while many people want to eat less fat, no one wants to sacrifice flavor to do so. The good news is that there are a number of techniques you can employ to cut back on fat very successfully.

Start with ingredients that are naturally low in fat, such as vegetables, fruits, grains, legumes, and fish. Meats and poultry should be chosen

fruits and vegetables, the sneaky way

A simple way to add more vegetables and fruits to your diet is to use them in sauces, purees, salsas, chutneys, compotes, and relishes. Dried fruits are wonderful in salads, sauces, stuffings, desserts, and as a topping for hot and cold breakfast cereals. Use vegetable and fruit juices in dressings, hot sauces, soups, and as a cooking liquid—some of the best chefs do. Simmering or boiling vegetable and fruit juices before using them will allow some of their water content to evaporate and further intensify their flavors. This technique, known as "reduction," is widely used by chefs to concentrate flavor in soups, sauces, and other liquids.

the right tools

Special equipment for low-fat cooking is not necessarily essential, but it can make the process simpler. When you cook with small amounts of fat, nonstick pans or well-seasoned cast-iron cookware prevents food from sticking while still browning it nicely. For low-fat baking, use silicone baking mats or parchment paper to line baking sheets, eliminating the need for additional oil.

Try a defatting pitcher when the volume of liquid to be defatted is small and time does not allow for chilling and removing fat. These pitchers have a spout opening from the bottom, which allows the liquid to be poured out once the fat has risen to the top. For defatting large amounts of liquid, try special defatting ladles. They are constructed with a raised rim above small slots, which allow the fat to flow through and collect in the bowl of the ladle.

based on the leanness of particular cuts and should be trimmed of as much surface fat as possible before cooking. In general, the breasts of poultry and the tenderloin, loin, and top round cuts from meats are the leanest choices.

Consider the grade of the meat you are buying. The USDA standards for grading meat rely upon factors such as marbling—the streaks of fat found within the "lean" meat. In the case of beef, Choice may be a better selection health-wise than Prime—the quality is still excellent, but there is generally less marbling throughout all the cuts.

Try game meat instead of "traditional" meats next time you shop. These meats have bold, interesting flavors and, in many cases, are substantially lower in fat and cholesterol than their domestic counterparts. Game breeds, such as ostrich, emu, venison, and bison, are farm-raised and sold in quality food stores these days for those of us who aren't lucky enough to know a hunter.

Fish and shellfish are good choices for a healthy diet because they are naturally low in calories and saturated fats. However, certain types of shellfish, such as squid, are known to be quite high in cholesterol. Others, such as shrimp, scallops, and lobster, are more moderate and very low in total fat.

Flavorful fat-dense foods, such as butter and cheese, still have a place in the healthy kitchen, but they should always be used in small amounts and with a definite purpose in mind. Bacon, for instance, provides a unique flavor. Cooking the bacon first and pouring off most of the fat before proceeding with the recipe allows you to minimize the amount of fat while retaining the flavor of the bacon.

The type of fat is as important a consideration as the amount. Mono- and polyunsaturated fats are healthier than saturated fat, so vegetable-based fats, such as canola and olive oils (which contain more unsaturated fat than saturated fat), are generally a better choice than butter or other animal-based fats (which tend to be more saturated). Vegetable margarines and shortenings, however, are not as healthy a choice as the liquid oils because, although they are usually made from unsaturated fats, the processing they undergo to make them solid at room temperature results in chemical changes that make the unsaturated fats more like saturated fats. A useful rule of thumb to remember is the softer the fat at room temperature, the more appropriate it is from a health standpoint.

the elements of flavor

The healthiest of meals won't mean much to anyone if it doesn't taste good. Flavorful food is created with quality ingredients that are maximized with the right preparation and cooking techniques. Then, all five of our senses provide us with perceptions that, when taken collectively, represent the "flavor."

seeing flavor

One of the first senses that begin to give you flavor clues is sight. Bright vivid colors please the eyes. You expect that the foods will be as flavorful as they are colorful. Colors hint at freshness and cooking technique. You would expect vibrantly green sugar snap peas to taste "from the garden" fresh. And slices of orange sweet potato bearing grill marks should have a sweet, smoky taste and a dense, melting texture.

Foods that are bubbling or steaming let you know that they are piping hot. Height adds another dimension to the plate and excites your imagination. By looking at the plate, you already know a great deal about how the food will feel and taste, even though you have yet to taste it.

hearing flavor

The fizzing of a glass of champagne, a sizzling platter of food, and the snapping and popping of a breakfast cereal newly doused in milk all send us flavor clues. If you are about to tuck into a crispy-looking piece of herb-breaded, baked chicken, you expect that first bite to be accompanied by a nice crunch. If the coating turns out to be quietly soggy, you will most likely feel disappointed,

regardless of the actual taste and aroma.

smelling flavor

The sense of smell plays an enormous role in our perception of flavor, as anyone who has ever had a head cold knows all too well. In fact, aroma is the dominant component of flavor. While we are able to physically perceive a few basic tastes, we are able to distinguish among hundreds of smells. For example, an orange and a tangerine share the same basic tastes of sweet and sour, but most people are able to tell the difference because each fruit has a set of characteristic aromas.

feeling flavor

When you touch a food, with your fingers or with a utensil, you receive a preview of its texture. A piece of poached salmon that softly flakes away under the gentle prodding of a fork hints at the tenderness of the fish. Part of the pleasure in eating comes from feeling the foods in your mouth as you chew.

tasting flavor

When you chew and swallow the first bite, you experience the full flavor of the dish. What we typically think of as "taste" or "flavor" is actually the interaction of taste and smell, combined with the feel

of the food in the mouth. Our sense of taste comes from the chemical receptors, referred to as taste buds, on our tongues. It is generally accepted that taste buds are tuned in to receive four primary tastes—sweet, salty, sour, and bitter. However, some researchers believe that there are other categories of taste, such as the metallic taste or the savory, meaty taste known by the Japanese word umami. Additionally, our mouths feel such sensations as the burn of hot chiles, the cooling effect of mint, astringency from tannins in tea or wine, and the fizz of a carbonated beverage, among others.

The temperature at which foods are served also affects our ability to perceive tastes. We are most sensitive to taste in the temperature range of 72°–105°F. Sweet and sour sensations seem to be enhanced at the upper end of this temperature range, while salty and bitter tastes are more pronounced at the lower end. A classic example of this temperature-flavor difference is Potato-Leek Soup. When served hot, the sweetness of the leeks tends to stand out over the thick, creamy potato base. The same soup served cold, as Vichyssoise, will be refreshingly salty and the starchy quality of the potatoes will be more apparent.

beyond salt

Aromatic ingredients—onions, garlic, ginger, shallots, and scallions—are fundamental in chefs' kitchens and should be in yours. These ingredients infuse any dish with distinctive aroma and flavor.

Chiles, such as Anaheim, poblano, serrano, jalapeño, and habanero, are increasingly available in fresh, dried, and smoked forms; these add a wonderful heat and piquancy to foods. Pungent ingredients, such as mustard and horseradish, are a sure-fire way to add a kick to your cooking without using large quantities of salt.

Don't overlook citrus fruits and flavored vinegars. These ingredients are bright and sharp tasting, giving a refreshing taste to foods without increasing their sodium content.

Whenever possible, remove unnecessary fat throughout the cooking process. Soups and stews, for instance, can be made a day before they are needed and refrigerated overnight. This allows the fat to rise to the top and solidify, making for easy removal. After browning or roasting meats or poultry, the extra fat in the pan should be poured off before additional ingredients are added.

Poultry skin, which helps prevent the loss of natural juices, may be left on during roasting and baking and then removed. As long as it is not eaten, it will not add a significant amount of fat to the meat.

Some recipes call for more fat than is necessary. Too much fat can actually mask the other ingredient flavors. Kitchen experiments focused on reducing added fats have shown that the reduced-fat version is often as flavorful as the original, and in some cases, an improvement over it. In incremental steps, try reducing the fat in a favorite recipe to determine how much fat is actually necessary.

Replace high-fat ingredients with reduced or nonfat versions whenever you can. Try some of the high-quality reduced-fat, or light, dairy products now available, such as sour cream, cheese, and milk. Evaporated skim milk, for instance, can be used to simulate the effect of heavy cream in soup recipes because of its similar color, flavor, and texture. In most recipes calling for eggs, some of the egg yolks can often be omitted or replaced with an egg white, or an egg substitute may be used.

Many sauces, both cold and hot, are high in fat and make perfect candidates for fat replacement. Because these sauces are crucial to the overall flavor, appearance, and texture of the foods they complement, they should be modified in a way that does not diminish their appeal. Gravy, traditionally thickened with fat and flour, can instead be lightly thickened with arrowroot or cornstarch. Emulsified vinaigrettes, normally made with 3 parts of oil to 1 part vinegar, can be made by replacing 2 parts of the oil with a starch-thickened broth or juice, resulting in a lower-fat dressing that actually coats foods better than a regular vinaigrette.

cutting salt, but stocking the pantry   Use salt with care and purpose. Most people consume far more sodium than they really need, so before you reach for the saltshaker, you should always attempt to build as much flavor as possible into a dish by using ingredients that are low in sodium and high in natural flavor.

the art of the plate

If you have ever said "It looks too good to eat!" when you were at a restaurant, then you've witnessed the final part of the chef's process: the presentation. Chefs have long understood the art of presentation—and changed with the shifting moods of the dining-out population. The following useful tips never go out of style and you needn't be a chef or an artist to make any meal more inviting.

- Warm or chill the plate. Hot food served on a hot plate will retain an optimal temperature longer. Use your oven on the lowest setting for about 10 minutes (be sure the plates are heatproof first). Cold foods, such as salads, stay fresher longer if they are served on chilled plates. Refrigerate plates for about 20 minutes to chill them.

- Make the food easy to eat. If you're serving a chicken breast, remove the bone, and then thinly slice the meat. For a pretty presentation, you can fan the chicken slices on the plate, overlapping them slightly. When serving salad, tear the lettuces into bite-size pieces. When making soup, be sure that all the solids in the soup are small enough to fit in a soupspoon.

- Think about layering. Rather than serving your menu family-style, can any of the dishes be layered or paired on a plate? Pasta, rice, or couscous are obvious choices for a base on which you can place meat, poultry, or fish.

- Don't try to make the food look perfect. It's more inviting to present plates with a slightly more relaxed and natural style.

When you do use salt, add it in small doses throughout the cooking process rather than just at the end. When salt is added early in the cooking process, foods are in contact with the salt longer, allowing for deeper salt penetration and better overall flavor. Salting should never be an automatic reaction, however. Salt should be added in very small increments and you should always taste the food before adding more.

Whenever it is appropriate, let the sodium in ingredients such as anchovies, capers, olives, pickles, prepared mustard, smoked foods, soy sauce, and Parmesan cheese take the place of the salt called for in a recipe. These ingredients, which contribute additional flavors beyond their salty flavor, should be added first so that you can taste for overall seasoning before deciding if additional salt is necessary. Sodium may be heavily concentrated in brined ingredients such as pickles and capers, so rinse them off— they still will be salty.

Without some measure of salt, many foods taste bland and unappetizing. By combining and contrasting spices, herbs, and other distinctive flavoring agents, you can reduce the sodium level in dishes while enhancing the flavors of the main ingredients at the same time.

portion: a deck of cards Serve appropriate portions of food. Most sensible eating plans limit portion sizes to help control both calories and fat. A single portion size for meats, poultry, and fish should weigh in at 4 ounces. Most adults should have only 2 or 3 servings per day.

A 4-ounce portion is about the size of a deck of cards, which may appear meager when you are used to larger cuts. Artful presentation is an important tool in making meals look satisfying, as is adding a variety of grains and vegetables to round out the plate. Stuffing a serving of meat, fish, or poultry with vegetables and/or grains makes for a far more generous portion. Thinly slicing and fanning out cooked meat or poultry on the plate is a terrific way to present a healthful-sized portion. Pounding out or "butterflying" a piece of meat or poultry before cooking is another technique that makes the portion go a long way.

chapter 2

appetizers and hors d'oeuvres

spinach-avocado dip

A blend of spinach and buttermilk fills in for some of the much maligned, fat-laden avocado in this guacamole-inspired dip. Serve it with baked tortilla chips or lightly toasted pita wedges.

makes 4 servings

2 cups packed spinach leaves, cleaned

1/4 cup low-fat buttermilk

1/2 red onion, finely chopped

1 tablespoon canned chopped green chiles, drained

1 teaspoon fresh lime juice

1/4 medium avocado, peeled and sliced

2 plum tomatoes, chopped

1/4 cup chopped cilantro

1 **Cook the spinach** in a pot of boiling water for 1 minute. Drain, rinse under cold water, drain again, and squeeze dry.

2 **Place the spinach,** buttermilk, half of the onion, the chiles, and the lime juice in a food processor and pulse until the spinach is finely chopped and the mixture is well combined (do not overblend).

3 **Mash the avocado** in a bowl. Stir in the spinach mixture, the tomatoes, cilantro, and the remaining onion.

0 *POINTS* per serving

Per serving

44 Calories | 2 g Total Fat | 0 g Saturated Fat | 1 mg Cholesterol | 57 mg Sodium
5 g Total Carbohydrate | 3 g Dietary Fiber | 2 g Protein | 45 mg Calcium

vegetable spread

This rich, earthy spread is similar to pâté and perfect for pre-dinner nibbles. Tofu gives this spread a smooth texture; spread it on crackers, toasted French bread, or crispbreads.

makes 4 servings

1 **Place the tofu** in a single layer between two small flat plates. Weight the top with a heavy can. Let stand 30–60 minutes (do not press for longer than 60 minutes). Pour off and discard the water.

2 **Heat the oil** in a large nonstick skillet, then add the onion. Sauté until softened. Add the mushrooms and sauté until wilted. Add the beans and walnuts and sauté until heated through, about 3 minutes.

3 **Transfer the mixture** to a food processor. Add the parsley, sage, allspice, salt, and pepper; pulse until fairly smooth. Transfer to a bowl.

4 **Coarsely shred the tofu** and squeeze to remove any excess moisture. Stir the tofu into the onion mixture. Refrigerate, covered, until chilled, at least 2 hours. Garnish with the parsley sprigs, if desired.

$1/4$ pound reduced-fat firm tofu, halved lengthwise

1 teaspoon vegetable oil

1 medium onion, finely chopped

$3/4$ cup finely chopped mushrooms

1 cup chopped steamed green beans

$1/4$ cup chopped walnuts

2 tablespoons chopped flat-leaf parsley

1 teaspoon chopped sage

$1/4$ teaspoon ground allspice

$1/4$ teaspoon salt

Freshly ground pepper

Parsley sprigs (optional)

Per serving

95 Calories | 6 g Total Fat | 0 g Saturated Fat | 0 mg Cholesterol | 173 mg Sodium
7 g Total Carbohydrate | 2 g Dietary Fiber | 5 g Protein | 41 mg Calcium

2 *POINTS* per serving

tomatillo salsa

This twist on tomato salsa is as versatile as the traditional one, but has a crunchier texture and more tart flavor. Tomatillos, which look like small green tomatoes in a paper-like husk, are actually related to gooseberries. They have a firm flesh and an herb-like, lemony flavor; look for them in the specialty produce section of your supermarket. Serve the salsa with baked tortilla chips, vegetables, or over grilled chicken or fish. (See photo on page 15.)

makes 6 servings

3 medium tomatillos, chopped
(remove papery husk and rinse
before chopping)

1 small tomato, chopped

1/2 red onion, finely chopped

1/4 cup chopped cilantro

1 medium jalapeño pepper,
seeded and chopped
(wear gloves to prevent irritation)

2 teaspoons fresh lime juice

1 large garlic clove, minced

1/2 teaspoon chopped oregano

1/2 teaspoon salt

1/4 teaspoon ground cumin

1/4 teaspoon crushed
black peppercorns

Combine all of the ingredients in a serving bowl, cover, and refrigerate until chilled.

---

0 *POINTS* per serving

Per serving
17 Calories | 0 g Total Fat | 0 g Saturated Fat | 0 mg Cholesterol | 180 mg Sodium
4 g Total Carbohydrate | 1 g Dietary Fiber | 1 g Protein | 7 mg Calcium

deviled ham-stuffed eggs

During the 1940s, canned deviled ham mixed with cream cheese or sour cream was standard Midwestern party fare. We've updated this nostalgic favorite, pairing it with another classic cocktail hors d'oeuvre, deviled eggs. Stuffing the hard-cooked eggs with homemade deviled ham and leaving out the yolks is the low-fat modern twist. For extra kick, we've added pepperoncini, or pickled peppers.

makes 12 servings

1 **Pop out the yolks** from each of the eggs and reserve for another use or discard; set the egg halves aside.

2 **Mince the ham** in a food processor. Add the pepperoncini and pulse three times, until minced. Add the mayonnaise, mustard, and paprika. Pulse just until blended. (Or finely chop the ham and the pepperoncini by hand; stir in the remaining ingredients.) Spoon the ham mixture into each egg half. Refrigerate, covered, up to 4 hours before serving.

6 hard-cooked large eggs, peeled and halved lengthwise

1/4 pound lean reduced-sodium ham

2 tablespoons pickled pepperoncini, drained

3 tablespoons light mayonnaise

1 teaspoon yellow mustard

1/2 teaspoon paprika

Chef's Tip

For perfectly cooked hard-boiled eggs, place eggs in enough cold water to cover. Bring to a rolling boil, then immediately cover and remove from the heat. Let sit for 20 minutes without uncovering, then drain and rinse under cold water to stop the cooking. Peel immediately.

Per serving

33 Calories | 2 g Total Fat | 0 g Saturated Fat | 6 mg Cholesterol | 153 mg Sodium
1 g Total Carbohydrate | 0 g Dietary Fiber | 3 g Protein | 3 mg Calcium

1 *POINT* per serving

scallion-studded corn cakes

These bite-size, corn-crunchy pancakes are a thoroughly American take on Russian *blini*—the small buckwheat pancakes often topped with caviar and sour cream. Although the flavor won't be as pronounced, you can use frozen instead of fresh corn if you're pressed for time or if fresh corn is out of season. Try serving these cakes with Spinach-Avocado Dip (page 10).

makes 4 servings

1 cup fresh corn kernels (from about 2 medium ears)

1/2 red bell pepper, seeded and chopped

2 scallions, chopped

3/4 cup fat-free buttermilk

1 large egg, lightly beaten

1 tablespoon corn oil

1 teaspoon fresh thyme leaves

1 1/4 cups all-purpose flour

2 teaspoons sugar

1 teaspoon baking powder

1 teaspoon salt

Freshly ground pepper

1/2 cup light sour cream (optional)

1 **Combine the corn,** bell pepper, scallions, buttermilk, egg, oil, and thyme in one bowl. Combine the flour, sugar, baking powder, salt, and ground pepper in another bowl. Slowly pour the corn mixture into the flour mixture, stirring until just combined. Allow the batter to rest 5 minutes.

2 **Spray a large nonstick skillet** with nonstick spray and set over medium heat. Pour the batter by 1/4-cup measures into the skillet. Spread out to 3-inch rounds with the back of a spoon. Cook just until bubbles appear on the surface of the pancakes, 2–3 minutes. Flip and cook until lightly browned, 2–3 minutes more. Repeat with the remaining batter, making a total of 8 corn cakes. Serve with the sour cream, if using.

5 *POINTS* per serving

Per serving (2 corn cakes)

268 Calories | 6 g Total Fat | 1 g Saturated Fat | 54 mg Cholesterol | 729 mg Sodium
47 g Total Carbohydrate | 3 g Dietary Fiber | 9 g Protein | 94 mg Calcium

clockwise from top right: scallion-studded corn cakes, spinach-avocado dip (page 10); shrimp cocktail on skewers (page 18); tomatilla salsa (page 12); and turkey empanadas (page 20)

salmon cakes with cucumber relish

A bit of smoked salmon mixed with the canned salmon boosts the flavor of these savory fish cakes. Serve them alongside a green salad tossed with the reserved liquid from the relish.

makes 4 servings

1 large Idaho potato, peeled and cut into 1/2-inch cubes

1/2 teaspoon salt

1 (6-ounce) can salmon, drained and flaked

1/2 cup plain dried bread crumbs

2 ounces smoked salmon, minced (about 1/4 cup)

1/4 cup fat-free milk

1 tablespoon coarse-grained or yellow mustard

1 tablespoon mayonnaise

1 tablespoon chopped drained capers

1 tablespoon chopped fresh chives

1 tablespoon chopped fresh dill

1/2 teaspoon crushed pepper

1 small cucumber, peeled, seeded and cut into 1/4-inch cubes

1 tomato, peeled, seeded, and chopped (see Chef's Tip)

1 small red onion, chopped

1 jalapeño pepper, seeded and minced (wear gloves to prevent irritation)

4 teaspoons balsamic vinegar

1 tablespoon chopped cilantro

2 teaspoons olive oil

1 **Combine the potato,** salt, and enough water to cover in a large pot and bring to a boil. Reduce the heat and simmer, covered, until the potato is tender, about 15 minutes. Drain the liquid, return the pot to the stove, place over low heat, and gently toss the potato until the steam stops rising. Transfer the potato to a bowl, mash it until fairly smooth, and let it cool to room temperature.

2 **Combine the canned salmon,** bread crumbs, smoked salmon, milk, mustard, mayonnaise, capers, chives, dill, and pepper with the potato. Form into 8 cakes. Refrigerate, covered, at least 30 minutes or up to 6 hours before cooking.

3 **To make the cucumber relish,** toss the cucumber, tomato, onion, jalapeño, vinegar, cilantro, and oil in a bowl. Place the relish mixture in a fine mesh strainer over a bowl and drain briefly (reserve the liquid to toss with mixed greens or drizzle over vegetables, if desired).

4 **Spray a large nonstick skillet** with nonstick spray and set over medium-high heat. Add the salmon cakes and cook, turning once, until golden brown, about 4 minutes on each side. Serve the salmon cakes over the cucumber relish.

Chef's Tip

To prepare the tomato, bring a large pot of water to a boil. Have ready a bowl of ice water. Cut a shallow "X" into the bottom of the tomato. Submerge the tomato in boiling water for 30 seconds. Plunge into ice water, then remove immediately, and peel the tomato with a paring knife, starting at the "X." Cut the tomatoes in half horizontally and remove the seeds, then chop.

5 *POINTS* per serving

Per serving
243 Calories | 10 g Total Fat | 2 g Saturated Fat | 39 mg Cholesterol | 438 mg Sodium
23 g Total Carbohydrate | 3 g Dietary Fiber | 16 g Protein | 69 mg Calcium

seared scallops with beet vinaigrette

The daikon, a large, white Asian radish, has a refreshing and mild taste. If you can't find daikons in your local grocery store, you can substitute any other white radish. To add a more intense color and flavor to the vinaigrette, use a juicer to juice the raw beet, instead of cooking and pureeing it.

makes 4 servings

1   **To make the beet vinaigrette,** add the beet to a small pot of boiling water; simmer until tender, about 20 minutes. Drain; let cool slightly. When cool enough to handle, peel and chop it. Puree the beet and vinegar in a food processor or blender. Transfer to a small bowl and whisk in the oil, dill, salt, and pepper.

2   **Thoroughly dry the scallops** with paper towels. Spray a nonstick skillet with nonstick spray and heat over medium-high heat. Add the scallops and cook, turning once, until lightly browned on the outside and opaque in the center, about 2 minutes on each side.

3   **Toss the greens with** the vinaigrette, top with the carrot, daikon, and then the scallops. Serve immediately.

1 small beet

3 tablespoons cider vinegar

1 1/2 tablespoons extra-virgin olive oil

1/2 teaspoon dried dill

1/4 teaspoon salt

1/8 teaspoon freshly ground pepper

1 pound sea scallops, muscle tabs removed

2 cups mixed salad greens, washed and dried

1 small carrot, peeled and finely shredded

1 cup finely shredded daikon

Chef's Tip

Scallops often come with tabs of muscle still attached to them. The muscle is tough and should be removed before cooking. To remove, simply peel the muscle tab away from the scallop and discard.

Per serving

166 Calories | 6 g Total Fat | 1 g Saturated Fat | 37 mg Cholesterol | 371 mg Sodium
8 g Total Carbohydrate | 1 g Dietary Fiber | 20 g Protein | 60 mg Calcium

4 POINTS per serving

shrimp cocktail on skewers

The bold flavors of Mexico and the Southwest—lime, jalapeño, and cilantro—jazz up the usual cocktail sauce in this recipe. Consider serving this refreshing dish as an hors d' oeuvre when entertaining: The skewers make a beautiful presentation that can be prepared a day ahead. Save even more time by buying the shrimp precooked at the fish market the day you plan to serve them. (See photo on page 15.)

makes 8 servings

1 pound (about 24) large shrimp, peeled and deveined

Pinch salt

1 (12-ounce) jar cocktail sauce

1 tablespoon minced fresh cilantro

2 teaspoons fresh lime juice

1 jalapeño pepper, seeded and minced (wear gloves to prevent irritation)

Small romaine lettuce leaves, washed and dried

1 **Bring a large pot of water to a boil;** add the shrimp and salt and cook until the shrimp are just opaque in the center, 3–5 minutes. Drain in a colander and rinse under cold water to stop the cooking. Dry the shrimp on paper towels.

2 **Combine the cocktail sauce,** cilantro, lime juice, and jalapeño in a small serving bowl.

   Make Ahead: The shrimp and sauce can be refrigerated separately, covered, for up to 24 hours.

3 **Thread 3 shrimp** on each of eight 7-inch bamboo skewers. Place the bowl of cocktail sauce in the center of a large plate and arrange the romaine leaves around it; top the leaves with the shrimp skewers.

Chef's Tip

To clean shrimp, remove the shells and the intestinal tract, or vein, a process known as "deveining." Shrimp shells pull easily away from the shrimp meat. The shells can be frozen for later use in shrimp stock or bisque. The vein, which runs along the back of the shrimp, is easy to locate. After the shell is removed, lay the shrimp on a cutting board with the curved outer edge (the back) of the shrimp on the same side as your cutting hand. Using a paring knife, make a shallow cut along the back of the shrimp from the head end to the tail. Use the edge of the knife to scrape out the vein, which may be either clear or dark.

2 POINTS per serving

Per serving

97 Calories | 1 g Total Fat | 0 g Saturated Fat | 86 mg Cholesterol | 338 mg Sodium
9 g Total Carbohydrate | 0 g Dietary Fiber | 12 g Protein | 56 mg Calcium

spicy chicken-peanut dumplings

Used primarily in Asian cooking, wonton skins are thin sheets of dough that serve as wrappers for tasty packages of ingredients in small treats such as egg rolls and dumplings. They are available in the refrigerator case of Chinese groceries, gourmet shops, and many large supermarkets. Make sure the wonton skins are soft before you buy them by giving them a gentle squeeze; otherwise, they may not be pliable and could tear easily. Serve these savory dumplings with reduced-sodium soy sauce for dipping.

makes 4 servings

1 **Combine the chicken,** scallions, cilantro, peanuts, egg white, salt, ginger, and pepper sauce in a bowl.

2 **Place the wonton skins** on a clean, dry work surface. Drop 1 scant tablespoon of the filling into the center of each wonton skin. Brush the edges with water, then fold into a half-circle. Press the filling to release any trapped air; press the edges to seal. Repeat this process to make a total of 20 dumplings.

3 **Arrange the dumplings** in a steamer rack; set in a saucepan over 1 inch of boiling water. Cover tightly and steam until the dumplings are cooked through, about 7 minutes.

$1/2$ pound ground chicken breast meat

16 scallions, minced

$1/2$ cup minced cilantro

$1/4$ cup unsalted dry-roasted peanuts, coarsely chopped

1 egg white

$1/2$ teaspoon salt

$1/2$ teaspoon ground ginger

$1/4$ teaspoon hot pepper sauce

20 (3-inch round) wonton skins

Per serving (5 dumplings)

245 Calories | 6 g Total Fat | 1 g Saturated Fat | 36 mg Cholesterol | 561 mg Sodium
28 g Total Carbohydrate | 3 g Dietary Fiber | 21 g Protein | 78 mg Calcium

5 _POINTS_ per serving

turkey empanadas

A South American delicacy, the word *empanada* is derived from the Spanish verb *empanar*, which means "to bake in pastry." In this lightened version, we use lean ground turkey in the filling and phyllo instead of pastry dough to cut down on fat and calories, without relinquishing any of the pleasing flavor and texture. The filling may be prepared up to one day ahead. (See photo on page 15.)

makes 12 servings

2 teaspoons canola oil

1 medium onion, chopped

1 garlic clove, minced

1/2 teaspoon ground allspice

1 pound ground skinless turkey breast

1 teaspoon dried oregano

1 teaspoon salt

12 (12 × 17-inch) sheets phyllo, at room temperature

1/4 cup fat-free egg substitute

1 **Heat a large nonstick skillet.** Swirl in the oil, then add the onion, garlic, and allspice. Sauté until the onion just begins to brown, about 7 minutes. Add the turkey, oregano, and salt. Cook the turkey, breaking it apart with a wooden spoon, until browned. Refrigerate, covered, until the mixture is firm, at least 1 hour.

2 **Preheat the oven** to 375°F. Line a baking sheet with parchment or with foil sprayed with nonstick spray.

3 **Cover the sheets of phyllo** with plastic wrap to keep them from drying out. Remove one sheet and spray it with nonstick spray. Repeat this process, stacking the phyllo, for a total of 3 layers. Cut the phyllo stack into three 5 1/2 × 12-inch strips. Put about 1/4 cup of the turkey filling about 3 inches from the right long end of one strip, to the left of the center. Fold the bottom right corner of the dough over the filling to make a triangle, then continue to fold up like a flag. Repeat with the 2 remaining strips and then the remaining phyllo sheets to make 12 empanadas. Transfer the empanadas to the baking sheet and brush with the egg substitute. Bake until golden brown, 20–25 minutes.

2 *POINTS* per serving

Per serving

121 Calories | 3 g Total Fat | 1 g Saturated Fat | 22 mg Cholesterol | 317 mg Sodium
11 g Total Carbohydrate | 1 g Dietary Fiber | 11 g Protein | 13 mg Calcium

vietnamese summer rolls

We call these "summer rolls" because they're served cold and have a fresh, light taste. A key ingredient in the dipping sauce, *nuoc mam*—a dark, pungent, salty sauce made from fermented fish—is a staple in Vietnamese kitchens. You can find it or the Thai version called *nam pla*, as well as rice paper wrappers, in Asian specialty stores.

1 To make the dipping sauce, whisk together the fish sauce, sugar, lemon juice, vinegar, water, garlic and chili sauce in a small bowl. Cover and refrigerate until the rolls are assembled, or up to 2 days.

2 To make the filling, cook the vermicelli in a large pot of boiling water until just tender, 1–2 minutes. Drain the noodles, rinse with cold water, and drain again. Refill the pot with water and bring it to a boil. Add the shrimp and cook until opaque in the center, about 2 minutes. Transfer the shrimp to a bowl of cold water to cool. Peel, clean, and then slice the shrimp in half lengthwise.

3 Toss the carrots with 1/2 teaspoon of the salt in a medium bowl and let stand 10 minutes. Drain off any liquid. Add the noodles, lettuce, lemon juice, 1 1/2 teaspoons of the sugar, and remaining 1/4 teaspoon salt; toss.

4 To assemble the rolls, combine the remaining 1 tablespoon sugar with the warm water in a large shallow bowl or pie plate and dissolve. Moisten 1 wrapper in the sugar water and place it on a clean kitchen towel. Place about 1/2 cup of the noodle mixture, 2 shrimp halves, and a few cilantro leaves in the center. Fold in each end of the wrapper and roll to completely enclose the filling. Repeat to make 10 rolls, rewarming the sugar water if necessary. Serve each roll, sliced in half, with some dipping sauce.

makes 10 servings

DIPPING SAUCE

1/4 cup Vietnamese fish sauce (nuoc mam)

1/3 cup sugar

3 tablespoons fresh lemon juice

3 tablespoons rice vinegar

2 tablespoons water

1 large garlic clove, minced

2 teaspoons chili sauce

SUMMER ROLLS

6 ounces rice vermicelli or rice sticks

10 medium shrimp

1 large carrot, peeled and grated

3/4 teaspoon salt

2 cups shredded iceberg lettuce

3 1/2 tablespoons fresh lemon juice

1 1/2 tablespoons sugar

1 cup warm water

10 (8 1/2-inch round) rice paper wrappers

1/3 cup cilantro leaves

Chef's Tip

Summer rolls are best served immediately, but they can be stored for up to 2 hours in the refrigerator. Cover with a damp paper towel and wrap tightly with plastic wrap to keep them moist.

Per serving (1 roll with about 1 tablespoon sauce)
161 Calories | 0 g Total Fat | 0 g Saturated Fat | 11 mg Cholesterol | 473 mg Sodium
36 g Total Carbohydrate | 1 g Dietary Fiber | 5 g Protein | 13 mg Calcium

3 *POINTS* per serving

working with rice paper

Moisten one wrapper at a time by dipping in warm water.

Fold the two long ends of the wrapper over the filling.

Tuck in the end closest to you and roll up completely to enclose the filling.

wild mushroom–goat cheese strudel

Shiitake mushrooms are delicious in this savory pastry, but any full-flavored mushroom or mushroom combination works well, so experiment with your favorite exotic varieties—cremini, porcini, oyster mushrooms, or chopped portobellos, for example. Substitute white mushrooms for some of the exotic varieties to keep the cost down.

makes 10 servings

1 **Heat the broth** in a large skillet, then add the shallots and garlic. Cook, stirring, until the shallots are translucent, 3–5 minutes. Add the mushrooms and cook until the mushrooms are shriveled and their juices have reduced, about 5 minutes. Add the wine and cook, scraping up the browned bits from the bottom of the skillet, until nearly dry. Spread the mixture on a baking sheet to cool. Once the mushrooms are cooled, combine them with the goat cheese and pepper.

2 **Preheat the oven** to 350°F.

3 **Cover the sheets** of phyllo with plastic wrap to keep them from drying out. Remove one sheet and spray it with nonstick spray. Repeat the process with a second sheet, top with a third sheet, and brush with 1/2 tablespoon of the butter. Mound half of the mushroom mixture along one long edge. Roll the strudel tightly, enclosing the mushroom mixture. Brush the top with 1/2 tablespoon of the butter. Repeat to make another strudel.

4 **Place the strudels** on a baking sheet. Score the tops, with a knife, to indicate 5 equal portions for each strudel. Bake the strudels until golden brown, 15–20 minutes. Cool on a rack for 10–15 minutes. Cut the strudels into 10 portions and serve warm.

1/4 cup low-sodium vegetable or chicken broth

1/2 cup minced shallots

4 garlic cloves, minced

1 pound wild mushrooms, quartered

1/2 cup dry white wine

1/2 cup crumbled reduced-fat goat cheese

1/4 teaspoon freshly ground pepper

6 (13 × 18-inch) sheets phyllo, room temperature

2 tablespoons unsalted butter, melted

Per serving

105 Calories | 5 g Total Fat | 1 g Saturated Fat | 12 mg Cholesterol | 104 mg Sodium
12 g Total Carbohydrate | 1 g Dietary Fiber | 2 g Protein | 7 mg Calcium

2 POINTS per serving

eggplant, goat cheese, and tomato tart

Who knew eggplant could be this elegant? A lovely presentation and a hint of tart flavor from slices of creamy goat cheese raise the humble vegetable to a new level of sophistication in this recipe. Try it as the first course at your next dinner party.

makes 4 servings

1 (1 1/2-pound) eggplant, peeled and sliced 1/4-inch thick

1 1/4 teaspoons salt

Freshly ground pepper

2 teaspoons olive oil

1 cup sliced mushrooms

1 (28-ounce) can plum tomatoes, drained and chopped

2 tablespoons capers, drained

2 tablespoons chopped fresh basil leaves, or 1 teaspoon dried

1 tablespoon chopped fresh oregano, or 1/2 teaspoon dried

1 tablespoon chopped fresh thyme, or 1/2 teaspoon dried

2 garlic cloves, minced

3 ounces goat cheese (such as Montrachet), thinly sliced

1 Sprinkle the eggplant slices on both sides with the salt and place in a colander. Put a plate on top of the eggplant and weight it with a large can. Let the eggplant drain for 30–60 minutes. Quickly rinse the eggplant; pat dry with paper towels.

2 Meanwhile, preheat the broiler. Spray a nonstick baking sheet and a 9-inch ceramic pie plate with nonstick spray. Place the eggplant slices on the baking sheet and sprinkle with pepper. Broil 5 inches from the heat until lightly browned, 5–10 minutes. Remove the eggplant from the broiler and set aside. Set the oven control to 450°F and adjust the racks to divide the oven in half.

3 Heat the oil in a nonstick skillet, then add the mushrooms. Sauté until wilted and almost dry. Add the tomatoes, capers, basil, oregano, thyme, garlic, the remaining 1/4 teaspoon salt, and another grinding of pepper. Cook, stirring frequently, until the mixture has thickened, 5–10 minutes. Remove from the heat and set aside.

4 Layer half of the eggplant slices in the pie plate, overlapping as necessary. Top with half of the tomato mixture, then all the remaining eggplant. Spoon the remaining tomato mixture over the eggplant. Arrange the goat cheese slices evenly on top. Bake until the cheese has melted, about 10 minutes.

5 Remove the tart from the oven and set the oven control to Broil. Broil the tart 5 inches from the heat until the cheese is golden brown, 5 minutes.

3 *POINTS* per serving

Per serving

153 Calories | 7 g Total Fat | 0 g Saturated Fat | 14 mg Cholesterol | 920 mg Sodium
18 g Total Carbohydrate | 8 g Dietary Fiber | 4 g Protein | 104 mg Calcium

roasted pepper–arugula salad with prosciutto

Slightly salty prosciutto is a wonderful counterpoint to the sweet roasted peppers in this dish. Aged Monterey Jack cheese is drier, firmer, and sharper than unaged Jack; look for it in specialty cheese shops or use Parmigiano-Reggiano or Asiago in its place. Cheese shavings make a dramatic presentation, and they're easy to make. Use a vegetable peeler or a cheese slicer and carefully shave off curls.

makes 6 servings

2 red bell peppers

1 green bell pepper

1 yellow bell pepper

3/4 pound asparagus, peeled, trimmed, and cut into 3-inch pieces

2 tablespoons balsamic vinegar

1 tablespoon extra-virgin olive oil

1/4 teaspoon Dijon mustard

1 bunch arugula, cleaned

2 ounces prosciutto, thinly sliced

1 ounce aged Monterey Jack cheese, shaved

1 Preheat the broiler. Place the peppers in a roasting pan and broil 5 inches from the heat, turning frequently with tongs, until shriveled and darkened, 10–20 minutes. Place the peppers in a medium bowl, cover with plastic wrap, and let steam for 10 minutes. When cool enough to handle, peel, seed, and cut into 2 × 3-inch pieces.

2 Bring 1 inch of water to a boil in a skillet; add the asparagus. Reduce the heat and simmer, uncovered, until crisp-tender. Drain and set aside.

3 To make the vinaigrette, whisk together the vinegar, oil, and mustard.

4 To assemble the salad, arrange the arugula with the roasted peppers and asparagus scattered on top. Tear the prosciutto into long strips and arrange over the salad. Drizzle with the dressing, add the cheese shavings, and serve.

Per serving

105 Calories | 6 g Total Fat | 2 g Saturated Fat | 9 mg Cholesterol | 227 mg Sodium
9 g Total Carbohydrate | 2 g Dietary Fiber | 7 g Protein | 149 mg Calcium

2 *POINTS* per serving

portobello–white bean salad

The meaty taste and texture of portobello mushrooms gives this salad a hearty warmth. You can make the bean salad up to a day ahead of time if you like, but be sure to let it stand at room temperature at least 1 hour before serving.

makes 4 servings

BEAN SALAD

1 (15-ounce) can cannellini beans, rinsed and drained (about 1 1/2 cups)

1 small carrot, peeled and finely chopped

1 stalk celery, finely chopped

1/2 red bell pepper, seeded and finely chopped

1/2 yellow bell pepper, seeded and finely chopped

1 scallion, finely chopped

1 tablespoon chopped fresh chives

1 tablespoon chopped fresh parsley

2 teaspoons extra-virgin olive oil

2 teaspoons lemon juice

1/2 teaspoon salt

1/4 teaspoon ground pepper

4 medium (about 5-inch diameter) portobello mushrooms

2 teaspoons olive oil

1/2 cup shredded radicchio

2 teaspoons chopped cilantro

1 To make the bean salad, combine the beans, carrot, celery, bell peppers, scallion, chives, parsley, oil, lemon juice, salt, and pepper in a large nonreactive bowl. Cover and let stand at room temperature for up to 2 hours (refrigerate if not serving within 2 hours).

2 To prepare the mushrooms, preheat the oven to 350°F. Place the mushrooms on a baking sheet and brush the tops with the olive oil. Cover with foil and bake until tender, 15–20 minutes. Remove mushrooms from the oven and uncover. Raise the oven setting to Broil.

3 Broil the mushrooms 5 inches from the heat, until they are lightly browned and the excess moisture has evaporated, about 2 minutes on each side. Slice the mushrooms into 1/2-inch strips.

4 Divide the bean salad among 4 plates and arrange the mushroom strips around each salad. Top with the radicchio and cilantro.

3 *POINTS* per serving

Per serving

181 Calories | 6 g Total Fat | 1 g Saturated Fat | 0 mg Cholesterol | 302 mg Sodium
27 g Total Carbohydrate | 8 g Dietary Fiber | 9 g Protein | 93 mg Calcium

chapter 3

salads

spinach-strawberry salad

This savory-sweet salad, full of bright colors and vivid flavors, packs a nutrition punch as well: The vitamin C in the strawberries helps make the iron in the spinach more available for the body to use. Aged goat cheese, which has a drier texture and deeper flavor than the softer fresh types, beautifully complements the tangy salad.

makes 4 servings

1 tablespoon cider vinegar

2 teaspoons vegetable oil

1 teaspoon Dijon mustard

$1/2$ teaspoon honey

Pinch crumbled dried rosemary

Freshly ground pepper

1 (10-ounce) bag triple-washed spinach, rinsed and torn

2 cups strawberries, hulled and halved

$1/4$ sweet onion, very thinly sliced

$2/3$ cup crumbled aged goat cheese

Whisk together the vinegar, oil, mustard, honey, rosemary, and pepper in a large bowl. Add the spinach, strawberries, and onion; gently toss to coat. Sprinkle the salad with the cheese and serve at once.

Chef's Tip

Fresh spinach, even the triple-washed kind, is often gritty. To clean the spinach leaves, immerse them in cold standing water and swish gently to free the grit. Let soak for a minute or two while the grit settles to the bottom. Lift the spinach out of the water and repeat the rinsing with clean water until the spinach is free of grit, usually three changes of water. Drain and dry in a salad spinner. Store the cleaned spinach in a loosely closed plastic bag in the refrigerator for up to 3 days.

3 _POINTS_ per serving

Per serving

144 Calories | 10 g Total Fat | 5 g Saturated Fat | 20 mg Cholesterol | 154 mg Sodium
8 g Total Carbohydrate | 8 g Dietary Fiber | 8 g Protein | 238 mg Calcium

romaine and grapefruit salad with walnuts and stilton

Tangy English Stilton cheese and grapefruit combine with sweet ruby port and walnuts in this refreshing salad. If Stilton is unavailable, substitute a good-quality blue-veined cheese with a creamy consistency, such as Roquefort. All the components of this salad, including the dressing, can be prepared ahead and combined just before serving.

1 **Bring the port** and broth to a boil in a small saucepan. Slowly add the arrowroot mixture; stir constantly until thickened, about 1 minute. Remove from the heat; stir in the vinegar and grapefruit juice and let cool completely. Gradually whisk in the oil.

2 **Gently toss the romaine** with the dressing in a large bowl. Arrange the lettuce on chilled plates; top with the grapefruit sections, cheese, and walnuts. Serve at once.

makes 4 servings

2 tablespoons ruby port wine

1 1/2 tablespoons vegetable broth

1/2 teaspoon arrowroot, dissolved in 1 teaspoon water

2 teaspoons red wine vinegar

2 teaspoons grapefruit juice

2 teaspoons olive oil

4 cups thinly sliced romaine lettuce, rinsed

1 white or pink grapefruit, cut into sections

1/3 cup crumbled Stilton cheese

1/3 cup chopped toasted walnuts

Chef's Tip

To toast the walnuts, place them in a small skillet over medium-low heat. Cook, shaking the pan and stirring constantly, until lightly browned and fragrant, 3–5 minutes. Watch them carefully when toasting; walnuts can burn quickly. Transfer the nuts to a plate to cool.

Per serving

145 Calories | 11 g Total Fat | 3 g Saturated Fat | 8 mg Cholesterol | 163 mg Sodium
4 g Total Carbohydrate | 2 g Dietary Fiber | 6 g Protein | 86 mg Calcium

3 *POINTS* per serving

winter greens with blue cheese and pine nuts

Slightly sweet Port Wine Vinaigrette (page 52) is the perfect contrast to sharp blue cheese and slightly bitter greens in this warm winter salad. Feel free to substitute a dash of oil and vinegar if you don't have time to make the dressing.

makes 4 servings

1 small red onion, sliced 1/4-inch thick

1/2 cup Port Wine Vinaigrette (page 52)

12 Belgian endive spears

1 1/2 cups torn arugula, rinsed

1 1/2 cups torn spinach, rinsed

1 cup torn frisée (curly endive), rinsed

1/2 cup torn radicchio, rinsed

1/2 cup crumbled blue cheese

2 tablespoons pine nuts, toasted

1 **Spray the broiler rack** with nonstick spray; preheat the broiler. Broil the onion slices 5 inches from the heat until browned and tender, 2–3 minutes per side. Keep warm.

2 **Heat the vinaigrette** in a small saucepan; keep warm.

3 **Arrange the endive,** arugula, spinach, frisée, and radicchio on warm plates. Arrange the onion slices over the greens. Sprinkle on the blue cheese and pine nuts. Drizzle the salads with the warm dressing and serve at once.

Chef's Tips

To clean the greens, immerse them in cold standing water and swish gently to free the grit. Let soak for a minute or two while the grit settles to the bottom. Lift the greens out of the water and repeat the rinsing with clean water until the greens are free of grit, usually three changes of water. Drain and dry in a salad spinner. Store the cleaned greens in a loosely closed plastic bag in the refrigerator for up to 3 days.

To toast the pine nuts, place them in a dry small skillet over medium-low heat. Cook, shaking the pan and stirring constantly, until the nuts are lightly browned, 3–5 minutes. Watch them carefully when toasting; pine nuts can burn quickly. Transfer the nuts to a plate to cool.

4 *POINTS* per serving

Per serving

179 Calories | 14 g Total Fat | 4 g Saturated Fat | 13 mg Cholesterol | 294 mg Sodium
7 g Total Carbohydrate | 2 g Dietary Fiber | 6 g Protein | 134 mg Calcium

minted carrot salad with lemon vinaigrette

This refreshing side dish is simple to prepare and a great choice to serve at a brunch or luncheon. Select only the freshest carrots, since they are served raw; organic carrots, with the tops still attached, are your best bet. Look for fresh-looking tops with no wilting, and remove them before storing the carrots in the refrigerator crisper.

1 **To create the dressing,** whisk together the lemon juice, oil, and sugar in a small bowl. Combine the carrots, raisins, and mint in a non-reactive bowl.

2 **Drizzle the carrots** with the dressing and toss to coat. If you have time, let the salad stand at room temperature for 30 minutes to blend the flavors.

makes 4 servings

2 tablespoons fresh lemon juice

2 teaspoons olive oil

1 teaspoon sugar

4 carrots, peeled and shredded

1 cup golden raisins

3 tablespoons chopped mint

Per serving

184 Calories | 2 g Total Fat | 0 g Saturated Fat | 0 mg Cholesterol | 33 mg Sodium
39 g Total Carbohydrate | 5 g Dietary Fiber | 2 g Protein | 46 mg Calcium

3 *POINTS* per serving

chinese long bean salad with tangerines and mustard-sherry vinaigrette

Chinese long beans are also known as yard-long beans. They are part of the same plant family as the black-eyed pea. For a dramatic presentation, serve them long or, if you prefer, cut into small pieces. They can be found in Asian groceries, but green beans may be substituted if Chinese long beans are unavailable. Serve this slightly sweet-and-sour salad with simple grilled meat, fish, or poultry.

makes 4 servings

1/2 pound Chinese long beans, trimmed and cut into 1 1/2-inch lengths

2 tangerines

1/2 cup thinly sliced Vidalia onion

1/4 cup sunflower seeds, toasted

1/4 teaspoon salt

1/8 teaspoon freshly ground pepper

1/2 cup low-sodium vegetable broth

1 teaspoon cornstarch, dissolved in 2 teaspoons water

1 1/2 tablespoons olive oil

1 tablespoon sherry vinegar

1 tablespoon fresh orange juice

1 tablespoon Dijon mustard

1/2 tablespoon packed light brown sugar

1 shallot, minced

1 teaspoon minced garlic

1 **Place the beans** in a steamer basket and set in a saucepan over 1 inch of boiling water. Cover tightly and steam until just tender, 7–9 minutes.

2 **Using a sharp paring knife,** slice away the top and bottom ends of the tangerines. Place on a cutting board on end and slice the rind away, removing all traces of pith. Working over a large bowl to catch the juices, cut the tangerine sections out from between the membranes, letting each one fall into the bowl as you cut it free. Discard any seeds.

3 **Add the beans,** onion, and sunflower seeds to the tangerine sections. Season with the salt and pepper; set aside.

4 **Bring the broth** to a boil in a saucepan. Whisk in the cornstarch mixture and stir constantly until thickened, about 1 minute. Remove from the heat and let cool.

5 **Combine the oil,** vinegar, orange juice, mustard, brown sugar, shallot, and garlic in a small bowl; whisk into the thickened broth. Pour the vinaigrette over the bean mixture and toss lightly; serve warm or at room temperature (or refrigerate, covered, up to 2 days).

Chef's Tip

To toast the sunflower seeds, place them in a dry skillet over medium-low heat. Cook, shaking the pan and stirring constantly, until the seeds are lightly browned. Watch them carefully when toasting; sunflower seeds can burn quickly. Transfer the seeds to a plate to cool.

3 *POINTS* per serving

Per serving
168 Calories | 10 g Total Fat | 1 g Saturated Fat | 1 mg Cholesterol | 261mg Sodium
17 g Total Carbohydrate | 4 g Dietary Fiber | 5 g Protein | 60 mg Calcium

chinese long bean salad with tangerines and mustard-sherry vinaigrette

roasted corn, peppers, and jícama salad

This colorful, crunchy salad is best served at room temperature. Roasting the corn first gives it a sweet, mellow flavor. Jícama (HEE-kah-mah), also known as the Mexican potato, is a root vegetable with a sweet flavor and a texture like that of a radish. Use a sharp paring knife to trim its thin skin just before using.

makes 6 servings

1 medium ear of corn

1 medium jícama, peeled and cut into thin strips

1 medium red onion, thinly sliced

1 small red bell pepper, cut into thin strips

1 small green bell pepper, cut into thin strips

1 small jalapeño pepper, seeded, deveined, and minced (wear gloves to prevent irritation)

2 tablespoons red wine vinegar

2 tablespoons vegetable oil

2 tablespoons water

1/2 teaspoon dry mustard

1/2 teaspoon salt

1 garlic clove, minced

Freshly ground pepper

1 **Preheat the oven** to 400°F. Loosen, but do not remove the husk from the corn. Remove the corn silk. Tie the husk closed again around the ear of the corn with a strip of husk and dampen with water. Place the corn on a baking sheet and roast until tender, about 25 minutes. Let cool slightly, then remove the husk and cut the corn from the cob.

2 **Combine the corn,** jícama, onion, bell peppers, and the jalapeño in a large bowl.

3 **Whisk together the vinegar,** oil, water, mustard, salt, garlic, and pepper in a small bowl. Add the dressing to the vegetables and toss to coat.

2 *POINTS* per serving

Per serving
85 Calories | 5 g Total Fat | 1 g Saturated Fat | 0 mg Cholesterol | 246 mg Sodium
10 g Total Carbohydrate | 3 g Dietary Fiber | 1 g Protein | 16 mg Calcium

mexican corn salad

Prepare this salad during the peak of corn season. Roast some extra corn and freeze it. Then, on a cold winter day, make this salad again for a reminder of summertime. If you're in a hurry, a bottled, roasted pepper can be substituted for freshly roasted bell pepper.

makes 6 servings

4 medium ears of corn

1 teaspoon olive oil

1 shallot, minced

1 garlic clove, minced

1 small jalapeño pepper, seeded, deveined, and minced (wear gloves to prevent irritation)

4–5 plum tomatoes, seeded and chopped

2 tomatillos, finely chopped

1/2 small jícama, peeled and chopped

1/2 roasted red bell pepper, chopped

1/2 tablespoon chopped cilantro

Pinch salt

1 **Preheat the oven** to 400°F. Loosen, but do not remove the husks from the corn. Remove the corn silk. Tie the husks closed again around the ears of the corn with strips of husk and dampen with water. Place the corn on a baking sheet and roast until tender, about 25 minutes. Let cool slightly, then remove the husks and cut the corn from the cob.

2 **Heat the oil** in a large nonstick skillet, then add the shallot, garlic, and jalapeño. Sauté until the shallot is translucent, 2–3 minutes.

3 **Add the corn,** tomatoes, tomatillos, jícama, and red pepper. Cook the vegetables until most of the liquid from the tomatoes has evaporated, 2–3 minutes. Sprinkle with the cilantro and salt. Serve warm or at room temperature.

Chef's Tips

Tomatillos, which are relatives of the gooseberry, are available in specialty stores and many supermarkets. Select firm tomatillos enclosed in paperlike husks (which should be removed before using the tomatillos). They can be eaten raw in salsas or salads.

To roast the bell pepper, spray the broiler rack with nonstick spray; preheat the broiler. Broil the pepper 5 inches from the heat, turning frequently with tongs, until the skin is shriveled and darkened, 10–20 minutes. Place the pepper in a small bowl, cover with plastic wrap, and let steam for 10 minutes. When cool enough to handle, peel and seed.

Per serving

83 Calories | 1 g Total Fat | 0.2 g Saturated Fat | 0 mg Cholesterol | 155 mg Sodium
18 g Total Carbohydrate | 4 g Dietary Fiber | 3 g Protein | 22 mg Calcium

1 *POINT* per serving

warm salad of wild mushrooms and fennel

There is a wonderful assortment of exotic mushrooms available in most supermarkets now. Cremini, oyster, chanterelle, and shiitake mushrooms all work well in this recipe, but select what is fresh and in season.

makes 4 servings

1 small fennel bulb, thinly sliced

$2/3$ cup torn radicchio, rinsed

1 head garlic, cloves separated and peeled

$1^1/_2$ tablespoons extra-virgin olive oil

$2^1/_2$ cups wild mushrooms, sliced or quartered

$1^1/_4$ cups low-sodium chicken broth

$1/_2$ cup chopped sun-dried tomatoes (not oil-packed)

6 kalamata olives, pitted and sliced

2 tablespoons minced fresh sage

$1^1/_2$ tablespoons capers, drained

3 tablespoons fresh lemon juice

$1/_3$ medium red bell pepper, sliced

Freshly ground pepper

1 **Combine the fennel** in a small saucepan with enough water to cover and bring to a boil. Reduce the heat, cover, and simmer until the fennel is barely tender, about 5 minutes. Drain, cool, and gently toss the fennel with the radicchio in a bowl.

2 **Combine the garlic cloves** with enough water to cover them by 1 inch in the sauce pan and bring to a boil. Drain the garlic and repeat the process using fresh water. Reserve the garlic.

3 **Heat the oil** in a nonstick skillet, then add the garlic. Sauté until golden brown, 4–5 minutes. Add the mushrooms and sauté until tender, about 8 minutes. Add the broth; cook, scraping up the browned bits from the bottom of the pan, until the broth has almost completely evaporated, 5–10 minutes. Remove from the heat and stir in the tomatoes, olives, sage, and capers.

4 **Arrange the fennel** and radicchio on plates and top with the mushroom mixture. Drizzle the salads with the lemon juice. Sprinkle with the red bell pepper and freshly ground pepper; serve at once.

Chef's Tip

In this recipe, whole garlic cloves are blanched twice before being browned in oil. This technique mellows and softens the garlic cloves enough to be eaten whole. To peel the garlic cloves, lightly crush them with the side of a large knife. The peels should easily slip off.

3 _POINTS_ per serving

Per serving

160 Calories | 8 g Total Fat | 1 g Saturated Fat | 2 mg Cholesterol | 400 mg Sodium
20 g Total Carbohydrate | 4 g Dietary Fiber | 7 g Protein | 96 mg Calcium

warm salad of wild mushrooms and fennel

asian buckwheat noodle salad

Don't let the long list of ingredients deter you from making this salad. It only takes a little measuring and chopping to prepare everything, and the full nutty flavor of this salad is well worth the effort. To make the salad into an entrée, top each serving with $1/3$ cup of shredded cooked chicken breast that has been tossed with a little Asian sesame oil and crushed red pepper.

makes 4 servings

3 tablespoons low-sodium vegetable broth or water

$1^1/2$ tablespoons rice vinegar

$3^1/2$ teaspoons reduced-sodium tamari or soy sauce

1 teaspoon minced shallot

1 teaspoon whole-grain mustard

1 garlic clove, minced

1 tablespoon + 1 teaspoon peanut oil

$1^1/2$ teaspoons chopped fresh chives

$1^1/2$ cups sliced shiitake mushrooms

$1/8$ teaspoon coarsely ground pepper

8 ounces buckwheat (soba) noodles

$1/2$ teaspoon Asian (dark) sesame oil

4 scallions, thinly sliced

$1^1/4$ cups bean sprouts

1 carrot, peeled and shredded

$2/3$ cup thinly sliced snow peas

2 cups mixed greens, rinsed

2 tablespoons pickled ginger

2 teaspoons sesame seeds, toasted

1 **To prepare the dressing,** combine the broth, vinegar, 2 teaspoons of the tamari, the shallot, mustard, and garlic in a small bowl. Gradually whisk in 1 tablespoon of the oil and stir in the chives.

2 **Heat the remaining** 1 teaspoon peanut oil in a large nonstick skillet. Add the mushrooms and sauté until tender, about 4 minutes. Season with the remaining $1^1/2$ teaspoons tamari and the pepper. Let cool completely.

3 **Cook the noodles** according to package directions. Drain the noodles, rinse under cold water, and drain once more. Toss the noodles with the sesame oil in a large bowl. Add the mushrooms, scallions, bean sprouts, carrot, and snow peas. Pour in the dressing and gently toss to coat.

4 **Arrange the mixed greens** on plates and top with the noodle salad. Garnish with the pickled ginger and sesame seeds; serve at once.

Chef's Tip

Often served with sushi, spicy sweet-and-sour pickled ginger adds an essential flavor element to this salad. It is preserved in sweetened vinegar and usually appears pink in color. Find it in Asian groceries and large supermarkets (in the Asian ingredient section).

6 *POINTS* per serving

Per serving
301 Calories | 8 g Total Fat | 1 g Saturated Fat | 0 mg Cholesterol | 807 mg Sodium
51 g Total Carbohydrate | 5 g Dietary Fiber | 13 g Protein | 75 mg Calcium

curried rice salad

Toasting the pumpkin seeds and curry powder releases the fragrance of the seeds and spices and adds a lovely flavor to this salad. Use leftover rice to make this salad, or if making rice specifically for the salad, start with 1¼ cups of uncooked rice.

makes 6 servings

1 **Toast the pumpkin seeds** in a dry small skillet over medium-low heat, stirring frequently, until they begin to pop and are lightly browned, 2–3 minutes. Transfer the seeds to a plate to cool. In the same skillet, lightly toast the curry powder over low heat, stirring constantly, until fragrant, 1–2 minutes. Transfer to a large nonreactive bowl.

2 **Whisk in the broth,** oil, and vinegar. Add the rice, peas, scallions, raisins, pumpkin seeds, apple, salt, and pepper; toss to combine and serve at once.

1½ tablespoons pumpkin seeds

4 teaspoons curry powder

¼ cup low-sodium vegetable broth

2 tablespoons extra-virgin olive oil

2 tablespoons red wine vinegar

2 cups cooked long-grain white rice

½ cup green peas, thawed if frozen, cooked if fresh

2 scallions, thinly sliced

2 tablespoons golden raisins

1 small Granny Smith apple, cored and chopped

¼ teaspoon salt

¼ teaspoon freshly ground pepper

Per serving

156 Calories | 7 g Total Fat | 1 g Saturated Fat | 0 mg Cholesterol | 105 mg Sodium
21 g Total Carbohydrate | 0 g Dietary Fiber | 4 g Protein | 21 mg Calcium

4 *POINTS* per serving

lentil, olive, and orange salad

The lentil, popular in stews and soups, takes on a new taste in this refreshing but satisfying salad. Lentils come in several varieties: red, yellow, brown, and French green. Whatever the variety, lentils are quick-cooking, around 20 minutes for most types. Prepare the other salad ingredients while the lentils cook.

makes 4 servings

1 tablespoon fresh lemon juice

1 tablespoon extra-virgin olive oil

2 garlic cloves, minced

1/2 teaspoon ground cumin

1/4 teaspoon salt

Pinch ground cloves

2 cups cooked lentils

2 navel oranges, peeled and sectioned

1 small red onion, chopped

1/4 cup sliced pimiento-stuffed green olives

2 tablespoons chopped fresh parsley

Lettuce or spinach leaves (optional)

Mix the lemon juice, oil, garlic, cumin, salt, and cloves in a bowl. Gently stir in the lentils, orange sections, onion, olives, and parsley. Serve the lentil salad over the lettuce (if using).

4 *POINTS* per serving

Per serving

197 Calories | 5 g Total Fat | 1 g Saturated Fat | 0 mg Cholesterol | 340 mg Sodium
31 g Total Carbohydrate | 10 g Dietary Fiber | 10 g Protein | 63 mg Calcium

red lentil salad

Serve this colorful salad for dinner with grilled salmon, tuna, or sardines. Leftovers can be served over baby spinach leaves with a hard-boiled egg for a simple but nutritious lunch.

makes 6 servings

1. **Prepare the lentils** according to package directions. Let cool.

2. **Heat the oil** in a nonstick skillet, then add the bell pepper, onion, garlic, and jalapeño. Sauté until the onion is translucent, about 3 minutes. Let cool.

3. **Combine the lentils,** tomatoes, the bell pepper mixture, the orange, vinegar, and basil in a large bowl. Refrigerate the salad until well chilled, 1–1 1/2 hours.

1 cup packaged red lentils

2 tablespoons extra-virgin olive oil

1/2 small red bell pepper, chopped

1/2 red onion, chopped

1 tablespoon minced garlic

1/2 teaspoon minced jalapeño pepper (wear gloves to prevent irritation)

3–4 fresh plum tomatoes, peeled, seeded and chopped

1 small orange, peeled and chopped

1 tablespoon balsamic vinegar

1 tablespoon shredded fresh basil

Chef's Tip

To peel the tomatoes, bring a large pot of water to a boil. Have ready a bowl of ice water. Cut a shallow "X" into the bottom of each tomato. Submerge 1 tomato in boiling water for 10–15 seconds. Plunge into ice water, then remove immediately, and peel the tomato with a paring knife, starting at the "X." If the tomato does not peel easily, return it to the boiling water briefly, shock it in the ice water again, and peel. Repeat with the remaining tomatoes. Cut the tomatoes in half horizontally and remove the seeds, then finely chop. Set aside.

Per serving

108 Calories | 5 g Total Fat | 1 g Saturated Fat | 0 mg Cholesterol | 53 mg Sodium
14 g Total Carbohydrate | 4 g Dietary Fiber | 4 g Protein | 27 mg Calcium

2 *POINTS* per serving

italian calamari salad

Calamari (squid), so often deep-fried, are superb when cooked just briefly and served chilled—as they are in this flavorful salad. The flavors are authentically Italian, and you can find the ingredients at your supermarket.

makes 4 servings

³/₄ pound cooked calamari, sliced ¹/₄-inch thick

1 (7-ounce) jar roasted red peppers, drained and cut into 2-inch strips

1 (14-ounce) can artichoke hearts, drained and halved (about 1 cup)

6 scallions, sliced

20 small pitted black olives, halved

8 sun-dried tomato halves (not oil-packed), cut into thin strips

¹/₂ cup shredded basil

4 or 5 garlic cloves, minced

¹/₂ teaspoon salt

Freshly ground pepper

2 tablespoons red wine vinegar

2 teaspoons olive oil

2 cups arugula, rinsed

1 **Combine the calamari,** peppers, artichoke hearts, scallions, olives, sun-dried tomatoes, basil, garlic, salt, and pepper in a large nonreactive bowl. Add the vinegar and oil, and toss to coat. Refrigerate, covered, stirring the mixture occasionally, until the calamari and vegetables are marinated, 2–4 hours.

2 **Arrange the arugula** on plates and top with the calamari salad; serve at once.

Chef's Tips

Calamari are available cooked at some supermarket seafood counters. If purchasing them uncooked, select fresh, briny-smelling squid with clear eyes. Ask the fishmonger to clean and slice the squid. Or, prepare the squid by pulling out the tentacles and insides. Cut the tentacles above the eyes; discard the head and the beak inside it. From the sac remove the quill-like cartilage. Rinse the squid thoroughly and remove the skin from the sac. Cut the sac in ¹/₄-inch slices. Chop the tentacles into 2-inch pieces. Refrigerate for up to 1 day.

To cook the calamari, simmer in a little water until tender, 1–2 minutes (keep the cooking time brief, since squid becomes rubbery when overcooked).

4 *POINTS* per serving

Per serving
192 Calories | 6 g Total Fat | 1 g Saturated Fat | 227 mg Cholesterol | 1,044 mg Sodium
17 g Total Carbohydrate | 5 g Dietary Fiber | 19 g Protein | 126 mg Calcium

lobster and roasted red pepper salad

Rich tasting and gorgeous looking, this is an elegant salad that can be assembled in minutes. Serve it with crusty bread as a light dinner, or serve 6 as a first course. Look for cooked lobster meat at the market. If preparing fresh lobsters, two 1½-pound lobsters should yield enough meat for this salad. Cook the lobster (see page 151), remove the meat, and chill thoroughly. This can be done up to 2 days ahead of serving, but wait until serving time to assemble the salad.

Whisk together the lemon juice, thyme, and oil in a large nonreactive bowl. Add the lobster, peppers, and greens; gently toss to coat. Serve at once.

makes 4 servings

4 teaspoons fresh lemon juice

2 teaspoons chopped thyme

2 teaspoons extra-virgin olive oil

½-pound cooked lobster meat, cut into chunks and chilled, or surimi (imitation crabmeat)

1½ cups (about 4 large) roasted red bell peppers, thinly sliced

4 cups mixed greens, rinsed and torn

Chef's Tip

You can use bottled roasted red peppers, or if you prefer, roast your own: spray the broiler rack with nonstick spray; preheat the broiler. Broil the peppers 5 inches from the heat, turning frequently with tongs, until the skin is shriveled and darkened, 10–20 minutes. Place the peppers in a small bowl, cover with plastic wrap, and let steam for 10 minutes. When cool enough to handle, peel and seed.

Per serving

97 Calories | 3 g Total Fat | 0 g Saturated Fat | 41 mg Cholesterol | 327 mg Sodium
6 g Total Carbohydrate | 1 g Dietary Fiber | 13 g Protein | 65 mg Calcium

2 *POINTS* per serving

grilled chicken and pecan salad

Nutty, sweet, bitter, and tart elements combine in this meal-size salad. Substitute walnuts or almonds for the pecans, if you wish, but be sure to use walnut oil in the dressing—it contributes a great deal of flavor.

makes 4 servings

4 (1/4-pound) skinless boneless chicken breast halves

1/2 cup apple cider

1 tablespoon cider vinegar

1/2 teaspoon Worcestershire sauce

1/2 teaspoon hot pepper sauce

1/2 teaspoon chopped fresh thyme

1 tablespoon walnut oil

2 cups torn arugula, rinsed and dried

1 1/2 cups mixed salad greens, rinsed

1 cup thinly sliced Belgian endive

1 Granny Smith apple, cored and thinly sliced

1/4 cup pecans, toasted

1 **Spray the grill** or broiler rack with nonstick spray; prepare the grill or preheat the broiler. Grill or broil the chicken 5 inches from the heat, turning occasionally until cooked through, 10–12 minutes. Let cool. Thinly slice on the diagonal.

2 **Bring the cider to a boil** in a small saucepan and cook until it is reduced by two-thirds, about 5 minutes. Transfer the cider to a bowl; add the vinegar, Worcestershire sauce, hot pepper sauce, and thyme. Gradually whisk in the oil.

3 **Combine the arugula,** mixed greens, and endive in a large bowl; add the apple and half of the dressing, and gently toss to coat. Arrange the salad on plates and top with the chicken and pecans. Drizzle the chicken with the remaining dressing and serve at once.

Chef's Tip

To toast the pecans, place them in a dry skillet over medium-low heat. Cook, shaking the pan and stirring constantly, until lightly browned and fragrant, 3–5 minutes. Watch carefully; they can burn quickly. Transfer the nuts to a plate to cool.

7 *POINTS* per serving

Per serving
305 Calories | 12 g Total Fat | 2 g Saturated Fat | 96 mg Cholesterol | 105 mg Sodium
9 g Total Carbohydrate | 3 g Dietary Fiber | 37 g Protein | 71 mg Calcium

sesame chicken salad with ginger dressing

Warm sesame-crusted chicken is served over a bed of greens with a sweet and hot dressing in this Asian-inspired salad.

makes 4 servings

1. **To prepare the dressing,** combine the vinegar, soy sauce, honey, ginger, mustard, sesame oil, and red pepper in a small saucepan. Bring the mixture just to a boil, then remove from the heat.

2. **Combine the sesame seeds,** salt, and pepper on a piece of wax paper. Coat the chicken on both sides with the sesame seed mixture.

3. **Heat the vegetable oil** in a large nonstick skillet, then add the chicken. Cook, turning, until cooked through, 4–6 minutes per side. Transfer the chicken to a cutting board. Cut each chicken breast on the diagonal into four pieces.

4. **Arrange the greens** on plates. Keeping the chicken slices together, arrange each chicken breast over the greens. Drizzle each serving with the dressing and serve at once.

2 tablespoons rice vinegar

2 tablespoons reduced-sodium soy sauce

1 tablespoon honey

2 teaspoons minced peeled fresh ginger

1 teaspoon dry mustard

1 teaspoon Asian (dark) sesame oil

$1/4$ teaspoon crushed red pepper

3 tablespoons sesame seeds

$1/2$ teaspoon salt

Freshly ground pepper

4 ($1/4$-pound) skinless boneless chicken breast halves

1 tablespoon vegetable oil

4 cups rinsed mixed baby greens, or shredded rinsed romaine lettuce

Chef's Tip

Rice vinegar, made from fermented rice, is available in Asian markets, or the Asian food section of some supermarkets. It is mild tasting, with a sweet note.

Per serving

257 Calories | 11 g Total Fat | 2 g Saturated Fat | 72 mg Cholesterol | 629 mg Sodium
9 g Total Carbohydrate | 1 g Dietary Fiber | 29 g Protein | 100 mg Calcium

6 *POINTS* per serving

thai beef salad

This spicy salad is served warm over a bed of spinach for a hearty lunch or a light supper. Try thinly sliced cabbage as an alternative to spinach.

makes 4 servings

1/2 pound beef tenderloin or boneless sirloin, cut into 1/2-inch strips

1 medium onion, finely chopped

3 tablespoons reduced-sodium soy sauce

1 jalapeño pepper, seeded, deveined, and minced (wear gloves to prevent irritation)

2 garlic cloves, minced

1 teaspoon minced peeled fresh ginger

1 cup bean sprouts

1/4 cup minced fresh cilantro

2 teaspoons Asian (dark) sesame oil

1 (10-ounce) bag triple-washed spinach, rinsed and torn

1 **Spray a large nonstick wok** or skillet with nonstick spray and set over high heat. Add the beef and sauté until no longer pink, about 30 seconds. Add the onion, soy sauce, jalapeño, garlic, and ginger. Stir-fry until the onion is softened, 2–3 minutes. Remove from the heat. Add the bean sprouts, cilantro, and oil; toss to combine.

2 **Arrange the spinach** in bowls and top with the warm beef mixture.

3 *POINTS* per serving

Per serving

175 Calories | 9 g Total Fat | 2 g Saturated Fat | 44 mg Cholesterol | 537 mg Sodium
6 g Total Carbohydrate | 7 g Dietary Fiber | 19 g Protein | 84 mg Calcium

balsamic vinaigrette

The flavor of this vinaigrette depends on the quality of the balsamic vinegar used. A good-quality aged balsamic will have a mild acidity, a slightly sweet-and-sour note on the palate, and a syrupy consistency. In addition to salad dressing, try this vinaigrette as a marinade for grilled portobello mushrooms.

makes 8 servings

1/2 cup low-sodium vegetable or chicken broth

3/4 teaspoon arrowroot, dissolved in 1 teaspoon water

1/4 cup balsamic vinegar

1/4 cup extra-virgin olive oil

2 teaspoons finely chopped fresh basil

1/8 teaspoon salt

1 **Bring the broth to a boil** in a saucepan. Slowly add the arrowroot mixture; stirring constantly until thickened, about 1 minute. Remove the pan from the heat; stir in the vinegar, and let cool completely.

2 **Gradually whisk in the oil,** then season with the basil, and salt. Refrigerate the vinaigrette in an airtight container for up to 4 days.

Chef's Tip

The standard ratio of oil to vinegar (or another acidic ingredient) in a regular vinai-grette dressing is 3 to 1. To make a reduced-fat, vinaigrette-style dressing, up to 2 parts of the oil may be replaced with thickened chicken or vegetable broth, as this and the following recipes illustrate. The thickened broth has a neutral flavor and viscosity similar to oil, yet is virtually fat-free. The resulting reduced-fat dressing clings to greens as well as the full-fat version and has a comparable flavor. Arrowroot is the preferred starch for this technique because it results in a clear, translucent broth; cornstarch may be substituted, but the broth will be cloudy

Per serving (2 tablespoons)
74 Calories | 7 g Total Fat | 1 g Saturated Fat | 0 mg Cholesterol | 83 mg Sodium
3 g Total Carbohydrate | 0 g Dietary Fiber | 0 g Protein | 2 mg Calcium

2 POINTS per serving

lime-cilantro dressing

With the pronounced flavors of lime, sesame oil, and cilantro, this dressing works well with grilled seafood, such as shrimp or scallops, over tossed greens. It's also delicious drizzled over a whole roasted red snapper.

makes 8 servings

$1/2$ cup low-sodium vegetable broth

1 teaspoon arrowroot, dissolved in 2 teaspoons of water

$1/4$ cup fresh lime juice

$1/4$ teaspoon sugar

3 tablespoons peanut oil

1 tablespoon Asian (dark) sesame oil

$1/2$ teaspoon chopped fresh cilantro

$1/8$ teaspoon salt

1 **Bring the broth** to a boil in a saucepan. Slowly add the arrowroot mixture, stirring constantly until thickened, about 1 minute. Remove from the heat; stir in the lime juice and sugar; let cool completely.

2 **Gradually whisk** in the peanut and sesame oils, the cilantro, and salt. Refrigerate the dressing in an airtight container for up to 4 days.

2 *POINTS* per serving

Per serving (2 tablespoons)
66 Calories | 7 g Total Fat | 1 g Saturated Fat | 0 mg Cholesterol | 45 mg Sodium
1 g Total Carbohydrate | 0 g Dietary Fiber | 0 g Protein | 2 mg Calcium

peppercorn parmesan dressing

This dressing is delicious drizzled over bitter greens such as arugula and radicchio, or sprinkled inside a roast beef sandwich. Increase or reduce the amount of crushed peppercorns to suit your taste.

makes 8 servings

Combine the vinegar and oil in a small jar with a lid and shake. Add the cheese and pepper, seal the jar, and shake again. Refrigerate the dressing in an airtight container for up to 1 week.

$1/4$ cup balsamic vinegar

$1 1/2$ tablespoons extra-virgin olive oil

$1/2$ cup grated Parmesan cheese

1 tablespoon crushed black peppercorns

Per serving (2 tablespoons)

49 Calories | 4 g Total Fat | 1 g Saturated Fat | 4 mg Cholesterol | 93 mg Sodium
2 g Total Carbohydrate | 0 g Dietary Fiber | 2 g Protein | 71 mg Calcium

1 *POINT* per serving

blue cheese dressing

Although any quality blue cheese may be used in this sharp and creamy dressing, domestically produced Maytag blue cheese or Italian-produced Gorgonzola will produce the smoothest texture and boldest flavor. For a simple appetizer salad, serve the dressing as a dip with vegetable crudités or toss with a salad of frisée (curly endive), Belgian endive, roasted red peppers, and crisp-cooked, crumbled bacon.

makes 6 servings

^{1}/$_4$ cup + 2 tablespoons part-skim ricotta cheese

^{1}/$_4$ cup nonfat buttermilk

^{1}/$_4$ cup crumbled blue cheese

1 tablespoon cider vinegar

^{1}/$_2$ teaspoon Worcestershire sauce

^{1}/$_2$ teaspoon ketchup

2 teaspoons chopped fresh chives

Freshly ground pepper

Puree the ricotta, buttermilk, blue cheese, vinegar, Worcestershire sauce, and ketchup in a food processor or blender. Transfer to a small bowl; fold in the chives and pepper. Refrigerate the dressing in an airtight container for up to 2 days.

---

1 *POINT* per serving

Per serving (2 tablespoons)
44 Calories | 3 g Total Fat | 2 g Saturated Fat | 9 mg Cholesterol | 116 mg Sodium
2 g Total Carbohydrate | 0 g Dietary Fiber | 3 g Protein | 80 mg Calcium

horseradish and apple cream dressing

This tangy dressing makes an unusual dip for vegetables—or serve it as a spread with smoked fish or seafood sausage. If you do not plan to use the dressing right away, wait until just before serving to grate and add the apple.

makes 8 servings

1 **Puree the ricotta** in a food processor or blender. Add the yogurt cheese and vinegar; blend until smooth.

2 **By hand,** stir in the apple and horseradish. Season with a little lemon juice and pepper, if using. Refrigerate the dressing in an airtight container up to 2 days.

1/4 cup part-skim ricotta cheese

1/4 cup yogurt cheese

2 tablespoons red wine vinegar

1 small Granny Smith apple, peeled, cored and grated

2 1/4 teaspoons prepared horseradish, well drained

Lemon juice (optional)

Freshly ground pepper (optional)

Chef's Tip

To make the yogurt cheese, spoon 1/2 cup plain nonfat yogurt into a strainer lined with a coffee filter or cheesecloth and placed over a bowl. Cover and refrigerate at least 5 hours or overnight. Discard the liquid in the bowl.

Per serving (2 tablespoons)

27 Calories | 1 g Total Fat | 1 g Saturated Fat | 3 mg Cholesterol | 22 mg Sodium
3 g Total Carbohydrate | 1 g Dietary Fiber | 2 g Protein | 51 mg Calcium

0 *POINTS* per serving

port wine vinaigrette

Port wine gives this dressing its complex, deep flavor. The contrast of walnut oil to slightly sweet port makes this dressing an intriguing complement to most salads (see Winter Greens with Blue Cheese and Pine Nuts, page 30); it can also be used as a marinade for meats.

makes 8 servings

1/4 cup + 2 tablespoons vegetable broth

1/4 cup tawny port wine

2 teaspoons arrowroot

1/4 cup red wine vinegar

1/4 cup walnut oil

1/8 teaspoon salt

Pinch crushed black peppercorns

1 **Bring 1/4 cup of the broth** and the port to a boil in a saucepan. Whisk together the remaining 2 tablespoons broth and the arrowroot in a small cup. Slowly add the arrowroot mixture to the boiling broth mixture; stirring constantly until thickened, about 1 minute. Remove from the heat; stir in the vinegar, and let cool completely.

2 **Gradually whisk in the oil,** then season with the salt and pepper. Refrigerate the vinaigrette, in an air-tight container for up to 4 days.

Chef's Tip

Originally from Portugal, port is a sweet fortified wine now produced in many other countries. Vintage ports are of a single vintage, meaning that they are made from grapes harvested in a specific year, and are wood-aged from two to more than 50 years. They are usually the most expensive and should be saved for sipping, not cooking. Tawny ports are wood-aged up to 40 years and have a smooth, rich flavor. Ruby ports, the least expensive type, are usually wood-aged about two years and have the strongest fruit flavor. Blended from different vintages, tawny and ruby ports are both used frequently for cooking.

Per serving (2 tablespoons)

2 *POINTS* per serving

77 Calories | 7 g Total Fat | 1 g Saturated Fat | 0 mg Cholesterol | 41 mg Sodium
2 g Total Carbohydrate | 0 g Dietary Fiber | 0 g Protein | 2 mg Calcium

chapter 4

soups

asparagus soup

Fresh asparagus is readily available year-round, so you can enjoy this elegant first course anytime. If you're only cooking for two, the leftover soup does double duty as a refreshingly different sauce, drizzled over a main dish of grilled chicken breast.

makes 4 servings

1 1/2 pounds asparagus, trimmed

1 teaspoon unsalted butter

1/3 cup finely chopped onion

1 garlic clove, minced

3 cups low-sodium chicken broth

1/3 cup long-grain rice

1/3 cup evaporated fat-free milk

1/2 teaspoon grated lemon zest

1/2 teaspoon salt

2 tablespoons light sour cream

1 **Cut the tips** from 12 asparagus spears and reserve. Coarsely chop the spear bottoms and the remaining spears; reserve separately.

2 **Melt the butter** in a saucepan, then add the onion and garlic. Sauté until the onion is tender, 3–4 minutes. Stir in the chopped asparagus, the broth, and the rice; bring to a boil. Reduce the heat and simmer, partially covered, until the asparagus and rice are tender, 30–35 minutes.

3 **Meanwhile, fill a saucepan** with enough water to cover the reserved asparagus tips; bring to a boil. Add the asparagus tips; simmer, covered, until tender, 5–7 minutes. Drain in a colander and rinse under cold water to stop the cooking.

4 **Transfer the soup** to a blender or food processor and puree, in batches if necessary to prevent overflows. Strain the puree by pressing against the sieve with a spoon, then return it to the saucepan. Stir in the milk, zest, and salt; return to a simmer.

5 **To serve,** ladle into 4 bowls; top each with 1/2 tablespoon of the sour cream and 3 of the asparagus tips.

---

2 *POINTS* per serving

Per serving

145 Calories | 2 g Total Fat | 1 g Saturated Fat | 5 mg Cholesterol | 766 mg Sodium
24 g Total Carbohydrate | 3 g Dietary Fiber | 11 g Protein | 108 mg Calcium

hot and spicy tofu soup with thai flavors

Thailand's cuisine is both delicious and visually appealing. Thai dishes offer a layering of flavors including sweet, salty, and sour or tart tastes plus the heat of chiles and the pungency of garlic. You'll find an intriguing flavor combination in this soup. The Asian sesame oil used here has much stronger flavor than regular sesame oil. It and the other ingredients are available in supermarkets or Asian markets.

1 **Heat 1 tablespoon of the oil** in a large nonstick skillet over medium heat, then add the ginger and garlic. Sauté until softened, about 1 minute. Add the green beans, carrot, and bell pepper; cook, stirring frequently, until the vegetables are softened, about 5 minutes.

2 **Combine the water,** chili sauce, soy sauce, the remaining 1 teaspoon oil, and the crushed red pepper in a small bowl; stir into the vegetable mixture. Stir in the broth and tofu and bring to a boil. Reduce the heat and simmer, stirring constantly, until heated through, about 1 minute.

makes 4 servings

1 tablespoon + 1 teaspoon Asian sesame oil

1 tablespoon minced peeled fresh ginger

3 garlic cloves, minced

1/4 pound green beans, trimmed and cut into 1-inch pieces

1/2 medium carrot, peeled and thinly sliced

1/2 medium red bell pepper, thinly sliced

1/4 cup water

3 tablespoons chili sauce

1 tablespoon reduced-sodium soy sauce

1/4 teaspoon crushed red pepper

3 1/2 cups low-sodium vegetable or chicken broth

1/2 pound firm tofu, cut into 1-inch cubes

Per serving

142 Calories | 7 g Total Fat | 1 g Saturated Fat | 0 mg Cholesterol | 790 mg Sodium
12 g Total Carbohydrate | 3 g Dietary Fiber | 9 g Protein | 137 mg Calcium

3 POINTS per serving

beet-fennel-ginger soup

Richly colored and full of complex flavors, this easy-to-make soup may also be served hot. The ginger, though initially subtle, lingers in both flavor and heat after finishing the soup. The soup can be made 1 day ahead and refrigerated, in an airtight container.

makes 4 servings

2 1/2 cups low-sodium vegetable broth

1/4 medium head savoy cabbage, chopped

1 large beet, peeled and chopped

1/2 fennel bulb, trimmed and chopped

1 garlic clove, minced

1 teaspoon minced peeled fresh ginger

1/4 teaspoon lemon juice

1/4 teaspoon salt

Freshly ground pepper

4 tablespoons plain nonfat yogurt

1 **Combine the broth,** cabbage, beet, fennel, garlic, and ginger in a saucepan and bring to a boil. Reduce the heat and simmer, covered, until the beet is tender, about 10 minutes. Remove from the heat and let cool slightly.

2 **Transfer the mixture** to a blender or food processor and puree, working in batches if necessary to avoid overflows. Pour the soup into a large bowl. Season with the lemon juice, salt, and pepper. If necessary, thin the soup with enough cold water to reach a pourable consistency. Refrigerate, covered, until chilled, 3–4 hours or overnight. Serve, topped with the yogurt.

0 *POINTS* per serving

Per serving
42 Calories | 0 g Total Fat | 0 g Saturated Fat | 0 mg Cholesterol | 517 mg Sodium
8 g Total Carbohydrate | 2 g Dietary Fiber | 2 g Protein | 41 mg Calcium

beet-fennel-ginger soup

japanese winter vegetable soup

This is a classic, home-style Japanese soup. Mirin, also referred to as rice wine, is a staple in Japanese kitchens. Substitute sweet sherry if you can't find mirin at your local wine store or Asian grocery. Miso—fermented soybean paste—comes in several varieties. In general, lighter-colored miso is used for lighter soups, while the darker varieties are used in dishes where more robust flavor is desired. It's your choice in this recipe. Look for it in health food stores or Asian markets.

makes 4 servings

1 pound firm reduced-fat tofu, halved lengthwise

2 teaspoons vegetable oil

2 cups water

1 cup low-sodium vegetable or chicken broth

2 large all-purpose potatoes, peeled and cubed

2 carrots, peeled and cut into $1/4$-inch cubes

1 cup sliced daikon

1 onion, chopped

$1/2$ cup mirin

$1/4$ cup miso

1 tablespoon sugar

1 **Place the tofu** in a single layer between two small flat plates. Weight the top with a heavy can. Let stand 30–60 minutes (do not press for longer than 60 minutes). Pour off and discard the water. Cut the tofu into cubes.

2 **Heat a large nonstick skillet.** Swirl in the oil, then add the tofu. Sauté until golden, 5–6 minutes. Add the water and broth; bring to a boil. Stir in the potatoes, carrots, daikon, and onion; return to a boil. Reduce the heat and simmer until the potatoes are tender, about 20 minutes.

3 **Combine the mirin,** miso, and sugar with $1/4$ cup of the vegetable cooking liquid in a small bowl. Stir until the miso dissolves, then add the mixture to the skillet. Heat, gently stirring just until warmed—do not boil the mixture. Divide the soup into bowls and serve.

6 *POINTS* per serving

Per serving

302 Calories | 4 g Total Fat | 1 g Saturated Fat | 0 mg Cholesterol | 911 mg Sodium
54 g Total Carbohydrate | 5 g Dietary Fiber | 12 g Protein | 84 mg Calcium

sweet potato soup

Sweet potato soup is smooth, rich and satisfying. It's simple to prepare and makes an elegant first course for a fall dinner party or Thanksgiving feast.

makes 4 servings

1 tablespoon sliced almonds

3 cups low-sodium chicken broth

1/3 cup finely chopped onion

1/4 cup finely chopped celery

1 small garlic clove, minced

1 pound sweet potatoes, peeled, cut into 1-inch pieces

1 (2-inch) piece of cinnamon stick

Pinch ground nutmeg

2 tablespoons evaporated fat-free milk

1 teaspoon pure maple syrup

1/4 teaspoon salt

2 tablespoons plain nonfat yogurt

1 **To toast the almonds,** place them in a skillet over medium-low heat; cook, shaking the pan and stirring constantly, until golden brown and fragrant, 3–5 minutes.

2 **Heat 2 tablespoons** of the broth in a saucepan; add the onion, celery, and garlic. Cook until softened, about 5 minutes. Add the remaining broth, the sweet potatoes, cinnamon stick, and nutmeg; bring to a boil. Reduce the heat and simmer, covered, until the potatoes are tender, about 15 minutes. Discard the cinnamon stick.

3 **Transfer the sweet potato mixture** to a blender or food processor and puree, in batches if necessary to prevent overflows. Return the puree to the saucepan. Stir in the milk, syrup, and salt; return to a boil. If necessary, thin the soup with a small amount of water. Serve, topped with the yogurt and sprinkled with the almonds.

Per serving

160 Calories | 1 g Total Fat | 0 g Saturated Fat | 0 mg Cholesterol | 635 mg Sodium
33 g Total Carbohydrate | 4 g Dietary Fiber | 6 g Protein | 74 mg Calcium

2 *POINTS* per serving

zucchini soup with cheddar rusks

A rusk is a slice of bread that is baked or broiled until it becomes crisp and golden brown. In this recipe, rusks are topped with a sprinkle of cheddar cheese for added flavor and richness. As in French onion soup, the rusk tops the soup where it softens and absorbs the flavors of the soup.

makes 4 servings

1 bacon slice, minced

1/2 cup finely chopped onion

1 garlic clove, minced

1 medium zucchini, cut into 1/2-inch cubes

2 cups low-sodium chicken broth

1 plum tomato, peeled, seeded, and chopped

3 tablespoons canned tomato puree

1 tablespoon tarragon or cider vinegar

4 (1/2-inch) slices French or Italian bread

1/4 cup grated cheddar cheese

1/2 tablespoon minced basil leaves

1/4 teaspoon salt

Freshly ground pepper

1 **Cook the bacon** in a saucepan until crisp, about 5 minutes. Add the onion and garlic and sauté until the onions are a light golden brown, 8–10 minutes.

2 **Add the zucchini** and cook, covered, until it starts to become softened, about 5 minutes. Add the broth, tomato, tomato puree, and vinegar; raise the heat and bring the soup to a boil. Reduce the heat to low and simmer until all the vegetables are very tender, 15–20 minutes.

3 **Meanwhile, to prepare the rusks,** preheat the broiler. Broil the bread slices 5 inches from the heat, turning once, until golden brown on both sides, about 4 minutes. Top with the cheese and continue broiling until the cheese bubbles and begins to brown, about 1 minute.

4 **Just before serving the soup,** add the basil and season with salt, pepper, and, if desired, more vinegar. Serve the soup, each topped with a cheddar rusk.

Chef's Tips

Large zucchini can have bitter seeds; cut the zucchini in half lengthwise, scoop out and discard the seeds with a metal spoon. Then the zucchini can be cubed. For smaller zucchini, the whole squash can be used, seeds and all.

For a vegetarian soup, omit the bacon and use a teaspoon or two of olive oil to sauté the onion and garlic in Step 1. Replace the chicken broth with vegetable broth and add a tablespoon of minced sun-dried tomatoes along with the basil in Step 4.

3 POINTS per serving

Per serving

165 Calories | 5 g Total Fat | 3 g Saturated Fat | 11 mg Cholesterol | 468 mg Sodium
22 g Total Carbohydrate | 3 g Dietary Fiber | 8 g Protein | 109 mg Calcium

curried apple-squash soup

This mildly spicy soup is perfect for an early fall lunch. It is easy to make and can be prepared up to a day ahead.

makes 6 servings

1 Heat $^1/_4$ **cup of the broth** in a saucepan, then add the onion, celery, and half of the garlic. Cook until softened, about 5 minutes. Add the remaining $2^3/_4$ cups broth, the curry powder, cinnamon, and nutmeg; bring to a boil. Add the squash; reduce the heat and simmer 8 minutes. Add the apples; simmer until the apples and squash are tender, 7–8 minutes.

2 **Transfer the mixture** to a blender or food processor and puree, working in batches if necessary to prevent overflows. Pour into a large bowl and stir in the salt. Refrigerate, covered, until chilled, 3–4 hours or overnight.

3 cups low-sodium chicken broth

1 onion, finely chopped

1 stalk celery, finely chopped

1 garlic clove, minced

$1^1/_4$ teaspoons curry powder

$^1/_2$ teaspoon ground cinnamon

$^1/_4$ teaspoon ground nutmeg

$1^1/_2$ pounds (about $^1/_2$ medium) butternut squash, peeled, seeded, and cut into 1-inch cubes

2 Granny Smith apples, cored, peeled, and chopped

$^1/_2$ teaspoon salt

variation

To add a zesty kick to this dish, top it with a mixture of lime, thyme, and garlic, a refreshing counterpoint to the sweetness of the soup. Combine 1 minced garlic clove, 1 teaspoon grated lime zest, and $^1/_4$ teaspoon minced thyme in a small bowl. Sprinkle mixture over soup, just before serving.

Chef's Tip

To peel the squash, cut in half crosswise, separating the narrow top part of the squash from the round bottom part. This step makes it easier to handle the squash. Remove the seeds. Use a very sharp, sturdy vegetable peeler or a sharp knife to cut the skin away from the squash.

Per serving

94 Calories | 0 g Total Fat | 0 g Saturated Fat | 1 mg Cholesterol | 502 mg Sodium
22 g Total Carbohydrate | 5 g Dietary Fiber | 3 g Protein | 66 mg Calcium

1 *POINT* per serving

chilled plum soup

This delicate fruit soup of apple juice, plums, honey, and lemon juice is infused with aromatic spices. Serve it as a refreshing first course or dessert.

makes 4 servings

1 tablespoon slivered almonds

2 cups apple juice

4 medium plums, pitted and chopped

2 tablespoons honey

1 thyme sprig

1 (1/4-inch) slice peeled fresh ginger

4 black peppercorns

1/4 teaspoon cinnamon

Pinch allspice

1 1/2 teaspoons fresh lemon juice

4 tablespoons light sour cream

1 **Toast the almonds** in a skillet, shaking the pan and stirring constantly, until lightly browned, 3–5 minutes.

2 **Combine the apple juice,** plums, honey, thyme, ginger, peppercorns, cinnamon, and allspice in a medium saucepan; bring to a boil. Reduce the heat and simmer until the plums are tender, 12–15 minutes.

3 **Discard the ginger,** thyme, and peppercorns. Transfer the plum mixture to a blender or food processor and puree. Stir in the lemon juice. Refrigerate, covered, until chilled, 3–4 hours or overnight. Serve, topped with the sour cream and sprinkled with the almonds.

4 *POINTS* per serving

Per serving

230 Calories | 2 g Total Fat | 1 g Saturated Fat | 3 mg Cholesterol | 16 mg Sodium
54 g Total Carbohydrate | 3 g Dietary Fiber | 2 g Protein | 34 mg Calcium

tortilla soup

Toasted corn tortillas thicken this lightly spicy and thoroughly satisfying soup. Use leftover roasted or grilled chicken, or buy one pre-roasted at your supermarket.

makes 4 servings

1 **Preheat the oven** to 200°F. Thinly slice one of the tortillas; place on a baking sheet with the remaining tortillas. Bake until crisp, 15–20 minutes. Crush the whole tortillas into small pieces.

2 **Heat 2 tablespoons** of the broth in a saucepan, then add the onion and garlic. Cook until softened, about 2 minutes. Add the remaining broth, the crushed tortillas, the tomato puree, cilantro, cumin, chili powder, bay leaf, and salt. Bring the mixture to a boil, reduce the heat, and simmer 20 minutes. Discard the bay leaf. Transfer the mixture to a blender or food processor and puree, working in batches if necessary to avoid overflows.

3 **To serve,** ladle the soup into 4 bowls; top each serving with equal amounts of tortilla strips, chicken, avocado, and cheese.

3 (6-inch) corn tortillas

4 cups low-sodium chicken broth

1 large onion, chopped

2 garlic cloves, minced

$1/2$ cup tomato puree

1 tablespoon chopped cilantro

1 teaspoon ground cumin

1 teaspoon chili powder

1 bay leaf

$1/2$ teaspoon salt

1 (4-ounce) roasted or grilled boneless chicken breast half, skinned and cut into thin strips

$1/4$ cup chopped avocado

4 tablespoons shredded cheddar cheese

Per serving

186 Calories | 6 g Total Fat | 2 g Saturated Fat | 30 mg Cholesterol | 958 mg Sodium
20 g Total Carbohydrate | 5 g Dietary Fiber | 16 g Protein | 103 mg Calcium

3 *POINTS* per serving

michigan white bean soup

Great Northern beans—large, white, and delicate tasting—are grown in the Midwest and can be used in any recipe calling for white beans. For a quick, weeknight version of this nourishing soup, use 2 cups of drained and rinsed canned beans—there is no need to soak them. Reduce the broth to 3 cups and simmer for only 15 minutes. The soup, in either version, is terrific served with warm semolina bread.

makes 4 servings

3/4 cup dried great Northern beans, picked over, rinsed, and drained

5 cups low-sodium chicken broth

1 bacon slice, chopped

1/4 cup finely chopped leek, rinsed

1/4 cup finely chopped red onion

2 garlic cloves, minced

1 small bay leaf

1 thyme sprig

1/2 teaspoon red wine vinegar

Freshly ground pepper

1 **Combine the beans** with enough cold water to cover by 3 inches in a saucepan. Bring the water to a boil and then remove the pan from the heat. Cover and let stand 1 hour; drain.

2 **Combine the beans** and broth in the saucepan; bring to a boil. Reduce the heat and simmer gently, partially covered, until the beans are almost tender, about 45 minutes.

3 **Meanwhile, cook the bacon** in a nonstick skillet until crisp, about 6 minutes. Add the leek, onion, and garlic. Sauté until the onion is softened, about 3 minutes.

4 **Add the onion mixture,** the bay leaf, and thyme to the beans. Simmer until the beans are completely tender, 15–20 minutes. Discard the bay leaf and thyme. Season with the vinegar and pepper.

2 POINTS per serving

Per serving

142 Calories | 1 g Total Fat | 0 g Saturated Fat | 1 mg Cholesterol | 804 mg Sodium
22 g Total Carbohydrate | 6 g Dietary Fiber | 12 g Protein | 69 mg Calcium

indian lentil soup

Unlike other dried legumes, lentils don't need to be soaked. In fact, this lightly spicy, one-pot soup can be ready to eat in just an hour whenever the craving strikes.

makes 4 servings

1 **Heat the oil** in a medium saucepan, then add the onion. Sauté until softened, about 5 minutes. Add the ginger, garlic, cumin, and coriander; cook, stirring, 1 minute.

2 **Stir in the water,** tomatoes, lentils, and salt; bring to a boil. Reduce the heat and simmer until the lentils are soft, 35–45 minutes. Transfer 2 cups of the lentil mixture to a blender or food processor and puree. Stir the puree into the lentils and simmer until the soup is heated through, 3–5 minutes. Just before serving, stir in the lemon juice and sprinkle with the cilantro.

1 tablespoon olive oil

1 medium onion, chopped

2 tablespoons minced peeled fresh ginger

4 garlic cloves, minced

1 teaspoon ground cumin

1/2 teaspoon ground coriander

4 cups water

1 (14-ounce) can crushed tomatoes (no salt added)

1 cup dried green lentils, picked over, rinsed, and drained

1/2 teaspoon salt

2 teaspoons fresh lemon juice

1/4 cup chopped cilantro

Per serving
234 Calories | 4 g Total Fat | 1 g Saturated Fat | 0 mg Cholesterol | 340 mg Sodium
37 g Total Carbohydrate | 17 g Dietary Fiber | 15 g Protein | 58 mg Calcium

4 *POINTS* per serving

wonton soup

The wontons in this Chinese restaurant favorite get their mildly sweet taste from *hoisin* (Chinese barbecue) sauce. You'll easily master the versatile technique for making them. Experiment with wrapping vegetable or meat fillings to make dumplings for your next cocktail party. Look for hoisin and tamari (a dark, mellow-flavored kind of soy sauce) in the Asian food section of your supermarket. Wonton skins can be found in the refrigerator case.

makes 4 servings

4 cups low-sodium chicken broth

1 (1/4-pound) skinless boneless chicken breast half

1/4 cup julienned carrot

1 1/2 ounces soft tofu (about 1/4 cup)

1/4 cup chopped scallions

3 garlic cloves, minced

1 tablespoon minced peeled fresh ginger

1 tablespoon hoisin sauce

12 (3-inch square) wonton skins

1 tablespoon tamari or soy sauce

1 star anise

1 thin slice fresh ginger

1/4 cup shredded bok choy leaves

1/4 cup julienned leek (white part only), rinsed

1 **Bring the broth** to a boil in a saucepan, and then add the chicken. Reduce the heat and simmer, covered, until the chicken is cooked through, about 8 minutes. Strain and reserve the broth. When the chicken is cool enough to handle, shred it into thin, 1-inch strips.

2 **Meanwhile, fill a small saucepan** with enough water to cover the carrot; bring to a boil and add the carrot. Simmer, covered, until tender-crisp, 2 minutes. Drain the carrot in a colander and rinse under cold water to stop the cooking; set aside.

3 **To prepare the filling,** combine the chicken, tofu, scallions, garlic, minced ginger, and hoisin sauce in a bowl. Mash together the mixture with a fork. Drop a tablespoon of the filling into the center of each wonton skin. Brush the edges with water, then fold the wrapper into a triangle. Press the filling to release any trapped air, and then press the edges to seal the wontons. Bring together the two points of the triangle, then twist and press the points together. Repeat with the remaining filling and wonton skins to make 12 wontons.

4 **Combine the reserved broth,** the tamari, star anise, and ginger slice in a saucepan; bring to a boil. Reduce the heat and simmer, covered, 20 minutes. Remove and discard the star anise and ginger.

5 **Meanwhile, cook the wontons** in a large pot of simmering water until they rise to the surface, about 3 minutes; drain.

6 **Add the bok choy,** leek, and carrot to the broth and bring just to a simmer, then remove the pan from the heat. To serve, divide the wontons, vegetables, and soup among 4 bowls.

3 *POINTS* per serving

Per serving
158 Calories | 2 g Total Fat | 0 g Saturated Fat | 28 mg Cholesterol | 1,112 mg Sodium
19 g Total Carbohydrate | 1 g Dietary Fiber | 16 g Protein | 25 mg Calcium

cutting julienne

Cut the vegetable into 2-inch pieces. Trim the vegetable so that the sides are straight, making it easier to produce even cuts. (The trimmings can be used for stocks, soups, purees, or any preparation where the shape is not important.)

Slice the vegetable lengthwise, using parallel cuts about $1/8$-inch thick.

Stack the slices, aligning the edges, and make parallel cuts of the same thickness through the stack.

amish-style chicken and corn soup

Despite its plain image, Amish cooking is notable for its clever use of herbs and spices. Here, saffron gives the soup a deep golden color as well as a subtle flavor. If you prefer, the soup can be prepared without the saffron.

makes 4 servings

4 cups low-sodium chicken broth

1 chicken leg quarter (drumstick and thigh), skinned

$1/2$ medium onion, chopped

$1/2$ carrot, peeled and chopped

$1/2$ celery stalk, coarsely chopped

$1/2$ teaspoon crushed saffron threads (optional)

$1/2$ cup corn kernels (fresh or frozen)

$1/2$ cup cooked egg noodles

$1/2$ celery stalk, cut into small cubes

$1/2$ tablespoon chopped parsley

1 **Combine the broth,** chicken leg, onion, carrot, chopped celery, and the saffron, if using, in a saucepan. Bring the mixture to a boil, reduce the heat and simmer, covered, 45 minutes, occasionally skimming off any scum that accumulates on the surface.

2 **Remove the chicken** with tongs and transfer to a plate. Strain the broth through a fine sieve. When the chicken is cool enough to handle, remove the bones and cut the meat into $1/4$-inch cubes.

3 **Add the chicken meat,** corn, noodles, cubed celery, and parsley to the broth. Bring the soup to a simmer and serve immediately.

Chef's Tip

This soup can be completed through Step 2 in advance. The broth and chicken meat can be refrigerated for 2–3 days, or frozen for up to 3 months. Store them in separate airtight containers and label and date them. To serve, heat the broth to a full boil, then add the meat and remaining ingredients to complete the soup.

3 _POINTS_ per serving

Per serving

143 Calories | 5 g Total Fat | 2 g Saturated Fat | 36 mg Cholesterol | 184 mg Sodium
13 g Total Carbohydrate | 1 g Dietary Fiber | 13 g Protein | 35 mg Calcium

amish-style chicken and corn soup

seafood minestrone

You can make this quick and easy minestrone chock full of seafood: Just cut an 8-ounce fillet of catfish or another white fish into $3/4$-inch chunks and add it to the soup with the mussels and shrimp. Although it's best eaten right away, you can reheat the soup up to a day later; thin with a little water first, as the soup will thicken when cooled.

makes 4 servings

8 medium mussels, scrubbed and debearded

2 tablespoons dry white wine

3 cups fish broth or clam juice

$1/2$ bacon slice, thinly sliced

1 small leek, rinsed and chopped

1 small onion, sliced

2 garlic cloves, minced

2 teaspoons Italian herb seasoning

$3/4$ cup canned red kidney beans, rinsed and drained

3 plum tomatoes, chopped

3 tablespoons Arborio rice

1 ($1/2$-inch) lemon slice

1 bay leaf

Freshly ground pepper

4 medium shrimp, peeled, deveined and chopped

$1/4$ teaspoon salt

1 **Combine the mussels,** wine, and 3 tablespoons of the broth in a saucepan. Bring to a simmer and cook, covered, until the mussels open, about 4 minutes. Transfer the mussels to a bowl with a slotted spoon. Discard any mussels that don't open. Return any liquid from the mussels back to the saucepan. Strain the mixture and set aside. Remove the mussels from their shells; coarsely chop them and refrigerate until needed.

2 **Cook the bacon** in a saucepan until crisp, about 6 minutes. Add the leek, onion, garlic, and Italian seasoning and sauté until the vegetables are softened. Stir in the remaining broth, the reserved mussel cooking broth, the beans, tomatoes, rice, lemon, bay leaf, and pepper; bring to a boil. Reduce the heat, cover, and simmer until the rice is tender, about 15 minutes.

3 **Add the chopped mussels,** shrimp, and salt; simmer until the shrimp are pink, about 3 minutes. Discard the bay leaf and lemon slice.

Chef's Tips

The hairy filaments that protrude from a mussel are known as a "beard." To remove, pinch the filaments between thumb and forefinger and pull firmly. Wait to debeard mussels until as close to cooking time as possible. Scrub mussels thoroughly under running water before cooking.

To clean shrimp, remove the shells and the intestinal tract, or vein, a process known as "deveining." After the shell is removed, lay the shrimp on a cutting board with the curved outer edge (the back) of the shrimp on the same side as your cutting hand. Using a paring knife, make a shallow cut along the back of the shrimp from the head end to the tail. Use the edge of the knife to scrape out the vein, which may be either clear or dark.

3 *POINTS* per serving

Per serving
159 Calories | 2 g Total Fat | 0 g Saturated Fat | 17 mg Cholesterol | 855 mg Sodium
26 g Total Carbohydrate | 3 g Dietary Fiber | 9 g Protein | 63 mg Calcium

crab and wild mushroom chowder

The stems of meaty, full-flavored shiitake mushrooms are typically too tough to eat. Reserve them to make a quick-cooking mushroom stock, which adds extra-rich flavor to this impressive soup. Sweet lump crabmeat is the finishing touch for this chowder. Buy the freshest you can find, and pick through it to remove any bits of shell, being careful not to break up the lumps too much.

makes 4 servings

1 **Remove the stems** from the mushrooms and chop them. Thinly slice the mushroom caps. Reserve in separate piles. Combine the arrowroot and 2 tablespoons of the broth in a small bowl.

2 **Melt the butter** in a saucepan, then add the onion, celery, and garlic. Sauté until the vegetables are tender. Add the remaining broth to the vegetables; bring to a simmer. Add the potato and simmer, covered, until tender, 15–20 minutes. Whisk the arrowroot mixture and stir into the broth. Simmer until the mixture thickens, about 2 minutes. Remove from the heat; stir in the milk, sherry, salt, and pepper.

3 **Meanwhile, bring the water** to a boil in a small saucepan. Add the reserved mushroom stems; reduce the heat and simmer 5 minutes. Strain the liquid into a medium skillet, discarding the stems. Bring to a simmer and add the reserved sliced mushrooms. Cook, stirring occasionally, until softened, about 5 minutes. Stir the mushrooms and their broth into the soup. Serve, topped with the crabmeat.

$1/2$ pound shiitake mushrooms

1 tablespoon + 2 teaspoons arrowroot

2 cups low-sodium chicken broth

1 teaspoon unsalted butter

$1/3$ cup finely chopped onion

3 tablespoons finely chopped celery

1 garlic clove, minced

1 medium all-purpose potato, peeled and chopped

$1/4$ cup evaporated fat-free milk

$1 1/2$ teaspoons dry sherry

$1/2$ teaspoon salt

$1/2$ teaspoon coarsely ground pepper

$1/3$ cup water

$1/4$ pound cooked lump crabmeat, picked over

Per serving

140 Calories │ 2 g Total Fat │ 1 g Saturated Fat │ 32 mg Cholesterol │ 684 mg Sodium
22 g Total Carbohydrate │ 3 g Dietary Fiber │ 10 g Protein │ 88 mg Calcium

2 POINTS per serving

oyster bisque

This creamy classic is a perfect lunch or warming start to dinner on a cold day. Rice thickens this dish, allowing us to leave out the cream, trimming the fat without sacrificing the soup's creamy texture. This can be prepared slightly ahead of time, but wait to add the oysters until just before serving time.

makes 4 servings

1/2 medium carrot, peeled and thinly sliced

1 celery stalk, thinly sliced

2 teaspoons canola oil

1 medium onion, finely chopped

1/4 cup long-grain rice

1 1/2 cups low-sodium chicken broth

1 1/2 cups water

1/2 cup fat-free milk

Pinch cayenne

One 8-ounce can oysters, drained (reserve 1/2 cup liquid)

Pinch salt

Minced flat-leaf parsley

1 **Fill a small saucepan** with enough water to cover the carrot and celery; bring to a boil. Simmer the carrot and celery, covered, until just tender, 1–2 minutes then drain.

2 **Heat the oil** in a saucepan, then add the onion. Sauté until the onion softens, about 5 minutes. Add the rice and cook, stirring constantly, 2 minutes. Stir in 1 cup of the broth and 1 cup of the water; bring to a boil. Reduce the heat and simmer, covered, until the rice is tender, about 15 minutes.

3 **Transfer the rice mixture** to a blender or food processor and puree. Combine the puree, the cooked carrot and celery, the remaining 1/2 cup broth and 1/2 cup water, the milk, and cayenne in the saucepan. Cook, stirring constantly, until heated through (do not boil). Stir in the oysters with the reserved liquid and the salt; cook, gently stirring until the edges of the oysters just begin to curl and the soup is heated through. Serve, sprinkled with the parsley.

3 *POINTS* per serving

Per serving

178 Calories | 6 g Total Fat | 1 g Saturated Fat | 22 mg Cholesterol | 283 mg Sodium

18 g Total Carbohydrate | 3 g Dietary Fiber | 12 g Protein | 63 mg Calcium

chapter 5

pizzas, sandwiches, and wraps

pizza dough, with variations

This dough is such a classic you will be able to make all kinds of pizzas, pitas, and grilled breads by experimenting with the crust variations and toppings.

makes 4 servings

1 cup warm (105°–115°F) water

$^1/_2$ tablespoon honey

2 teaspoons active dry yeast

2 cups + 2 tablespoons bread flour

$^3/_4$ teaspoon salt

Make It by Hand

Follow Step 1. Stir in $^1/_2$ cup of the remaining water, the remaining flour, and salt and mix until the dough starts to gather around the spoon, adding the remaining $^1/_4$ cup water if necessary. Turn out the dough on a lightly floured counter; knead until the dough is smooth and elastic, about 10 minutes. Continue with the recipe at Step 3.

---

1 **Mix $^1/_4$ cup of the water** with the honey, yeast, and enough of the bread flour to make a thin batter. Place the batter in a warm area and cover with plastic wrap or a damp towel. Allow the batter to sit for one hour, or until it becomes frothy and increases in bulk.

2 **Add $^1/_2$ cup of the water,** the remaining bread flour, and salt to the batter. Knead at medium speed in an electric mixer fitted with a dough hook, adding the remaining water as necessary until a smooth elastic dough develops, about 8–10 minutes. The dough should cleanly pull away from the sides of the bowl.

3 **Spray a large bowl** with nonstick spray; put the dough in the bowl. Cover loosely with plastic wrap and let the dough rise in a warm spot until it doubles in size, about 1 hour. When pressed with a finger, the dough should hold the impression for a few seconds.

4 **Turn out the dough** on a lightly floured counter; knead briefly to release the air in the dough. Divide the dough into 4 equal pieces and shape each into a ball. Place on a baking sheet; cover the balls with plastic wrap and let rise a second time in a warm spot, about $^1/_2$ hour.

Make Ahead: If not using immediately, wrap the dough balls tightly before the final rise in Step 4 and refrigerate or freeze. The dough will keep under refrigeration for 2 days or frozen for up to a month. Thaw the frozen dough, still wrapped, overnight in the refrigerator. Bring the chilled dough to room temperature and allow to rise before using.

continues on page 76

---

5 *POINTS* per serving

Per serving (1 pizza crust with no topping)

256 Calories | 1 g Total Fat | 0 g Saturated Fat | 0 mg Cholesterol | 438 mg Sodium
54 g Total Carbohydrate | 2 g Dietary Fiber | 8 g Protein | 12 mg Calcium

working with pizza dough

Knead dough by hand to release air bubbles before dividing into equal pieces.

When forming pizza rounds the dough will be very elastic. Roll a circle first then let it relax while you start rolling another one. The relaxed circle will respond better and maintain its shape during the second rolling.

Transfer to a cornmeal-lined baking sheet before topping. (The pizza is awkward to move after the toppings have been added.)

continued from page 74

variations

Whole-Wheat Pizza Dough: Use $1^3/4$ cups bread flour, $3/4$ cup whole-wheat flour, and double the amount of yeast.

Per serving (1 cooked pizza crust with no topping)

253 Calories | 1 g Total Fat | 0 g Saturated Fat | 0 mg Cholesterol | 440 mg Sodium 53 g Total Carbohydrate | 5 g Dietary Fiber | 9 g Protein | 17 mg Calcium

4 *POINTS* per serving

Buckwheat Pizza Dough: Use $1^3/4$ cups bread flour, $3/4$ cup buckwheat flour, and double the amount of yeast.

Per serving (1 pizza crust with no topping)

252 Calories | 1 g Total Fat | 0 g Saturated Fat | 0 mg Cholesterol | 441 mg Sodium 53 g Total Carbohydrate | 4 g Dietary Fiber | 9 g Protein | 18 mg Calcium

4 *POINTS* per serving

Pita Bread: Prepare Pizza Dough or one of the two variations above. Shape the dough as directed in Step 4, and bake on 2 baking sheets sprinkled with 1/4 cup cornmeal in a 500°F oven for 7–8 minutes. Once removed from the oven, the bread will deflate and a pocket will form.

Grilled Bread: Prepare Pizza Dough or one of the two variations above. Shape the dough as directed in Step 4 and grill until the bread puffs and blisters, 2–3 minutes per side.

pizza with roasted tomatoes and mozzarella

This pizza is a variation on Pizza Margherita, which was created at the turn of the last century, when Italy's Queen Margherita visited Naples. It features the red, white, and green colors of the Italian flag. In our version, the tomatoes are roasted first to deepen their flavor. (Chopped roasted tomatoes make a wonderful topping for pasta, by the way; make extra if you can and store the leftovers in the refrigerator for up to 3 days.)

1 To roast the tomatoes, preheat the oven to 275°F. Toss together the tomatoes, 1 tablespoon of the oil, and the salt in a bowl. Place the slices on a rack in a roasting pan; roast until dry, but still flexible, 2½–3 hours. Combine the remaining 1½ tablespoons oil, half of the basil, the oregano, and garlic in a bowl.

2 Raise the oven temperature to 500°F. Sprinkle 2 baking sheets with the cornmeal. With your fingers, flatten each pizza dough ball into an 8-inch round. Place the rounds on the baking sheets. Top each with the basil mixture and arrange the roasted tomato and mozzarella cheese around the outer edges. Spread the tomato sauce in the center of each pizza, leaving a 1-inch rim, then sprinkle with the remaining basil, the Parmesan cheese, and crushed peppercorns. Bake until the crusts are browned and crisp, 7–8 minutes.

makes 4 servings

1 pound plum tomatoes, sliced

2½ tablespoons extra-virgin olive oil

¼ teaspoon salt

5 fresh basil leaves, cut into thin strips

½ teaspoon chopped fresh oregano

3 garlic cloves, minced

¼ cup cornmeal

1 recipe Pizza Dough (page 74)

¼ pound part-skim mozzarella cheese, thinly sliced

¾ cup tomato sauce

4 teaspoons freshly grated Parmesan cheese

1 tablespoon crushed black peppercorns

Per serving (1 pizza)

487 Calories | 17 g Total Fat | 5 g Saturated Fat | 17 mg Cholesterol | 1,089 mg Sodium
68 g Total Carbohydrate | 4 g Dietary Fiber | 19 g Protein | 259 mg Calcium

10 POINTS per serving

new york pizza with roasted broccoli

Layering broccoli on a pizza is a great way to get kids to eat their veggies (it works for grown-ups, too). Here, the broccoli gets an added flavor dimension by roasting it first.

makes 4 servings

4 cups broccoli florets

2 tablespoons olive oil

2 garlic cloves, thinly sliced

1/4 teaspoon salt

Freshly ground pepper

1 recipe Pizza Dough (page 74)

1 cup part-skim shredded mozzarella cheese

1/2 cup prepared pizza sauce

1/4 cup grated Parmesan cheese

1 teaspoon dried oregano

1/2 teaspoon crushed red pepper (optional)

1 **Preheat the oven** to 500°F. Toss the broccoli with the olive oil, garlic, salt, and pepper in a bowl. Arrange the broccoli in a single layer on a baking sheet. Roast until the broccoli is tender and browned, about 10 minutes. Set aside.

2 **Spray 2 additional baking sheets** with nonstick spray. With your fingers, flatten each pizza dough ball into an 8-inch round. Place the rounds on the baking sheets. Top each with the broccoli and mozzarella cheese. Top with the sauce, then the Parmesan cheese, oregano, and crushed red pepper, if using. Bake until the crusts are golden and crisp, 8–10 minutes.

10 *POINTS* per serving

Per serving (1 pizza)
464 Calories | 15 g Total Fat | 5 g Saturated Fat | 20 mg Cholesterol | 939 mg Sodium
62 g Total Carbohydrate | 5 g Dietary Fiber | 21 g Protein | 357 mg Calcium

new york pizza with roasted broccoli, and caramelized onion and pancetta pizza (page 81)

pizza with wild mushrooms and goat cheese

Wild mushrooms and goat cheese combine to make an unusually delicious pizza topping. Choose an assortment of your favorite exotic mushroom varieties, available at most supermarkets.

makes 4 servings

1/4 cup cornmeal

1/2 pound assorted wild mushrooms, sliced

1 1/2 tablespoons low-sodium chicken broth

1 recipe Pizza Dough (page 74)

1/2 cup prepared pizza sauce

1 cup crumbled herbed goat cheese

4 teaspoons grated Parmesan cheese

4 garlic cloves, minced

2 teaspoons crushed black peppercorns

1 **Preheat the oven** to 500°F. Sprinkle 2 baking sheets with the cornmeal. Combine the mushrooms and broth in a nonstick skillet and cook, stirring as needed, until the mushrooms are tender and the liquid has evaporated, about 5 minutes.

2 **With your fingers,** flatten each pizza dough ball into an 8-inch round. Place the rounds on the baking sheets. Top each with the sauce, then arrange the mushrooms and goat cheese on top. Sprinkle with the Parmesan cheese, garlic, and crushed peppercorns. Bake until the crusts are browned and crisp, 7–8 minutes.

13 *POINTS* per serving

Per serving (1 pizza)
567 Calories | 24 g Total Fat | 11 g Saturated Fat | 141 mg Cholesterol | 1,045 mg Sodium
68 g Total Carbohydrate | 5 g Dietary Fiber | 22 g Protein | 141 mg Calcium

caramelized onion and pancetta pizza

Pancetta, an Italian bacon, is cured in salt and seasonings but not smoked.
Look for pancetta in specialty food markets; wrapped airtight and refrigerated,
it may be kept for up to 3 weeks. (See photo on page 79.)

makes 4 servings

1 **Sauté the pancetta** in a nonstick skillet until lightly browned.
Transfer to a plate, discard any fat, and wipe the skillet clean.
Return the skillet to the heat and add $1/4$ cup of the water, the
onions, and sugar. Cook, stirring occasionally, until the onions
are just beginning to color, about 12 minutes. Add the salt and
remaining $1/4$ cup water; cook, stirring occasionally, until the
onions are caramelized, about 30 minutes. Let cool 5–10 minutes;
stir in the pancetta, basil, and pepper.

2 **Preheat the oven** to 500°F. Sprinkle 2 baking sheets with the
cornmeal.

3 **With your fingers,** flatten each pizza dough ball into an 8-inch
round. Place the rounds on the baking sheets. Top each with the
onion mixture, tomatoes, mozzarella, and Parmesan cheeses.
Bake until the crusts are browned and crisp, about 10 minutes.

2 tablespoon chopped pancetta

$1/2$ cup water

8 onions, thinly sliced

Pinch sugar

Pinch salt

1 tablespoon chopped basil

Freshly ground pepper

$1/4$ cup cornmeal

1 recipe Pizza Dough (page 74)

3 plum tomatoes, chopped

$3/4$ cup shredded part-skim
mozzarella cheese

2 tablespoons freshly grated
Parmesan cheese

Per serving

462 Calories | 6 g Total Fat | 3 g Saturated Fat | 15 mg Cholesterol | 651 mg Sodium
82 g Total Carbohydrate | 7 g Dietary Fiber | 19 g Protein | 258 mg Calcium

9 _POINTS_ per serving

sun-dried tomato and provolone pizza with black olives

Provolone cheese blends effortlessly with tomato, basil, black olives, garlic, and olive oil—flavors reminiscent of the cooking of Provence, a region in southeastern France.

makes 4 servings

1/4 cup cornmeal

1/2 cup boiling water

4–5 sun-dried tomato halves (not oil-packed)

1 recipe Pizza Dough (page 74)

1 1/2 tablespoons extra-virgin olive oil

2/3 cup basil leaves

12 kalamata olives, pitted and sliced

3 garlic cloves, minced

3/4 cup grated provolone cheese

1 **Preheat the oven** to 500°F. Sprinkle 2 baking sheets with the cornmeal. Pour the boiling water over the sun-dried tomatoes in a bowl; set aside until softened, about 10 minutes. Drain and cut into slivers.

2 **With your fingers,** flatten each pizza dough ball into an 8-inch round. Place the rounds on the baking sheets and brush each with the oil. Scatter the tomatoes, basil, olives, and garlic over the rounds, then sprinkle with the cheese. Bake until the crusts are browned and crisp, 7–8 minutes.

10 *POINTS* per serving

Per serving (1 pizza)
489 Calories | 18 g Total Fat | 6 g Saturated Fat | 23 mg Cholesterol | 1,005 mg Sodium
64 g Total Carbohydrate | 4 g Dietary Fiber | 17 g Protein | 262 mg Calcium

cobb salad sandwiches

This enlightened version of the classic (but high-fat) Cobb salad is portable, since it's neatly tucked into a sourdough pita. You can certainly get the Cobb salad flavor from blue cheese dressing, but if you have Roquefort cheese on hand, crumble a few bits of it on top for more zing.

makes 4 servings

Spread the inside of each pita half with about $^1/_2$ tablespoon of the dressing; fill with the lettuce, tomatoes, turkey, and bacon. Drizzle the filling with the remaining dressing and serve.

4 large sourdough pitas, halved

4 tablespoons reduced-calorie blue cheese dressing, homemade (page 50) or bottled

8 Romaine lettuce leaves

2 large tomatoes, thinly sliced

$^1/_2$ pound thinly sliced lean turkey breast

4 slices bacon, crisp-cooked, drained, and crumbled

Per serving

284 Calories | 7 g Total Fat | 2 g Saturated Fat | 27 mg Cholesterol | 1,115 mg Sodium
41 g Total Carbohydrate | 3 g Dietary Fiber | 18 g Protein | 86 mg Calcium

6 *POINTS* per serving

roasted chicken and chutney sandwiches

These satisfying sandwiches transform boring leftover roast chicken into an exciting treat. The chutney is made with a refreshingly sweet-tart blend of cider, dried cranberries, and apples; it can be made a day ahead and refrigerated. You can also serve it alongside roasted or grilled chicken for dinner.

makes 4 servings

2 teaspoons vegetable oil

2 onions, chopped

1 teaspoon ground ginger

2 Granny Smith apples, peeled, cored, and chopped

$2/3$ cup dried cranberries or raisins

$1/2$ cup apple cider

$1/4$ cup cider vinegar

3 tablespoons packed dark brown sugar

$1/2$ cup shredded watercress

2 cups sliced skinless roast chicken breast

8 slices pumpernickel or raisin-pumpernickel bread

1 **Heat the oil** in a nonstick skillet, then add the onions and ginger. Sauté until the onions are tender and lightly browned, about 10 minutes. Add the apples, cranberries, cider, vinegar, and brown sugar. Reduce the heat and simmer, stirring occasionally, until the liquid evaporates and the chutney thickens, about 30 minutes. Cool the chutney to room temperature, then refrigerate until ready to use.

2 **Layer the watercress** and chicken on 4 slices of bread. Dollop each with 1 tablespoon of the chutney and top each with the remaining bread.

9 POINTS per serving

Per serving

477 Calories | 7 g Total Fat | 1 g Saturated Fat | 60 mg Cholesterol | 492 mg Sodium
76 g Total Carbohydrate | 8 g Dietary Fiber | 29 g Protein | 86 mg Calcium

moroccan chicken salad sandwiches

Chicken legs braised in Moroccan-style seasonings make an unusual, highly flavored sandwich filling. Prepare the chicken salad a day ahead and refrigerate for an effortless and satisfying supper or elegant picnic fare.

makes 4 servings

1 **Combine the lemon juice,** garlic powder, salt, paprika, pepper, cinnamon, cumin, and cayenne in a large zip-close bag; add the chicken. Squeeze out the air and seal the bag; turn to coat the chicken. Refrigerate, turning the bag occasionally, at least 30 minutes.

2 **Heat the oil** in a large skillet then add the chicken. Sauté, turning once, until browned, 3–4 minutes per side. Transfer to a plate. Drain the fat from the skillet; add the broth and cook, scraping up the browned bits from the bottom of the pan. Return the chicken to the skillet; add the olives and bring to a simmer. Reduce the heat, cover, and cook gently until the chicken is fork-tender, about 45 minutes. Allow the chicken to cool in the braising liquid.

3 **Remove the chicken** with a slotted spoon, reserving the braising liquid. Bone the chicken and place the meat in a large bowl.

4 **Skim any fat** from the braising liquid and add about 1/2 cup of the liquid to the chicken, along with the tomatoes, roasted pepper, cilantro, and parsley. Season with salt, if using. Toss to combine. Split the pitas in half and divide the chicken salad evenly among the pitas.

2 teaspoons fresh lemon juice

1/2 teaspoon garlic powder

1/2 teaspoon salt

1/4 teaspoon sweet paprika

Freshly ground pepper

1/4 teaspoon ground cinnamon

1/4 teaspoon ground cumin

1/8 teaspoon cayenne

2 1/4 pounds chicken legs (about 2–3 legs), skinned

1 tablespoon extra-virgin olive oil

1 cup low-sodium chicken broth

10 kalamata olives, pitted and chopped

2 large tomatoes, peeled, seeded, and chopped

1 roasted red bell pepper, chopped

1/2 teaspoon chopped fresh cilantro

1/2 teaspoon chopped fresh parsley

Salt, to taste (optional)

4 large whole-wheat pitas

Chef's Tip

To peel and seed the tomatoes, bring a large pot of water to a boil. Have ready a bowl of ice water. Cut a shallow "X" into the bottom of each tomato. Submerge 1 tomato in boiling water for 10–15 seconds. Plunge into ice water, then remove immediately and peel the tomato with a paring knife, starting at the "X." If the tomato does not peel easily, return it to the boiling water briefly, shock it in the ice water again, and peel. Repeat with the remaining tomato. Cut the tomatoes in half horizontally and squeeze out the seeds.

Per serving

452 Calories | 16 g Total Fat | 4 g Saturated Fat | 99 mg Cholesterol | 831 mg Sodium
42 g Total Carbohydrate | 6 g Dietary Fiber | 37 g Protein | 45 mg Calcium

10 *POINTS* per serving

smoked turkey and roasted pepper panini

Panini are small Italian breads that come in varying shapes and make tasty sandwiches. In this recipe, fill your favorite roll with slices of smoked turkey and piquant marinated bell pepper. Prepare the pepper a day ahead so it has time to absorb all the flavor of the marinade.

makes 4 servings

1 red bell pepper

1 tablespoon balsamic vinegar

1 tablespoon water

1 sprig fresh rosemary or
$1/2$ teaspoon dried rosemary

4 whole-wheat hard rolls, split

$1/2$ pound thinly sliced
smoked turkey

8 large basil leaves

1 **Spray the broiler rack** with nonstick spray; preheat the broiler. Broil the bell pepper 5 inches from the heat, turning frequently with tongs, until the skin is shriveled and darkened, about 10 minutes. Place the pepper in a bowl, cover with plastic wrap and let steam 10 minutes. When cool enough to handle, peel, seed, then slice the pepper into thin strips.

2 **Combine the vinegar,** water, and rosemary in a zip-close bag; add the pepper strips. Squeeze out the air and seal the bag; turn to coat the pepper. Refrigerate, turning the bag occasionally, at least 8 hours or overnight.

3 **Drain the pepper strips** and discard the marinade. To assemble the sandwiches, layer the rolls with the turkey, pepper strips, and basil.

5 *POINTS* per serving

Per serving
215 Calories | 9 g Total Fat | 2 g Saturated Fat | 54 mg Cholesterol | 964 mg Sodium
22 g Total Carbohydrate | 2 g Dietary Fiber | 14 g Protein | 76 mg Calcium

madeira glazed portobello sandwiches

Portobello mushrooms, which measure several inches in diameter, are mature cremini mushrooms. The caps are typically fully open and the stems tend to be tough. The portobellos can easily be prepared a day ahead, without sacrificing taste. Broil the mushroom caps and refrigerate them whole, then return to room temperature and slice when ready to make the sandwiches.

makes 4 servings

2 tablespoons Madeira

1 tablespoon olive oil

1 teaspoon dried basil

$1/2$ teaspoon dried oregano

Freshly ground pepper

$1/2$ pound portobello mushrooms, stems and gills removed

1 medium onion, sliced

4 (1-ounce) slices reduced-fat Swiss cheese

2 large sourdough rolls, split

1 **Spray the broiler rack** with nonstick spray; preheat the broiler.

2 **Combine the Madeira,** oil, basil, oregano, and pepper in a large bowl; add the mushrooms and toss to coat. Set aside 10 minutes to marinate.

3 **Spray a nonstick skillet** with nonstick spray and set over medium-high heat. Add the onion and sauté until softened, about 5 minutes.

4 **Broil the mushrooms** 5 inches from the heat, brushing with the marinade, until browned, about 4 minutes on each side. When cool enough to handle, thinly slice.

5 **Place 1 slice of cheese** on each of the 4 roll halves; broil until the cheese is melted, about 2 minutes. Top each with the mushrooms and onions and serve.

Chef's Tip

To remove the stem of a portobello, grasp it firmly near the base and slowly snap it off. It should break cleanly away from the cap. To remove the gills, which are bitter and produce an unappealing black liquid when cooked, scrape them away gently with the side of a spoon or butter knife.

Per serving

247 Calories | 10 g Total Fat | 4 g Saturated Fat | 15 mg Cholesterol | 311 mg Sodium
27 g Total Carbohydrate | 4 g Dietary Fiber | 14 g Protein | 269 mg Calcium

5 *POINTS* per serving

grilled garden sandwiches

A hint of Granny Smith apple, creamy ricotta, and fresh basil add excitement to this satisfying sandwich. With a ridged nonstick grill pan, you can grill the onions and bread indoors, without having to prepare an outdoor grill (if you prefer, you can also broil them on a baking sheet sprayed with nonstick spray). Be sure to allow enough time for the ricotta to drain.

makes 4 servings

³/4 cup part-skim ricotta cheese

1 large red onion, thinly sliced

8 slices whole-wheat bread

2 tablespoons vegetable broth

¹/4 pound mushrooms, sliced

¹/2 red bell pepper, cut into thin strips

¹/2 yellow bell pepper, cut into thin strips

¹/4 teaspoon salt

Freshly ground pepper

6 large fresh basil leaves, cut into thin strips

1 small English cucumber, thinly sliced

1 large Granny Smith apple, quartered and thinly sliced

1 plum tomato, thinly sliced

¹/2 medium zucchini, thinly sliced

1 **Spoon the ricotta** into a strainer lined with a coffee filter or cheesecloth and place over a medium bowl. Cover and refrigerate at least 8 hours or overnight. Discard the liquid in the bowl.

2 **Spray a ridged nonstick grill pan** with nonstick spray and set over medium-high heat. Grill the onion slices until tender, about 2 minutes per side. Transfer to a plate. Grill the bread slices; transfer to a plate and loosely cover to keep warm.

3 **Preheat the oven** to 350°F. Combine the broth, mushrooms, and bell peppers in a nonstick skillet. Cook over medium heat, stirring occasionally, until the vegetables are slightly tender and almost dry, about 5 minutes. Season with the salt and pepper.

4 **Spread the ricotta** on 4 slices of the bread. Sprinkle with the basil. Layer the cucumber, apple, and pepper mixture over the ricotta. Add the grilled onions, then the tomato and zucchini; top each sandwich with a slice of the remaining bread. Press the tops down firmly and place the sandwiches on a baking sheet. Bake, turning twice, until heated through, 20–25 minutes.

5 POINTS per serving

Per serving

278 Calories | 7 g Total Fat | 3 g Saturated Fat | 16 mg Cholesterol | 539 mg Sodium
45 g Total Carbohydrate | 8 g Dietary Fiber | 13 g Protein | 188 mg Calcium

vegetable burgers

These burgers are packed with the fresh flavors of vegetables and herbs with a subtle spiciness from the hot pepper sauce. Serve them on Kaiser rolls, topped with a little nonfat plain yogurt enhanced with roasted garlic and a sprinkle of bean sprouts—or with a salad and pickle. However you top them, they are a terrific tasting—and healthy— alternative to traditional hamburgers.

makes 4 servings

1 **Preheat the oven** to 475°F. Spray a baking sheet with nonstick spray. Combine the carrots, celery, onion, and bell pepper in a sieve and press with the back of a spoon to drain the excess juice. Place the carrot mixture in a large bowl and add the mushrooms, scallions, egg, walnuts, thyme, garlic, salt, pepper sauce, sesame oil, and pepper. Stir to thoroughly combine the mixture. Add 1/4 cup of the cracker meal, or more as needed, to make a firm mixture. Form into 4 burgers. Dredge each burger in any remaining cracker meal.

2 **Place the burgers** on the baking sheet and bake, turning once, until browned, about 12 minutes.

2 medium carrots, peeled and grated

1/2 celery stalk, grated

2 tablespoons grated onion

2 tablespoons minced red bell pepper

1/3 cup minced mushrooms

4 scallions, minced

1 egg, lightly beaten

1/4 cup walnut halves, finely ground

2 teaspoons chopped fresh thyme

1 garlic clove, minced

1/2 teaspoon salt

1/4 teaspoon hot pepper sauce

1/4 teaspoon sesame oil

1/8 teaspoon ground pepper

1/3 cup cracker or matzo meal

Chef's Tip

Grind the walnuts with a rolling pin or in a mini food processor; they should yield about 2 tablespoons.

Per serving

110 Calories | 4 g Total Fat | 1 g Saturated Fat | 53 mg Cholesterol | 328 mg Sodium
15 g Total Carbohydrate | 2 g Dietary Fiber | 4 g Protein | 32 mg Calcium

2 POINTS per serving

oyster po' boy with rémoulade

There are several explanations about its origin, but one popular theory reports that the po' boy sandwich—a true New Orleans specialty—was invented in 1920 by Benny and Clovis Martin at Martin Brothers Grocery, where it was offered to striking streetcar workers. In this version, oysters are rolled in fresh bread crumbs, sautéed, and served in French rolls with a classic rémoulade sauce.

makes 4 servings

RÉMOULADE

1/4 cup fat-free mayonnaise

1 scallion, minced

2 tablespoons minced celery

1 tablespoon minced fresh flat-leaf parsley

1 tablespoon minced dill pickle

1 tablespoon red wine vinegar

2 teaspoons Dijon mustard

2 teaspoons capers, drained, and finely chopped

1 teaspoon Worcestershire sauce

Hot pepper sauce (optional)

PO' BOYS

4 crusty French rolls, split

2 tablespoons all-purpose flour

1/4 teaspoon freshly ground pepper

1/4 teaspoon cayenne

24 medium oysters, shucked

1/4 cup fat-free egg substitute

1 tablespoon vegetable oil

1 tomato, thinly sliced

1/2 cup shredded iceberg lettuce

1 lemon, cut into wedges

1 **To prepare the rémoulade,** combine the mayonnaise, scallion, celery, parsley, pickle, vinegar, mustard, capers, Worcestershire sauce, and pepper sauce, if using, in a nonreactive bowl. Cover and let stand 30 minutes to blend the flavors.

2 **To prepare the po' boys,** with your fingers, pull out about 1 tablespoon of bread from each roll. Tear the removed bread into crumbs and place on a plate. Add the flour, pepper, and cayenne to the crumbs, tossing with your fingertips to combine. Dip the oysters, one at a time, into the egg substitute, then roll each in the crumb mixture.

3 Heat **1/2 tablespoon** of the oil in a large nonstick skillet, then add half of the oysters. Cook, turning once, until the oysters are browned and cooked through, about 3 minutes. Repeat with the remaining oil and oysters.

4 **Toast the roll halves.** Layer the oysters, tomato, and lettuce evenly on 4 halves and top with the remaining halves. Serve with the rémoulade and lemon wedges.

5 POINTS per serving

Per serving (1 sandwich with about 1 tablespoon sauce)

239 Calories | 7 g Total Fat | 1 g Saturated Fat | 19 mg Cholesterol | 664 mg Sodium
34 g Total Carbohydrate | 2 g Dietary Fiber | 10 g Protein | 92 mg Calcium

lobster and asparagus crêpes

Crêpes are delicate pancakes that can be served with a number of savory or sweet fillings. In this sumptuous interpretation—perfect for a special brunch—lobster-filled crêpes are accented by a delightful, fat-free Hollandaise-style sauce. Refer to the recipe for Classic Boiled Lobster (page 151) for instructions on cooking lobster.

makes 4 servings

1/2 cup fat-free milk

1/3 cup + 2 teaspoons all-purpose flour

1 egg

1 egg white

2 teaspoons canola oil

1/4 teaspoon salt

1 tablespoon minced fresh chives

24 thin asparagus spears, trimmed, cooked, and cooled

10 ounces cooked shelled lobster meat, cut into chunks

1/4 cup fat-free mayonnaise

1/4 cup hot water

1/4 teaspoon grated lemon zest

2 tablespoons fresh lemon juice

Pinch cayenne

1 **To make the crêpes,** combine the milk, flour, egg, egg white, oil, and salt in a blender; process until smooth. Transfer the batter to a 1-cup glass measure and stir in the chives. Let stand 30 minutes.

2 **Spray a crêpe pan** or 6-inch nonstick skillet with nonstick spray; heat over medium-high heat until a drop of water skitters. Pour in 2 tablespoons of the batter and swirl to cover the pan. Cook until lightly browned, about 30 seconds. Turn the crêpe over and cook until dry, about 5 seconds. Transfer the crêpe to a plate and cover with wax paper. Repeat, making 7 more crêpes, stirring the batter before each use and stacking the crêpes with wax paper to prevent them from sticking to each other.

3 **Preheat the oven** to 350°F. Spray a 9 × 13-inch baking dish with nonstick spray. Top each crêpe with 3 asparagus spears and one-eighth of the lobster; roll to enclose the filling. Place the crêpes seam-side down in the baking dish. Cover and bake until heated through, about 15 minutes.

4 **Meanwhile, to make the sauce,** with a wire whisk, combine the mayonnaise and water in a double boiler over simmering water. Cook, whisking constantly, until smooth and heated through, 1–2 minutes. Remove the pan from the heat; stir in the lemon zest, lemon juice, and cayenne. The sauce should be pourable; if necessary, thin with water, 1 teaspoon at a time, until the desired consistency is reached. Serve the crêpes with the sauce.

Per serving (2 crepes with about 2 tablespoons sauce)

201 Calories | 5 g Total Fat | 1 g Saturated Fat | 105 mg Cholesterol | 583 mg Sodium
17 g Total Carbohydrate | 3 g Dietary Fiber | 22 g Protein | 112 mg Calcium

4 *POINTS* per serving

spicy soft-shell crab sandwiches

During the period of time when crabs cast off their shells, before the new larger shells have hardened, the crustaceans are called soft-shell crabs—a tasty delicacy that can be eaten shell and all. Soft-shell crabs should still be alive when you purchase them; have your fishmonger clean them and plan to cook them within 4 hours.

makes 4 servings

2 tablespoons water

1 1/2 teaspoons rice vinegar or dry sherry

1 1/2 teaspoons reduced-sodium soy sauce

1/2 teaspoon cornstarch

1/2 teaspoon packed dark brown sugar

3 teaspoons peanut oil

4 small (3-ounce) soft-shell crabs, cleaned

1/2 teaspoon minced peeled fresh ginger

1 garlic clove, minced

2 scallions, cut into 2-inch lengths

1 1/2 teaspoons fermented black beans, rinsed, drained, and finely chopped

8 slices thin-sliced sandwich bread, toasted

1 **Combine the water,** vinegar, soy sauce, cornstarch, and brown sugar in a bowl.

2 **Heat 2 teaspoons** of the oil in a large nonstick skillet, then add the crabs, shell side down. Cook, turning once, until their shells turn reddish brown, 1–2 minutes per side. Transfer to a plate and keep warm.

3 **Return the skillet** to the heat. Swirl in the remaining 1 teaspoon oil, then add the ginger and garlic. Sauté until fragrant, about 15 seconds. Add the scallions and black beans; stir-fry until the scallions are softened, 3–4 minutes. Add the vinegar mixture, then the crabs; cook, stirring gently, until the sauce thickens and coats the crabs, about 2 minutes. Place the crabs on 4 slices of bread and top with the remaining bread.

Chef's Tip

Fermented black beans are soybeans that have been cooked, salted, and fermented. The process causes the beans to turn almost black and gives them an intense flavor some call meaty, others winelike. A small amount adds big flavor. Find the beans in plastic bags at Asian grocery stores; they'll last almost indefinitely in your refrigerator.

5 *POINTS* per serving

Per serving
213 Calories | 6 g Total Fat | 1 g Saturated Fat | 56 mg Cholesterol | 533 mg Sodium
23 g Total Carbohydrate | 1 g Dietary Fiber | 17 g Protein | 115 mg Calcium

spicy soft-shell crab sandwiches

asian beef in lettuce bundles

Wrapping in crisp, cool lettuce leaves is a refreshing way to serve beef flavored with Asian ingredients such as ginger and sesame. The dipping sauce may be prepared up to three days ahead and refrigerated; make a little extra as a deliciously different accent for vegetable crudités.

makes 4 servings

1/4 cup rice vinegar

1 tablespoon reduced-sodium soy sauce

2 teaspoons minced fresh mint

1 teaspoon minced peeled fresh ginger

1 teaspoon grated orange zest

1 teaspoon Asian (dark) sesame oil

8 large iceberg lettuce leaves

1/2 pound thinly sliced, lean roast beef, cut into 1/4-inch strips

1 cup bean sprouts, washed

1 medium cucumber, peeled, seeded, and shredded

8 large fresh mint leaves

1 **To make the dipping sauce,** combine the vinegar, soy sauce, minced mint, ginger, orange zest, and oil in a bowl; set aside.

2 **Arrange the lettuce leaves** on a work surface and top with the beef strips, bean sprouts, cucumber, and mint leaves. Fold the sides of each lettuce leaf over the filling, then, starting from the shortest end, roll the leaves to enclose the filling. Serve with the dipping sauce.

---

4 *POINTS* per serving

Per serving (2 bundles)
174 Calories | 9 g Total Fat | 3 g Saturated Fat | 46 mg Cholesterol | 183 mg Sodium
5 g Total Carbohydrate | 1 g Dietary Fiber | 17 g Protein | 26 mg Calcium

chapter 6

pasta

peppery noodles

These quick, peppery noodles are the consummate accompaniment for rich, hearty fare, such as pork roast or meatloaf. But don't use the pepper shaker for these noodles—crack whole peppercorns for unmatched flavor. Crack peppercorns using a mortar and pestle, or spread them on a cutting board and crush gently with the bottom of a clean, small, heavy pot or skillet.

makes 4 servings

1^1/$_2$ cups medium egg noodles

^{1}/$_2$ cup minced flat-leaf parsley

1 teaspoon cracked
black peppercorns

^{1}/$_4$ teaspoon salt

1 **Cook the noodles** according to package directions; drain, reserving ^{1}/$_4$ cup of the cooking liquid, and place the noodles in a large bowl.

2 **Add the cooking liquid,** parsley, peppercorns, and salt; toss to combine.

1 *POINT* per serving

Per serving
58 Calories | 1 g Total Fat | 0 g Saturated Fat | 14 mg Cholesterol | 153 mg Sodium
11 g Total Carbohydrate | 1 g Dietary Fiber | 2 g Protein | 16 mg Calcium

lemon-caper capellini

Super-thin capellini (also called angel hair pasta) is the ideal pasta for this delicate dish, which has just a hint of citrus. Substitute one teaspoon of chopped thyme for the parsley or add a little kick with a pinch of crushed red pepper.

makes 4 servings

1 **Cook the capellini** according to package directions. Drain and keep warm.

2 **Meanwhile, heat a large** nonstick skillet. Swirl in the oil, then add the garlic. Sauté until the garlic turns a rich, nutty brown, 2 to 3 minutes (take care to keep the heat fairly low so the garlic doesn't burn). Add the capellini, parsley, lemon juice, capers, and salt; toss to coat. Serve, sprinkled with the pepper.

6 ounces capellini

2 teaspoons olive oil

1–2 garlic cloves, minced

$^{1}/_{4}$ cup minced parsley

2 tablespoons fresh lemon juice

1 tablespoon capers, drained, and chopped

$^{1}/_{4}$ teaspoon salt

Freshly ground pepper

Per serving

184 Calories | 3 g Total Fat | 0 g Saturated Fat | 0 mg Cholesterol | 215 mg Sodium
33 g Total Carbohydrate | 1 g Dietary Fiber | 6 g Protein | 17 mg Calcium

4 *POINTS* per serving

orzo with spinach and asiago cheese

If you're looking for an alternative to rice, orzo may be the answer. *Orzo* is the Italian word for barley and also the name for a small, rice-shaped pasta. This pasta is often used for soups or side dishes like this one. Flavored with garlic, spinach, a touch of vinegar, and sharp Asiago cheese, it is a pleasing partner to simple grilled chicken or fish.

makes 4 servings

³/₄ cup orzo

2 teaspoons olive oil

1 small onion, chopped

1 small celery stalk, chopped

1 garlic clove, minced

1 cup packed and chopped spinach leaves, cleaned

¹/₄ cup reduced-sodium chicken broth

¹/₂ tablespoon red wine vinegar

¹/₄ cup grated Asiago cheese

Freshly ground pepper

1 **Cook the orzo** according to package directions.

2 **Meanwhile, heat a nonstick** saucepan. Swirl in the oil, then add the onion, celery, and garlic. Sauté until softened, 3 to 4 minutes. Stir in the spinach, half the broth, and the vinegar; cook, stirring frequently, until the liquid evaporates, 2 to 3 minutes longer. Stir in the orzo, cheese, the remaining broth, and the pepper.

3 *POINTS* per serving

Per serving

176 Calories | 4 g Total Fat | 1 g Saturated Fat | 4 mg Cholesterol | 147 mg Sodium
27 g Total Carbohydrate | 2 g Dietary Fiber | 7 g Protein | 90 mg Calcium

penne with creamy garlic-parmesan sauce

The whole family will love this easy weeknight pasta. To duplicate the flavor and richness of a heavy cream-and-cheese sauce, we whisked evaporated fat-free milk with flour to thicken it, and added whole garlic cloves—boiled and minced—to pump up the flavor.

makes 4 servings

8 garlic cloves, peeled

3 cups small broccoli florets

2¼ cups penne

2 cups evaporated fat-free milk

1 tablespoon + 1 teaspoon all-purpose flour

³/₄ cup shredded reduced-fat cheddar cheese

¹/₄ cup grated Parmesan cheese

Freshly ground pepper

¹/₄ teaspoon salt

1 **Cook the garlic** in a large pot of boiling water until softened, 3 minutes. With a slotted spoon, transfer the garlic to a cutting board, reserving the water in the pot. Mince the garlic; set aside.

2 **Cook the broccoli** in the same pot of boiling water until bright green and just softened, 3 minutes. With a slotted spoon, transfer the broccoli to a plate, reserving the water in the pot.

3 **Cook the penne** in the same pot of boiling water according to package directions.

4 **Meanwhile, with a wire whisk,** combine the milk and flour in a large nonstick skillet, blending until the flour is dissolved. Cook over medium heat, whisking constantly, until the mixture is bubbling and thickened, about 5 minutes; stir in the minced garlic.

5 **Reduce the heat** to low. Add the cheddar and Parmesan cheeses, the pepper, and salt to the milk mixture; cook, stirring constantly, until the cheeses are melted. Stir in the cooked broccoli and penne; cook, stirring frequently, just until heated through.

Per serving

446 Calories | 7 g Total Fat | 4 g Saturated Fat | 24 mg Cholesterol | 588 mg Sodium
67 g Total Carbohydrate | 4 g Dietary Fiber | 27 g Protein | 642 mg Calcium

9 *POINTS* per serving

spaghetti with creamy gorgonzola sauce

Rich and creamy, with a slightly pungent flavor, Gorgonzola is one of Italy's great cheeses. It's traditionally paired with fruit and wine, but also works beautifully in this sophisticated entrée. The addition of chopped dried figs adds a lovely touch of sweetness to the sauce.

makes 4 servings

6 ounces spaghetti

2 cups fat-free milk

2 tablespoons all-purpose flour

1/4 teaspoon salt

Freshly ground pepper

Pinch cayenne

1/4 cup crumbled Gorgonzola cheese

1/4 cup grated Parmesan cheese

2 large dried figs, coarsely chopped

1/4 cup minced chives

1 **Cook the spaghetti** according to package directions; drain and keep warm in a large bowl.

2 **Meanwhile, with a wire whisk,** combine the milk and flour in a large skillet, blending until the flour is dissolved. Add the salt, pepper, and cayenne; cook over medium heat, whisking constantly, until the mixture is bubbling and thickened, about 5 minutes.

3 **Add the Gorgonzola** and Parmesan cheeses to the milk mixture; cook, stirring constantly, until the cheese melts. Stir in the figs and chives.

4 **Pour the cheese** mixture over the warm spaghetti; toss to combine.

6 *POINTS* per serving

Per serving
294 Calories | 5 g Total Fat | 3 g Saturated Fat | 12 mg Cholesterol | 434 mg Sodium
48 g Total Carbohydrate | 3 g Dietary Fiber | 14 g Protein | 284 mg Calcium

spaghetti with creamy gorgonzola sauce

linguine with olives, basil, and red and yellow tomatoes

The summer months are the ideal time to try this recipe, when an abundance of colorful tomatoes can be found in the market or your garden. If you prefer to use plum instead of cherry tomatoes, simply chop them coarsely. This dish also works with most noodle pastas, such as spaghetti, fettuccine, or capellini.

makes 4 servings

8 ounces linguine

1 tablespoon extra-virgin olive oil

3/4 teaspoon minced garlic

1 cup red cherry tomatoes, halved

1 cup yellow cherry tomatoes, halved

2 scallions, thinly sliced

1/4 cup oil-cured olives, pitted and sliced

1 tablespoon shredded fresh basil

1/4 teaspoon salt

Freshly ground pepper

1/4 cup grated Parmesan cheese

1 **Cook the linguine** according to package directions. Drain and keep warm.

2 **Heat a large** nonstick skillet. Swirl in the oil, then add the garlic. Sauté until fragrant, about 30 seconds. Add the red and yellow tomatoes and cook just until heated through. Add the linguine, scallions, and olives. If the mixture seems dry, add 1 to 2 tablespoons of water. Cook, stirring, until heated through. Stir in the basil, salt, and pepper. Serve, sprinkled with the Parmesan cheese.

6 _POINTS_ per serving

Per serving
294 Calories | 7 g Total Fat | 2 g Saturated Fat | 5 mg Cholesterol | 447 mg Sodium
46 g Total Carbohydrate | 5 g Dietary Fiber | 11 g Protein | 132 mg Calcium

linguine with olives, basil, and red and yellow tomatoes

capellini with grilled vegetables

The taste and texture of grilled vegetables and pasta are always a marvelous combination. You can use your broiler if you prefer. We offer a colorful mix of bell pepper, red onion, zucchini, yellow squash, and fennel, plus a handful of fresh herbs tossed in. You can grill the vegetables up to 1 hour ahead and let them stand at room temperature.

makes 4 servings

1 medium zucchini, halved lengthwise

1 yellow squash, halved lengthwise

1 red, yellow, or green bell pepper, seeded and quartered

1/2 fennel bulb, trimmed and halved

1 small red onion, thickly sliced

8 ounces capellini (angel hair pasta)

2 teaspoons extra-virgin olive oil

1 small shallot, minced

1 small garlic clove, minced

1/4 cup dry white wine

1 tablespoon soy sauce

2 tablespoons chopped chervil, tarragon, chives, or parsley, or a combination

1/4 teaspoon salt

Freshly ground pepper

1 **Spray the grill** or broiler rack with nonstick spray; prepare the grill or preheat the broiler.

2 **Spray the zucchini,** squash, bell pepper, fennel, and onion with nonstick spray. Grill or broil the vegetables 5 inches from the heat, turning frequently, until tender. When the vegetables are cool enough to handle, cube the bell pepper, zucchini, squash, and fennel, leaving the onion in rings.

3 **Meanwhile, cook the capellini** according to package directions.

4 **Heat a large** nonstick skillet. Swirl in the oil, then add the shallot and garlic. Sauté until fragrant, 1 minute. Add the grilled vegetables and the wine; cook until heated through. Stir in the soy sauce, herbs, salt, and pepper. Add the capellini and toss. If the mixture seems dry, add 1 to 2 tablespoons water.

3 *POINTS* per serving

Per serving

160 Calories | 3 g Total Fat | 0 g Saturated Fat | 0 mg Cholesterol | 411 mg Sodium
27 g Total Carbohydrate | 4 g Dietary Fiber | 5 g Protein | 36 mg Calcium

rigatoni in wild mushroom broth with spring vegetables

This dish is essentially a lightened version of pasta primavera. Instead of the classic cream sauce and fresh fettuccine noodles, we substitute heartier rigatoni, simmered in a vegetable broth that has been enriched with wild mushrooms and a touch of sherry. There are still plenty of spring vegetables in the dish—baby carrots, scallions, and crisp sugar snap peas.

makes 4 servings

3 plum tomatoes

2 cups baby carrots

1 cup sugar snap peas, trimmed

8 ounces rigatoni

2 cups low-sodium vegetable broth

2 scallions, thinly sliced

1 tablespoon minced shallot

1 teaspoon minced garlic

6 ounces assorted wild mushrooms, chopped

3 tablespoons dry sherry

Freshly ground pepper

1/4 cup grated Parmesan cheese

2 tablespoons chopped fresh basil

1 tablespoon chopped fresh parsley

1 **To prepare the tomatoes,** bring a large pot of water to a boil. Have ready a bowl of ice water. Cut a shallow "X" into the bottom of each tomato. Submerge 1 tomato in boiling water for 10 to 15 seconds. Plunge into ice water, then remove immediately, and peel the tomato with a paring knife, starting at the "X." If the tomato does not peel easily, return it to the boiling water briefly, shock it in the ice water again, and peel. Repeat with the remaining tomatoes. Cut the tomatoes in half horizontally and remove the seeds, then chop. Set aside.

2 **Bring the water back** to a boil; add the carrots. Boil until tender, about 5 minutes. With a slotted spoon, transfer the carrots to a colander, reserving the water in the pot. Rinse the carrots under cold water to stop the cooking; drain and transfer to a medium bowl. Cook the sugar snap peas in the same way, just until tender; rinse, drain, and transfer to the same bowl.

3 **Cook the rigatoni** in the same pot of boiling water according to package directions; drain and keep warm.

4 **Meanwhile, bring 2 tablespoons** of the broth to a simmer in a large nonstick saucepan; add the scallions, shallot, and garlic. Simmer gently until the shallot is translucent, about 2 minutes. Stir in the remaining broth, the mushrooms, sherry, and pepper. Reduce the heat and simmer 15 minutes. Add the rigatoni, carrots, peas, and tomatoes; simmer until heated through. Serve, sprinkled with the cheese, basil, and parsley.

Per serving

336 Calories | 4 g Total Fat | 1 g Saturated Fat | 5 mg Cholesterol | 681 mg Sodium
60 g Total Carbohydrate | 7 g Dietary Fiber | 13 g Protein | 151 mg Calcium

6 *POINTS* per serving

bow ties with grilled asparagus, morels, and spring peas

Fresh morel mushrooms are alluring delicacies of spring. They have an intense smoky, earthy, nutty flavor that is prized among wild mushrooms. Although morels are expensive, a little goes a long way, so they're well worth the cost. If they are not available, substitute one portobello mushroom: Scrape its gills off with a spoon, then cut it into chunks.

makes 4 servings

³/₄ pound asparagus, trimmed

2 teaspoons olive oil

¹/₄ cup snow peas

¹/₄ cup sugar snap peas

2 cups bow-tie pasta (farfalle)

1 teaspoon unsalted butter

¹/₂ cup fresh morel mushrooms, halved, rinsed well, patted dry

2 teaspoons minced shallot

¹/₃ cup thawed frozen peas

2 tablespoons vegetable broth

1¹/₂ teaspoons minced fresh marjoram

¹/₄ teaspoon salt

Freshly ground pepper

1 scallion, thinly sliced

2 tablespoons aged Monterey Jack cheese

1 **Spray the grill** or broiler rack with nonstick spray; prepare the grill or broiler.

2 **Toss the asparagus** with the oil in a bowl. Grill or broil the asparagus 5 inches from the heat, turning frequently, until tender. Remove the asparagus from the grill, cut into 1-inch pieces, and return to the bowl.

3 **Meanwhile, bring a large pot** of water to a boil. Add the snow peas and boil just until bright green and almost tender, about 3 minutes. With a slotted spoon, transfer the snow peas to a colander, reserving the water in the pot. Rinse the snow peas under cold water to stop the cooking; drain and transfer to the bowl with the asparagus. Cook the sugar snap peas in the same way, just until bright green and almost tender; rinse, drain, and transfer to the same bowl.

4 **Cook the bow ties** in the same pot of boiling water, according to package directions; drain and keep warm.

5 **Meanwhile, heat a large** nonstick skillet. Swirl in the butter and cook until it begins to turn brown, then add the morels and shallot. Sauté until the shallot is translucent, about 2 minutes. Add the reserved asparagus mixture, the green peas, the broth, marjoram, salt, and pepper. Cook, stirring, until the vegetables are tender and the liquid has almost evaporated, about 5 minutes. Add the bow ties; toss to coat. Serve, sprinkled with the scallions and cheese.

6 *POINTS* per serving

Per serving

299 Calories | 5 g Total Fat | 2 g Saturated Fat | 5 mg Cholesterol | 241 mg Sodium 51 g Total Carbohydrate | 5 g Dietary Fiber | 13 g Protein | 87 mg Calcium

bow ties with grilled asparagus, morels, and spring peas

paglia e fieno with smoked salmon, peas, and capers

Paglia e Fieno, which is Italian for "straw and hay," refers to thin, long flat ribbons of yellow and green pasta. Our version combines plain and spinach fettuccine with thin strips of smoked salmon and a small amount of crème fraîche—a thick, velvety-rich and mildly tangy cream found in most supermarkets.

makes 4 servings

4 ounces spinach fettuccine

4 ounces plain fettuccine

2 cups low-sodium chicken broth

2 teaspoons unsalted butter

1/2 cup thawed frozen peas

1/4 teaspoon salt

Freshly ground pepper

2 tablespoons crème fraîche

1–2 teaspoons fresh lemon juice

1/4 pound smoked salmon, cut into thin strips

2 scallions, thinly sliced

1 tablespoon capers, rinsed and drained

Fresh chervil leaves (optional)

1 **Cook the spinach** and regular fettuccine according to package directions. Drain and keep warm.

2 **Meanwhile, bring the broth** to a boil in a large nonstick skillet; cook until the broth is reduced by half. Reduce the heat to a simmer; add the butter, peas, salt, and pepper. Stir in the crème fraîche and lemon juice; simmer until the peas are heated through. Add the fettuccine; remove from the heat and toss with the smoked salmon, scallions, and capers. Serve, garnished with the chervil (if using).

6 *POINTS* per serving

Per serving

300 Calories | 6 g Total Fat | 3 g Saturated Fat | 15 mg Cholesterol | 790 mg Sodium
46 g Total Carbohydrate | 4 g Dietary Fiber | 15 g Protein | 40 mg Calcium

linguine with white clam sauce

Add a cup of drained chopped canned tomatoes, and this dish becomes Linguine with Red Clam Sauce, another delightful Italian restaurant staple. Though some purists may consider it heresy, you could toss the clam sauce with 4 cups cooked farfalle (bow ties) or medium shells instead of the linguine.

makes 4 servings

1. **Cook the linguine** according to package directions, omitting salt; drain and keep warm.

2. **Heat a nonstick** saucepan. Swirl in the oil, then add the garlic and sauté until golden, 1 to 2 minutes. Stir in the clams, clam juice, parsley, lemon juice, red pepper, salt, and pepper; cook until heated through, 3 to 4 minutes. Toss with the linguine and serve.

$3/4$ pound linguine

3 tablespoons olive oil

4 garlic cloves, minced

1 (10-ounce) can minced clams, drained

1 (8-ounce) bottle clam juice

$1/3$ cup chopped fresh flat-leaf parsley

2 tablespoons fresh lemon juice

$1/2$ teaspoon crushed red pepper

$1/2$ teaspoon salt

Freshly ground pepper, to taste

Per serving

490 Calories | 13 g Total Fat | 2 g Saturated Fat | 35 mg Cholesterol | 485 mg Sodium
68 g Total Carbohydrate | 2 g Dietary Fiber | 24 g Protein | 82 mg Calcium

10 *POINTS* per serving

rigatoni with eggplant and sun-dried tomatoes

The shape of rigatoni is best suited to a chunky, zesty sauce, like this terrific combination of sun-dried tomatoes, eggplant, spinach, and pine nuts with plenty of garlic. If you want to choose another pasta, try penne rigate (with ridges) or fusilli to catch all the flavorful juices.

makes 6 servings

1/2 cup boiling water

14 sun-dried tomato halves (not oil-packed)

4 teaspoons olive oil

1 (1 1/2-pound) eggplant, peeled and cut into 1/2-inch cubes

4 garlic cloves, minced

1 (10-ounce) package frozen chopped spinach, thawed and squeezed dry

2 medium tomatoes, chopped

1 cup low-sodium vegetable broth

3 tablespoons pine nuts

2 tablespoons minced fresh basil, or 2 teaspoons dried basil

Freshly ground pepper

4 1/2 cups hot cooked rigatoni

1/4 cup grated Parmesan cheese

1 **Pour the boiling water** over the sun-dried tomatoes in a heatproof bowl; set aside until softened, about 20 minutes.

2 **Meanwhile, heat a large** nonstick saucepan or Dutch oven. Swirl in the oil, then add the eggplant. Sauté until it softens and releases some liquid, about 5 minutes. Add the garlic and cook, stirring constantly, until the garlic is lightly browned, about 1 minute.

3 **Add the spinach,** chopped tomatoes, broth, pine nuts, basil, pepper, and the sun-dried tomatoes and their liquid; bring the mixture to a boil. Reduce the heat and simmer, covered, stirring as needed, until the vegetables are softened, about 5 minutes. Place the rigatoni in a bowl; top with the eggplant mixture and toss to coat. Serve, sprinkled with the cheese.

5 *POINTS* per serving

Per serving
267 Calories | 7 g Total Fat | 2 g Saturated Fat | 3 mg Cholesterol | 272 mg Sodium
42 g Total Carbohydrate | 6 g Dietary Fiber | 11 g Protein | 144 mg Calcium

penne with broccoli rabe and hot turkey sausage

Super-nutritious broccoli rabe is now available year round in many supermarkets. Its pungent, slightly bitter flavor may not be suitable to all tastes; milder greens such as kale or Swiss chard would make an equally delicious substitute. When choosing broccoli rabe, select firm, small stems with compact heads. The florets should be tightly closed and dark green—not yellow.

makes 4 servings

3 cups penne

1 red bell pepper, chopped

2 Italian-style hot turkey sausages, casings removed

1 tablespoon olive oil

2 garlic cloves, minced

1 bunch broccoli rabe, cleaned and chopped

$1/3$ cup water

1 (14$1/2$-ounce) can diced tomatoes

$1/4$–$1/2$ teaspoon crushed red pepper

1 **Cook the penne** according to package directions.

2 **Meanwhile, spray a large** nonstick saucepan with nonstick spray and set over medium-high heat. Add the bell pepper and sausages. Sauté, breaking the sausages apart with a spoon, until the bell pepper is softened and the sausages are browned, about 5 minutes. Drain off any fat. Transfer to a plate; keep warm.

3 **Reheat the saucepan.** Swirl in the oil, then add the garlic. Sauté until fragrant, about 30 seconds. Add the broccoli rabe and cook, stirring, until wilted, adding the water to prevent sticking. Reduce the heat and simmer, loosely covered, until the broccoli rabe is tender, about 3 minutes. Transfer to a plate. Combine the bell pepper and sausages, penne, tomatoes, and crushed red pepper in the saucepan; cook until heated through, about 2 minutes. Gently stir in the broccoli rabe.

Per serving

453 Calories | 13 g Total Fat | 3 g Saturated Fat | 15 mg Cholesterol | 585 mg Sodium
69 g Total Carbohydrate | 5 g Dietary Fiber | 17 g Protein | 62 mg Calcium

9 *POINTS* per serving

pad thai

Enjoy a bowl of Thailand's most famous noodle dish—made easy! There are no hard-to-find ingredients in this version, just plenty of savory mushrooms, soy sauce, garlic, lime juice, and hot chile paste. Scallions, bean sprouts, and peanuts add crunch; feel free to toss in shredded carrots or cucumber to bulk up the vegetables. For ingredients, check the Asian foods aisle in supermarkets, gourmet shops, or Asian markets.

makes 4 servings

4 ounces rice vermicelli, rice sticks, or spaghetti

1 cup water

10 dried Chinese black mushroom caps (about 1 ounce)

2 teaspoons vegetable oil

8 scallions, minced

1 garlic clove, minced

1 teaspoon hot chile paste

1/4 cup fresh lime juice

2 tablespoons reduced-sodium soy sauce

1 tablespoon sugar

3 egg whites

1 cup bean sprouts

1/4 cup dry-roasted peanuts, chopped

Fresh cilantro leaves (optional)

1 **Cook the vermicelli** in a large pot of boiling water until just tender, 1 to 2 minutes. With a strainer or tongs, transfer the noodles to a large bowl of cold water to cool, then drain. (If using spaghetti, cook according to package directions, rinse in a colander under cold water, and set aside.)

2 **Meanwhile, bring the water** to a boil in a small saucepan; add the mushrooms, cover and remove from the heat. Let stand 20 minutes to soften. Drain the mushrooms, discarding the liquid and squeezing out the excess water. Thinly slice the mushrooms and set aside.

3 **Heat a large nonstick skillet** or wok. Swirl in the oil, then add the scallions and the garlic. Sauté until fragrant, about 10 seconds. Add the chile paste; cook, stirring constantly, until fragrant, about 10 seconds. Add the lime juice, soy sauce, and sugar; cook, stirring, until the sugar dissolves, about 30 seconds.

4 **Add the mushrooms;** cook until they have absorbed some of the sauce, about 1 minute. Stir in the egg whites; cook, stirring gently, until they begin to set, about 30 seconds. Add the vermicelli and bean sprouts; cook, tossing gently, until mixed and heated through, 2 to 3 minutes. Serve, sprinkled with the peanuts and (if using) the cilantro.

5 *POINTS* per serving

Per serving

258 Calories | 8 g Total Fat | 1 g Saturated Fat | 0 mg Cholesterol | 428 mg Sodium
39 g Total Carbohydrate | 4 g Dietary Fiber | 11 g Protein | 47 mg Calcium

pad thai

gnocchi

Gnocchi (pronounced NYOK-kee, the Italian word for "dumplings") are light, tender nuggets of dough made from potatoes and flour. Delicious prepared in a number of ways—tossed with a light tomato sauce, crumbled sharp blue cheese, pesto, or simply a bit of butter—gnocchi make a versatile main dish or accompaniment to meat or poultry.

makes 4 servings

1 pound baking potatoes, scrubbed

1/2 cup all-purpose flour

1/4 teaspoon salt

1 **Preheat the oven** to 400°F. Poke a few holes in the potatoes with a fork. Bake until tender, about 1 hour. Let cool slightly, then peel. Press the pulp through a potato ricer or food mill; there should be about 1 1/2 cups potato pulp. While the pulp is still hot, stir in the flour and the salt.

2 **Line a baking sheet** with wax paper. Turn out the dough onto a lightly floured counter and knead until smooth but slightly sticky, about 5 minutes. Break off a lemon-size chunk of dough; keep the remaining dough covered with plastic wrap. Roll the dough into a 1-inch-thick rope. Cut into 1-inch pieces, then roll each piece off the back of the tines of a fork to make decorative grooves. As you complete the gnocchi, place them on the baking sheet, making sure they don't touch. Repeat with the remaining dough. Refrigerate, lightly covered with plastic wrap, up to 2 days. (You can also freeze them on the baking sheet, then transfer the frozen gnocchi to zip-close plastic bags and store up to 1 month. Frozen gnocchi may be cooked without thawing.)

3 **Cook the gnocchi** in a large pot of boiling water in batches, without crowding, until they float to the surface, 30 to 45 seconds. With a slotted spoon, transfer the gnocchi to a serving bowl. Repeat until all the gnocchi are cooked. Toss gently with the sauce of your choice. (See next recipe.)

3 *POINTS* per serving

Per serving
162 Calories | 0 g Total Fat | 0 g Saturated Fat | 0 mg Cholesterol | 139 mg Sodium
36 g Total Carbohydrate | 2 g Dietary Fiber | 4 g Protein | 8 mg Calcium

gnocchi with shiitakes, tomatoes, zucchini, and pesto

You can find pesto in jars or in the refrigerator case at your supermarket, but you can also make your own. It freezes well: Just spread the pesto in an ice-cube tray and transfer the frozen cubes to a zip-close plastic bag.

makes 4 servings

1 **Pour the boiling water** over the sun-dried tomatoes in a small bowl; set aside until softened, about 20 minutes. Coarsely chop and reserve in the soaking liquid.

2 **Meanwhile, heat a large** nonstick skillet. Swirl in the oil, then add the zucchini and the mushrooms. Sauté until tender, 5 to 6 minutes.

3 **Add the tomatoes** to the skillet with the reserved liquid, the gnocchi, and pesto. Cook, stirring frequently, just until heated through. Serve, sprinkled with the Parmesan cheese.

$1/4$ cup boiling water

7 sun-dried tomato halves (not oil-packed)

1 teaspoon olive oil

1 medium zucchini, sliced

$1/2$ pound shiitake mushrooms, halved

About 2 cups hot cooked Gnocchi (page 114), or 2 cups cooked frozen gnocchi

$1/4$ cup pesto

1 tablespoon grated Parmesan cheese

Chef's Tip

To make your own pesto, combine $2^{1}/2$ cups packed rinsed basil leaves, $1/4$ cup toasted pine nuts (see Chef's Tip, page 30), 3 tablespoons olive oil, and 1 teaspoon minced garlic in a blender or food processor. Puree to a coarse paste. With the machine running, gradually add 2 tablespoons water to make a smooth paste. Stir in $1/4$ cup freshly grated Parmesan cheese by hand.

Per serving

315 Calories | 11 g Total Fat | 2 g Saturated Fat | 4 mg Cholesterol | 253 mg Sodium
48 g Total Carbohydrate | 4 g Dietary Fiber | 9 g Protein | 100 mg Calcium

6 *POINTS* per serving

spaetzle

Spaetzle are tiny, delicate, pale-yellow German noodles made with flour, eggs, milk, and nutmeg. Traditionally tossed with butter, our lighter version remains scrumptious, as it is mixed with chopped chives instead.

makes 4 servings

1 2/3 cups all-purpose flour

4 egg whites

1/2 cup fat-free milk

Pinch nutmeg

1 tablespoon chopped fresh chives

1/4 teaspoon salt

Freshly ground pepper

1 **Bring a large** saucepan of water to a boil.

2 **Meanwhile, with a wire whisk,** beat the flour, egg whites, milk, and nutmeg in a bowl. Mix in a little more flour or milk, if needed, until the batter is heavy but pourable. Continue to beat 1 to 2 minutes more until the batter is smooth and slightly elastic.

3 **Drop half of the batter** through a colander, large-hole sieve, or potato ricer into the boiling water. Use a spatula to push the batter through. Keep the water at a simmer until the spaetzle float to the surface and are tender, about 1 minute. With a slotted spoon, remove the spaetzle to a clean colander; drain well. Repeat with the remaining batter. Transfer the spaetzle to a large bowl and toss with the chives, salt, and pepper.

3 POINTS per serving

Per serving

144 Calories | 0 g Total Fat | 0 g Saturated Fat | 0 mg Cholesterol | 137 mg Sodium 28 g Total Carbohydrate | 1 g Dietary Fiber | 7 g Protein | 32 mg Calcium

roasted vegetable lasagne

If you think making lasagne is a big production, think again. This version combines roasted eggplant, bell peppers, zucchini, fresh tomato, and garlic to make a smoky vegetable filling that's ready before you know it. Plus, convenient no-boil lasagne noodles will make assembling the dish a breeze.

makes 6 servings

1 (1½-pound) eggplant, peeled and chunked

2 medium zucchini, chunked

4 plum tomatoes, halved

1 yellow bell pepper, seeded and quartered

1 medium white onion, chunked

1 garlic bulb

1 cup part-skim ricotta cheese

2 tablespoons grated Parmesan cheese

2 tablespoons chopped fresh basil

1 egg white

Freshly ground pepper

8 no-boil lasagne noodles

1 cup shredded part-skim mozzarella cheese

1 **Preheat the oven** to 375°F. Spray 2 baking sheets and a 9-inch square baking dish with nonstick spray. Scatter the eggplant, zucchini, tomatoes, bell pepper and onion on the baking sheets; lightly spray the vegetables with some additional nonstick spray. Cut off the top 1½ inches of the garlic bulb then wrap the bulb in foil. Roast the vegetables until well-browned, about 45 minutes, tossing every 15 minutes. Roast the garlic at the same time until softened, about 45 minutes.

2 **When the vegetables** are cool enough to handle, squeeze the garlic pulp into a food processor. Peel the tomatoes and add to the food processor; puree. Pour the puree into a large bowl.

3 **Peel and finely chop** the bell pepper and add it to the puree. Finely chop the eggplant, zucchini, and onion, and add them to the puree. Gently toss to combine.

4 **Combine the ricotta,** Parmesan cheese, basil, egg white, and ground pepper in another bowl.

5 **To assemble the lasagne,** spread about ¼ cup of the vegetable mixture over the bottom of the baking dish; top with 2 lasagne noodles. Top with 1½ cups of the vegetable mixture, then with 2 more noodles. Spread the next layer with all the ricotta mixture; top with 2 more noodles. Spread with about 1 cup of the vegetable mixture, top with the last 2 noodles, then the remaining vegetable mixture; sprinkle with the mozzarella cheese. Cover the lasagne with aluminum foil and bake 30 minutes. Remove the foil and bake until the cheese is melted and browned, about 5 minutes longer.

Per serving

303 Calories | 8 g Total Fat | 4 g Saturated Fat | 25 mg Cholesterol | 191 mg Sodium
42 g Total Carbohydrate | 5 g Dietary Fiber | 18 g Protein | 295 mg Calcium

6 *POINTS* per serving

asparagus lasagne

Here is an elegant vegetarian alternative to traditional lasagne—and a showcase for asparagus in all its springtime glory. We've lightened up the classic béchamel sauce by using cornstarch to add body without fat. Be sure to cook the asparagus only briefly; overcooking will rob them of their subtle flavor.

makes 4 servings

3 cups water

1 1/2 pounds asparagus, trimmed and cut into 1/4-inch pieces

2 cups low-fat (1%) milk

1 tablespoon cornstarch

1 tablespoon all-purpose flour

1 1/2 teaspoons unsalted butter

3/4 teaspoon salt

Freshly ground pepper

1 bunch scallions, thinly sliced

1/4 cup + 2 tablespoons grated Parmesan cheese

8 no-boil lasagne noodles

1 cup part-skim ricotta cheese

1 **Preheat the oven** to 400°F. Spray a 9-inch square baking dish with nonstick spray. Bring the water to a boil in a saucepan. Add the asparagus and cook for 2 minutes. Drain; let cool.

2 **Meanwhile, with a wire whisk,** combine the milk, cornstarch, flour, butter, salt, and pepper in a saucepan; cook, whisking constantly, until the sauce thickens and comes to a boil, 3 to 4 minutes. Remove from the heat. Stir in the scallions and 1/4 cup of the Parmesan cheese.

3 **Spoon one-fourth** of the sauce into the baking dish; top with 2 lasagne noodles, then spread one-third of the ricotta and one-third of the asparagus over the noodles. Repeat the layers two times with the sauce, noodles, ricotta, and asparagus. Top with the last 2 noodles, then the remaining sauce. Cover the lasagne with aluminum foil and bake 45 minutes. Remove the foil and sprinkle with the remaining 2 tablespoons Parmesan cheese. Bake until the cheese is golden brown and bubbling, about 15 minutes longer. Let stand 10 minutes before serving.

12 *POINTS* per serving

Per serving
584 Calories | 12 g Total Fat | 6 g Saturated Fat | 34 mg Cholesterol | 747 mg Sodium
90 g Total Carbohydrate | 4 g Dietary Fiber | 29 g Protein | 466 mg Calcium

chapter 7

fish

seared salmon with a moroccan spice crust

Seared salmon with lentils, frisée, and glazed pearl onions come together to create a sophisticated meal. Glazing the onions is a simple task, but requires slow cooking and frequent turning. As the onions glaze, their flavor concentrates and becomes rich, sweet, and mellow.

makes 4 servings

12–16 white pearl onions

1 1/2 teaspoons unsalted butter

3/4 teaspoon sugar

1/4 teaspoon salt

1/4 teaspoon freshly ground pepper

1 1/2 teaspoons curry powder

1 1/2 teaspoons coriander seeds

1 1/2 teaspoons cumin seeds

1 1/2 teaspoons caraway seeds

1 1/2 teaspoons anise seeds

1 1/2 teaspoons black peppercorns

1 pound salmon fillet, cut into 4 pieces

1 cup cooked green (French) lentils

1 small head frisée (curly endive), rinsed and torn

1 **Fill a medium saucepan** with enough water to cover the onions and bring to a boil. Add the onions; simmer, covered, 3–4 minutes. Drain. When cool enough to handle, cut off the roots and peel away the tough skins.

2 **Melt the butter** in a nonstick skillet over medium-low heat, then add the onions. Cook, turning often, until golden brown, about 15 minutes. Add the sugar and cook, stirring, until the onions are glazed, about 5 minutes. Add the salt and pepper and keep warm.

3 **Combine the curry powder,** coriander, cumin, caraway, anise, and peppercorns in a small bowl. Coarsely grind the mixture in a spice grinder or mortar and pestle. Rub both sides of each salmon piece with a generous amount of the spice mixture.

4 **Spray a large nonstick skillet** with nonstick spray and set over high heat. Add the salmon and cook, turning once, until the fish is browned on the outside and opaque in the center, about 4 minutes per side.

5 **Divide and arrange** the lentils on each of 4 plates. Place the salmon in the middle of the lentils and garnish with the glazed onions and frisée.

Chef's Tip

Pearl onions are sweet and, ideally, bite-size. Select onions with paper-thin skin and no soft spots. Dampness will spoil onions, so store them in a cool, dry place. Frozen, peeled pearl onions can be substituted for fresh, in which case it is unnecessary to peel and trim the root ends as described in Step 1.

5 *POINTS* per serving

Per serving

263 Calories | 9 g Total Fat | 2 g Saturated Fat | 66 mg Cholesterol | 189 mg Sodium
17 g Total Carbohydrate | 4 g Dietary Fiber | 28 g Protein | 62 mg Calcium

seared salmon with a moroccan spice crust

grilled herbed salmon with southwest white bean stew

This hearty meal matches salmon with savory beans. The bean stew may be prepared a day ahead and refrigerated. To save time, prepare the grill while the salmon marinates.

makes 4 servings

$^1/_4$ cup fresh lime juice

1 tablespoon chopped fresh parsley

1 tablespoon chopped fresh chives

$1^1/_2$ teaspoons chopped fresh thyme

1 teaspoon crushed black peppercorns

1 pound salmon fillet, cut into 4 pieces

1 (15-ounce) can navy beans, rinsed and drained

1 cup low-sodium chicken broth or water

1 garlic clove, peeled

1 teaspoon olive oil

1 red onion, chopped

1 green bell pepper, chopped

1 small jalapeño pepper, seeded, and minced (wear gloves to prevent irritation)

3 garlic cloves, minced

$1^1/_2$ teaspoons ground cumin

2 tablespoons sherry vinegar

$^1/_2$ tomato, chopped

1 tablespoon chopped fresh cilantro

1 **Combine the lime juice,** parsley, chives, thyme, and pepper in a zip-close plastic bag; add the salmon. Squeeze out the air and seal the bag; turn to coat the salmon. Refrigerate 30 minutes.

2 **Combine the beans,** broth, and garlic in a saucepan. Simmer until the beans are heated through, 2–3 minutes. Drain the beans, reserving the cooking liquid, and discard the garlic clove.

3 **Puree about half** of the beans with $^1/_2$ cup of the cooking liquid. Combine the puree with the whole beans.

4 **Heat the oil** in a nonstick skillet, then add the onion, bell pepper, jalapeño, and the minced garlic. Add the cumin and sauté the mixture until fragrant, about 30 seconds. Combine with the beans and enough of the reserved cooking liquid to make a stew consistency. Add the vinegar and tomato; cook until just heated through.

5 **Spray the grill rack** with nonstick spray and prepare the grill, or spray a nonstick ridged grill pan with nonstick spray and set over high heat. Grill the salmon 5 inches from heat until opaque in the center, 5–6 minutes per side.

6 **Stir the cilantro** into the warm bean stew and serve at once with the salmon.

6 *POINTS* per serving

Per serving

303 Calories | 9 g Total Fat | 1 g Saturated Fat | 62 mg Cholesterol | 574 mg Sodium
26 g Total Carbohydrate | 2 g Dietary Fiber | 30 g Protein | 83 mg Calcium

salmon napoleon with vegetables

This elegant recipe takes its name from the heavenly layered French dessert. Here, phyllo is used to sandwich the salmon, vegetables, and yogurt sauce. Look for phyllo in the freezer section of your supermarket; fully thaw it before using.

makes 4 servings

1. **To prepare the yogurt sauce,** combine the yogurt cheese, dill, lemon juice, salt, and pepper in a bowl; cover and refrigerate.

2. **Preheat the oven** to 400°F. Spray a baking sheet with nonstick spray; set aside. Whisk together the egg white, 2 teaspoons of the water, and the oil in a bowl.

3. **Cover the sheets** of phyllo dough with plastic wrap. Place one sheet on a clean dry work surface; brush it lightly with the egg-white mixture and lay a second sheet over it. Brush the second sheet with the egg white mixture, and add a third sheet. Cut the dough into 8 equal rectangles. Carefully place the rectangles on the baking sheet and bake until lightly browned, about 15 minutes. Repeat with the remaining sheets of phyllo dough.

4. **Bring the remaining** 1/2 cup water to a boil in a skillet with a fitted lid. Add the leeks; and simmer, covered, for 2 minutes. Add the zucchini and simmer 2 minutes longer. Uncover and cook, stirring, until the water evaporates, about 2 minutes. Season the vegetables with a pinch of the pepper, toss with the margarine, and transfer to a bowl.

5. **To assemble the napoleons,** place 1 baked phyllo rectangle on each of 4 plates; layer each with one-fourth of the vegetable mixture, a second baked phyllo rectangle, and 2 tablespoons of the yogurt sauce. Scatter one-fourth of the salmon evenly over each, top with a third phyllo rectangle, and one-fourth of the roasted bell pepper strips. Cover each with a fourth rectangle. Divide the remaining yogurt sauce evenly over the napoleons; serve with the dill sprigs and lemon wedges (if using).

1 cup yogurt cheese
(see Chef's Tip, page 51)

2 tablespoons finely chopped fresh dill, or 1 teaspoon dried

2 tablespoons fresh lemon juice

1/4 teaspoon salt

Freshly ground pepper

1 egg white

1/2 cup + 2 teaspoons water

2 teaspoons olive oil

6 (12 × 17-inch) sheets phyllo dough, room temperature

2 medium leeks, sliced into matchstick-size pieces

2 medium zucchini, sliced into matchstick-size pieces

2 teaspoons reduced-calorie tub margarine or 1 teaspoon unsalted butter

2 cups flaked, cooked salmon

1 roasted yellow bell pepper, cut into 1/4-inch strips

Dill sprigs (optional)

1 lemon, cut into wedges (optional)

Per serving

325 Calories | 8 g Total Fat | 2 g Saturated Fat | 42 mg Cholesterol | 463 mg Sodium
38 g Total Carbohydrate | 2 g Dietary Fiber | 27 g Protein | 324 mg Calcium

7 POINTS per serving

bass and scallops en papillote

The French term *en papillote* refers to baking ingredients inside a parchment paper parcel shaped like a half-heart. As the food heats and creates steam, the papillote puffs up. In this recipe the papillote is filled with bass, scallops, julienned vegetables, and gremolata, a sprightly flavored garnish. Cut the parcels open at the table to release the savory aroma from the papillote. See page 67 for instructions on how to julienne the vegetables.

makes 4 servings

1 1/2 cups low-sodium vegetable broth

1/2 cup dry vermouth

1/4 pound celeriac, cut into julienne (about 1 cup);

1 large carrot, peeled and julienned

1/2 pound (about 4) red potatoes, thinly sliced

1 small cucumber, peeled, seeded, and julienned

1 1/2 tablespoons chopped fresh flat-leaf parsley

1 teaspoon grated lemon zest

2 oil-packed anchovy fillets, chopped (optional)

1 garlic clove, minced

1/2 pound sea bass, cut into 4 pieces

1/2 pound sea scallops, muscle tabs removed

1/2 teaspoon crushed black peppercorns

1 **Combine the broth** and vermouth in a saucepan and bring to a simmer. Add the celeriac and carrots; cook until tender, about 6 minutes; transfer to a plate with a slotted spoon. Return the broth to a boil; add the potatoes and simmer until barely tender, about 12 minutes. Drain the potatoes, discarding the broth; toss with the celeriac, carrots, and cucumber in a bowl.

2 **Preheat the oven** to 425°F. To prepare the gremolata, combine the parsley, lemon zest, anchovies (if using), and the garlic in a bowl.

3 **Fold four 12 × 16-inch sheets** of parchment paper in half. Starting at the folded edge, cut each paper into a half-heart shape. Unfold and spray the parchment paper with nonstick spray.

4 **Divide and arrange** the potato mixture on half of each piece of parchment. Top with the bass and scallops. Top with the gremolata and sprinkle with the pepper. Fold the parchment over the fish and vegetables, making a tight seal. Place the parchment parcels on a baking sheet and bake until they are puffy and browned, about 8 minutes. Serve, drizzled with any juices.

Chef's Tip

Celeriac, also called celery root, tastes like celery and parsley. It can be eaten both raw and cooked. Select small firm celeriac with a minimum of root knobs. Before using, prepare a medium bowl of acidulated water (cold water with a splash of vinegar or lemon juice). Peel the celeriac with a paring knife and dip it in the acidulated water to prevent browning. If you can't find celeriac at your supermarket, use 1 cup julienned celery stalks instead.

4 *POINTS* per serving

Per serving

242 Calories | 3 g Total Fat | 1 g Saturated Fat | 59 mg Cholesterol | 624 mg Sodium
23 g Total Carbohydrate | 3 g Dietary Fiber | 23 g Protein | 91 mg Calcium

assembling en papillote packages

Cut heart shapes out of folded parchment paper.

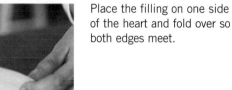

Place the filling on one side of the heart and fold over so both edges meet.

Crimp the edges, following the paper's shape, to form a tight seal.

baked bass with ginger nage

A la nage is a French cooking method of poaching and serving fish in court bouillon—a broth made from herbs, aromatic vegetables, wine, vinegar or lemon juice, and enough water to cover the fish. In this recipe, ginger and the stems of shiitake mushrooms are added to give depth and complexity to the bouillon.

makes 4 servings

2¹/₂ cups water

2 medium yellow onions, chopped

1 carrot, peeled and chopped

1 celery stalk, chopped

2 tablespoons thinly sliced peeled fresh ginger

5 shiitake mushrooms, stemmed and sliced

1 tablespoon cider vinegar

1 tablespoon dry white wine

¹/₄ teaspoon salt

1¹/₄ teaspoons black peppercorns

4 (¹/₄-pound) bass fillets

1 small red bell pepper, thinly sliced

4 medium scallions, thinly sliced

2 bok choy leaves, shredded

¹/₂ cup drained sliced water chestnuts

Chervil or cilantro sprigs

1 **To prepare the court bouillon,** combine the water, onion, carrot, celery, ginger, mushroom stems, vinegar, wine, and salt in a large saucepan. Bring to a boil, reduce the heat and simmer, covered, 20 minutes. Add the peppercorns and simmer 10 minutes more. Strain, discarding the vegetables; pour into a large ovenproof skillet with a fitted lid wide enough to accommodate the fish in a single layer.

2 **Preheat the oven** to 325°F.

3 **Bring the court bouillon** to a simmer; then add the fish. Add the mushroom caps, the bell pepper, scallions and bok choy; cover and bake 5 minutes. Add the water chestnuts. Bake until the fish is opaque in the center, about 3 minutes more.

4 **Serve the fish** and vegetables in the bouillon, garnished with the chervil sprigs.

3 *POINTS* per serving

Per serving

150 Calories | 5 g Total Fat | 1 g Saturated Fat | 77 mg Cholesterol | 227 mg Sodium
4 g Total Carbohydrate | 1 g Dietary Fiber | 22 g Protein | 116 mg Calcium

grilled halibut with roasted red bell peppers and warm potato salad

This recipe pairs mild-tasting, low-fat halibut with a potato salad that is as colorful as it is flavorful. To save time, prepare the grill while the potatoes are simmering. Sherry vinegar is a rich, full-flavored vinegar from Spain made from aged sherry wine. Find it in well-stocked supermarkets and specialty food shops.

makes 4 servings

1 **Bring the water** to a boil in a medium saucepan, then add the potatoes. Cook covered until the potatoes are tender, 20–30 minutes; drain. When the potatoes are cool enough to handle, cut them into $1/4$-inch slices. Whisk together 3 tablespoons of the oil, the cider vinegar, parsley, shallot, sugar, tarragon, mustard, $1/2$ teaspoon of the salt and $1/4$ teaspoon of the pepper in a bowl. Add the potatoes; gently toss and keep warm.

2 **Heat the rest of the oil** in a large nonstick skillet, then add the onion. Sauté until the onion is lightly browned, 2–3 minutes. Add the garlic and sauté until fragrant, 1 minute. Add the bell peppers, the sherry vinegar, capers, cumin, crushed red pepper, $1/8$ teaspoon of the salt, and the coriander. Heat through; keep warm.

3 **Spray the grill rack** with nonstick spray and prepare the grill, or spray a nonstick ridged grill pan with nonstick spray and set over medium-high heat.

4 **Season the halibut** with the remaining $1/4$ teaspoon of the pepper and $1/8$ teaspoon of the salt. Grill the halibut 5 inches from the heat until opaque in the center, about 2–3 minutes per side. Divide and arrange the potato salad on each of four plates, lay the grilled halibut over the potato salad. Top with the warm onion-bell pepper mixture.

8 cups water

$1 1/2$ pounds red potatoes

$3 1/2$ tablespoons extra-virgin olive oil

2 tablespoons cider vinegar

2 tablespoons chopped fresh parsley

1 tablespoon minced shallot

2 teaspoons sugar

2 teaspoons chopped fresh tarragon

2 teaspoons Dijon mustard

$3/4$ teaspoon salt

$1/2$ teaspoon coarsely ground pepper

1 onion, sliced

3 garlic cloves, thinly sliced

2 red bell peppers, roasted, peeled, and thinly sliced

2 yellow bell peppers, roasted, peeled, and thinly sliced

$1 1/2$ tablespoons sherry vinegar

1 tablespoon drained and chopped capers

$1/4$ teaspoon ground cumin

$1/8$ teaspoon crushed red pepper

Pinch ground coriander

1 pound halibut fillet, cut into 4 pieces

Per serving

422 Calories | 15 g Total Fat | 2 g Saturated Fat | 36 mg Cholesterol | 592 mg Sodium
45 g Total Carbohydrate | 8 g Dietary Fiber | 28 g Protein | 153 mg Calcium

9 *POINTS* per serving

seared cod in a rich broth with fall vegetables

This dish gets its rich, intense flavor from dried shiitake mushrooms, which are ground to a powder in a spice or coffee grinder and then used to coat the fish. The mushroom powder may be prepared ahead and stored in an airtight container; the vegetables may be prepared one day ahead and refrigerated. For instructions on cutting the vegetables into julienne, see page 67.

makes 4 servings

$^1/_2$ pound haricots verts or green beans, cut into 1-inch lengths

1 medium carrot, peeled and julienned

$^1/_2$ cup julienned rutabaga

1 medium white turnip, julienned

$^1/_2$ pound herb-flavored or plain fresh fettuccine

3 ounces dried shiitake mushrooms

$^3/_4$ pound cod fillet, cut into 4 pieces

$^1/_4$ teaspoon salt

$^1/_4$ teaspoon ground white pepper

$2^1/_2$ cups low-sodium vegetable broth

$1^1/_2$ teaspoons minced, peeled fresh ginger

$1^1/_2$ tablespoons snipped fresh chives

3 tablespoons thinly sliced scallions

$1^1/_2$ ounces enoki mushrooms, cut into $1^1/_2$-inch lengths (optional)

1 **Fill a large saucepan** with 3 inches water and bring to a boil. Add the haricots verts, carrot, and yellow and white turnips; simmer, covered, until the vegetables are tender-crisp, 3–5 minutes. Drain the vegetables in a colander and rinse under cold water to stop the cooking.

2 **Cook the pasta** according to package directions. Drain and rinse under cold water to stop the cooking.

3 **Grind 2 ounces** of the dried shiitake mushrooms to a powder in a spice or coffee grinder. Spread the powder on a piece of wax paper. Season the cod with a small amount of the salt and pepper, then dredge each piece in the ground mushrooms.

4 **Preheat the oven** to 450°F. Spray a large nonstick skillet with non-stick spray and set over medium-high heat for 3 minutes. Add the cod and cook until browned, about 2 minutes per side. Place the cod on a baking sheet and bake until opaque in the center, about 10 minutes.

5 **Meanwhile, bring the broth** to a simmer in a saucepan, then add the remaining dried shiitake mushrooms. Simmer until the broth has a rich mushroom flavor, 15 minutes. Strain the broth and discard the mushrooms. Add the pasta, the haricots verts-carrot mixture, and the ginger to the mushroom broth. Simmer until heated through. Transfer the pasta, vegetables, and broth to large soup plates. Arrange the pasta to make a bed for the cod in the center. Place the cod on the pasta and garnish with the chives, scallions, and (if using) the enoki mushrooms.

---

5 *POINTS* per serving

Per serving
292 Calories | 2 g Total Fat | 0 g Saturated Fat | 37 mg Cholesterol | 790 mg Sodium
48 g Total Carbohydrate | 11 g Dietary Fiber | 23 g Protein | 82 mg Calcium

cod in grape leaves

Grape leaves are commonly used in Greek and Middle Eastern recipes for wrapping foods while cooking and can be found canned in supermarkets or ethnic groceries. If grilling, the grape leaves will prevent the fish from sticking to the grill. This dish is just as tasty when prepared in the oven. Prepare the packets in the morning, refrigerate them until guests arrive, and cook them when the grill is hot. Make a few extras for a delicious cold meal later.

makes 4 servings

16 pickled grape leaves, drained

1¼ pounds boneless cod fillets

8 paper-thin lemon slices

4 teaspoons olive oil

½ teaspoon crumbled dried oregano

Freshly ground pepper

1 **Spray the grill rack** with nonstick spray and prepare the grill, or preheat the oven to 400°F. Soak 4–5 feet of kitchen twine in water for tying the cod packets.

2 **Rinse the grape leaves** well in cold water. Drain.

3 **Overlapping each leaf by half,** arrange the leaves into groups of three on a work surface. Put the cod fillets on the grape leaves; top each with the lemon slices, oil, oregano, and pepper. Wrap the fish in the leaves, enclosing completely; use additional leaves, if needed. Tie each packet crosswise and lengthwise with the twine.

4 **Grill or bake** until the fish is opaque in the center, about 15 minutes. If grilling, turn the fish often to avoid charring the leaves. Remove the twine before serving.

Per serving

179 Calories | 5 g Total Fat | 1 g Saturated Fat | 61 mg Cholesterol | 557 mg Sodium
6 g Total Carbohydrate | 2 g Dietary Fiber | 25 g Protein | 34 mg Calcium

4 *POINTS* per serving

thai monkfish with coconut sauce

Monkfish, a sweet-tasting and firm-textured fish, reminds some people of lobster. Here, it is seasoned with traditional Thai flavorings such as peanuts, ginger, and coconut. With its wonderful perfume, basmati or jasmine rice is the perfect accompaniment.

makes 4 servings

1/4 cup low-fat (1%) milk

1/2 teaspoon coconut extract

1 pound monkfish fillets, cut into 12 pieces

2 tablespoons chopped fresh cilantro

2 tablespoons fresh lime juice

4 teaspoons chunky peanut butter

1 tablespoon minced peeled fresh galangal (Thai ginger), or regular ginger

1 jalapeño pepper, seeded, and minced (wear gloves to prevent irritation)

2 garlic cloves, minced

3/4 teaspoon salt

Freshly ground pepper

4 lime slices

2 cups cooked basmati, jasmine, or white rice

1 **Spray the grill rack** with nonstick spray and prepare the grill, or preheat the oven to 400°F.

2 **To make the coconut sauce,** combine the milk and coconut extract in a small bowl.

3 **Cut four 12 × 24-inch pieces** of double-thickness, heavy-duty aluminum foil. Place 3 pieces of monkfish on each piece of foil. Then top each portion of fish with some coconut sauce, cilantro, lime juice, peanut butter, ginger, jalapeño, garlic, salt, pepper, and lime slices. Fold the foil into packets, making a tight seal.

4 **Grill the packets** 5 inches from the heat, or bake until the fish is opaque in the center, 25–30 minutes. Open the packets carefully when testing for doneness, as steam will escape. Serve with the rice and drizzle with any juices.

Chef's Tip

Galangal, also known as Thai ginger, is used widely in Asia to flavor dishes. It is a knobby, cream-colored root that tastes like a mixture of ginger and pepper. Find it in Asian markets.

5 *POINTS* per serving

Per serving

254 Calories | 5 g Total Fat | 1 g Saturated Fat | 29 mg Cholesterol | 492 mg Sodium
30 g Total Carbohydrate | 1 g Dietary Fiber | 21 g Protein | 39 mg Calcium

seared tuna with salsa cruda and orzo

In this simple dish, we prefer the fish rare; simply increase the cooking time if you like your fish more well-done. This dish makes an impressive entrée for guests, yet it's deceptively simple to prepare. Make the salsa cruda, an uncooked tomato salsa, first, so the juices of the ripe plum tomatoes and olives have time to mingle in the tangy vinaigrette. Don't add the basil or garlic until just before serving, though, to ensure the bright green color of the basil and fresh flavor of the garlic.

makes 4 servings

1 **To make the salsa cruda,** combine the tomatoes, olives, 1 tablespoon of the oil, the vinegar, 1/4 teaspoon of the salt, and the coarsely ground pepper in a bowl; let stand at room temperature to allow the flavors to blend.

2 **Cook the orzo** according to package directions. Rinse briefly under cool water; drain and toss with 2 teaspoons of the oil, the lemon juice, oregano, lemon zest, and 1/4 teaspoon of the salt.

3 **Season the tuna steaks** with the remaining 1/2 teaspoon salt and a grinding of the pepper. Heat the remaining teaspoon oil in a nonstick skillet, then add the tuna and cook, turning once, until browned but still red inside, about 2 minutes per side.

4 **Stir the basil** and garlic into the salsa. Evenly divide the orzo among 4 plates and top with the tuna. Spoon the salsa over the tuna and serve.

4 plum tomatoes, cut into 1/4-inch cubes

10 kalamata olives, pitted

2 tablespoons olive oil

2 tablespoons balsamic vinegar

1 teaspoon salt

Coarsely ground pepper

1/2 pound orzo pasta

2 teaspoons fresh lemon juice

1 teaspoon chopped fresh oregano, or 1/4 teaspoon dried

1/2 teaspoon grated lemon zest

Freshly ground pepper

4 (6-ounce) yellowfin tuna steaks, 3/4-inch thick

6 large fresh basil leaves, thinly sliced

1 garlic clove, minced

Per serving

482 Calories | 11 g Total Fat | 2 g Saturated Fat | 74 mg Cholesterol | 737 mg Sodium
48 g Total Carbohydrate | 3 g Dietary Fiber | 46 g Protein | 53 mg Calcium

10 *POINTS* per serving

grilled yellowfin tuna with citrus salad

Yellowfin tuna, also known as Ahi, has pale-pink flesh and a more intense flavor than albacore. Tuna is excellent grilled or broiled and, with this spicy citrus salad, makes a refreshing and easy meal. Roasted peanut oil, which is available in many supermarkets and health food stores, is more flavorful than regular peanut oil, so it imparts a unique toasty nut flavor to the citrus salad.

makes 4 servings

1/2 teaspoon arrowroot

1/3 cup low-sodium vegetable broth

1 medium pink grapefruit

1 medium orange

1 tablespoon minced jalapeño pepper (wear gloves to prevent irritation)

1 tablespoon roasted peanut oil

Freshly ground pepper

1/4 teaspoon salt

1 pound trimmed yellowfin tuna fillet, cut into 4 pieces

1/2 teaspoon finely grated lemon zest

1/2 teaspoon finely grated lime zest

1 cup very thinly sliced fennel bulb

1 red onion, very thinly sliced

2 teaspoons chopped fennel tops

1 **Dissolve the arrowroot** with 2 teaspoons of the broth in a small bowl. Bring the remaining broth to a boil in a small saucepan. Stir in the arrowroot mixture and cook, stirring, until thickened, about 30 seconds. Remove from the heat and let cool slightly.

2 **Using a sharp paring knife,** slice away the top and bottom ends of the grapefruit. Place on a cutting board on end and slice the rind away, removing all traces of pith. Working over a large bowl to catch the juices, cut the grapefruit sections out from between the membranes, letting each one fall into the bowl as you cut it free. Discard any seeds. Repeat with the orange.

3 **Add the jalapeño** and the juice from the citrus sections to the thickened broth. Whisk in the oil and season with pepper.

4 **Spray the grill rack** with nonstick spray and prepare the grill, or spray a nonstick ridged grill pan with nonstick spray and set over medium-high heat.

5 **Season the tuna** with the salt and pepper. Grill the fish 5 inches from the heat, until opaque in the center, 2–3 minutes per side.

continues on page 134

5 *POINTS* per serving

Per serving
244 Calories | 9 g Total Fat | 2 g Saturated Fat | 43 mg Cholesterol | 273 mg Sodium
12 g Total Carbohydrate | 3 g Dietary Fiber | 28 g Protein | 34 mg Calcium

grilled yellowfin tuna with citrus salad

continued from page 132

6 **Meanwhile, warm the dressing.** Add the grapefruit and orange sections and the lemon and lime zest; warm through (do not stir or the grapefruit will break apart). Divide and arrange the fennel on each of four plates and top with the onion. Arrange the citrus salad next to the fennel. Slice each portion of tuna and fan it around the other side of the fennel. Drizzle the plates with the dressing and sprinkle with the chopped fennel tops.

Chef's Tip

The success of this recipe depends in part on having very thinly sliced fennel and red onion. The perfect tool for such a cutting task is a mandoline. This hand-operated slicing machine comes with a variety of adjustable blades for cutting thick and thin slices, as well as julienne and waffle cuts. Professional-quality stainless steel mandolines retail for $150–$200, but plastic models with stainless steel blades are also available. They are much cheaper and do a perfectly acceptable job at a number of slicing tasks.

making citrus supremes

Segments of citrus fruit without membranes are called "suprêmes." Slice off the top and bottom ends of the orange. Place a flat end on a cutting board and slice off the rind and pith. Your knife should follow the natural curve of the fruit. A little flesh will adhere to the rind, but it should not be a very large amount.

Holding the fruit with one hand, slice next to the connective membrane on one side of a citrus segment. (Work over a bowl if you want to collect the juices.)

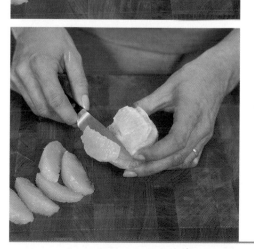

Twist the knife to turn the direction of your cut, and use a scooping motion to cut out the citrus suprême. Repeat from step 2 for each segment.

grilled swordfish with black-pepper pasta

The robust flavors of tomatoes, olives, and pepper coupled with swordfish steaks and pasta make a healthy yet hearty meal. If you can't find 1/4-pound steaks, buy 1/2-pound steaks and divide them in half. To save time, prepare the grill while you're cooking the vegetables. If you can't find black-pepper pasta, substitute it with plain fresh pasta.

makes 4 servings

2 tablespoons dried parsley

2 tablespoons dried chives

2 tablespoons dried thyme

1/2 pound black-pepper or plain fresh pasta

1 1/2 tablespoons olive oil

4 garlic cloves, minced

1 1/2 tablespoons minced shallot

2 1/2 medium tomatoes, chopped (about 1 1/4 cups)

6 kalamata olives, pitted and halved

1/4 cup + 1 tablespoon balsamic vinegar

1 tablespoon shredded fresh basil

1/2 teaspoon salt

4 (1/4-pound) swordfish steaks

1. **Combine the parsley,** chives, and thyme in a small bowl.

2. **Cook the pasta** according to package directions. Drain.

3. **Heat the oil** in a large nonstick skillet; add the garlic and shallot. Sauté until the shallot is translucent, about 3 minutes. Add the tomatoes and olives and sauté until heated through. Stir in the vinegar, basil and salt. Add the pasta and toss to combine; keep warm.

4. **Spray the grill rack** with nonstick spray and prepare the grill, or spray a nonstick ridged grill pan with nonstick spray and set over medium-high heat.

5. **Rub the swordfish** with a generous amount of the dried herb mixture. Grill 5 inches from the heat until the fish is opaque in the center, 3–4 minutes per side. Serve the swordfish over the pasta.

7 POINTS per serving

Per serving

305 Calories | 12 g Total Fat | 2 g Saturated Fat | 44 mg Cholesterol | 675 mg Sodium
23 g Total Carbohydrate | 3 g Dietary Fiber | 26 g Protein | 70 mg Calcium

grilled swordfish with black-pepper pasta

broiled swordfish with tomatoes, anchovies, and garlic

Swordfish, which is found in the waters off both the Atlantic and Pacific coasts, is wonderful grilled or broiled. The *Provençal* flavors in this quick, weeknight recipe add delightful contrast to the mild flavor and meaty texture of the fish.

makes 4 servings

¼ cup dry white wine

1 tablespoon chopped shallot

2 garlic cloves, minced

8 medium plum tomatoes, peeled, seeded, and chopped (about 3 cups)

4 anchovy fillets, minced

4 (4-ounce) swordfish steaks

1½ teaspoons olive oil

Freshly ground pepper

2 teaspoons shredded fresh basil

1 **Spray the broiler rack** with nonstick spray; preheat the broiler.

2 **Combine the wine,** shallots, and garlic in a nonstick skillet. Cook until the shallot is translucent, about 3 minutes. Stir in the tomatoes and anchovies and cook until just simmering, about 3 minutes. Keep warm.

3 **Brush the swordfish** with the oil; season with the pepper. Broil 5 inches from the heat, turning once, until the fish is browned on the outside and opaque in the center, about 6 minutes.

4 **Stir the basil** into the tomato mixture. Serve the swordfish on the tomato mixture.

Chef's Tip

To peel and seed the tomatoes, bring a large pot of water to a boil. Have ready a bowl of ice water. Cut a shallow "X" into the bottom of each tomato. Submerge 1 tomato in boiling water for 10–15 seconds. Plunge into ice water, then remove immediately, and peel the tomato with a paring knife, starting at the "X." If the tomato does not peel easily, return it to the boiling water briefly, shock it in the ice water again, and peel. Repeat with the remaining tomatoes. Cut the tomatoes in half horizontally and remove the seeds.

4 *POINTS* per serving

Per serving
203 Calories | 7 g Total Fat | 2 g Saturated Fat | 48 mg Cholesterol | 262 mg Sodium
7 g Total Carbohydrate | 2 g Dietary Fiber | 25 g Protein | 26 mg Calcium

indian-scented mako

Firm-fleshed mako shark is flavorful and moist. When it comes to curry powder make sure it is fresh to reap the most of its flavor boost. Look for steaks that are of even thickness for perfectly cooked fish. Substitute swordfish if mako is unavailable.

makes 4 servings

1 **Preheat the oven** to 375°F. Combine the ginger, garlic, curry powder, cumin, water, turmeric, and salt in a small bowl and blend to a paste. Rub over the fish.

2 **Arrange the fish** in a large baking dish. Cover with aluminum foil and bake until the fish is opaque in the center, about 12 minutes.

3 **Transfer the fish** with a slotted spatula to a serving platter; keep warm. Strain the pan juices into a small bowl; stir in the yogurt and cilantro. Top the fish with the yogurt mixture.

2 teaspoons minced peeled fresh ginger

2 garlic cloves, minced

1 teaspoon mild or hot curry powder

$1/2$ teaspoon ground cumin

$1/2$ teaspoon water

$1/8$ teaspoon turmeric

Pinch salt

4 (6-ounce) mako shark steaks

$1/4$ cup plain nonfat yogurt

2 tablespoons finely chopped fresh cilantro

Per serving

236 Calories | 8 g Total Fat | 2 g Saturated Fat | 87 mg Cholesterol | 184 mg Sodium
2 g Total Carbohydrate | 0 g Dietary Fiber | 37 g Protein | 98 mg Calcium

5 *POINTS* per serving

whole broiled fish, moroccan-style

This easy seasoning mixture, known as *chermoula* in Morocco, has vivid flavors that won't overwhelm the fish. Cooking a fish whole makes a dramatic presentation and helps enhance its taste. Try mild- to moderately flavored and medium-textured fish such as red snapper, striped bass, grouper, or tilapia in this recipe—whichever looks best at your fish market.

makes 4 servings

1 onion, finely chopped

1/2 cup finely chopped fresh flat-leaf parsley

1/2 cup finely chopped fresh cilantro

1/4 cup fresh lemon juice

1 tablespoon + 1 teaspoon olive oil

2 garlic cloves, minced

1 teaspoon ground cumin

1 teaspoon paprika

1/4 teaspoon turmeric

Pinch salt

2 small (2 pounds each) whole white-fleshed fish, gutted and scaled

Lemon wedges

1 **To prepare the chermoula,** combine the onion, parsley, cilantro, lemon juice, oil, garlic, cumin, paprika, turmeric, and salt in a large zip-close plastic bag. Add the fish, spooning some chermoula in the inner cavity of each fish. Squeeze out the air and seal the bag; turn to coat the fish. Refrigerate at least 6 hours or overnight.

2 **Spray the broiler rack** with nonstick spray; preheat the broiler.

3 **Brush the chermoula** off the outside of the fish, leaving some in the inner cavity. Broil or grill the fish 5 inches from the heat until opaque in the center, about 10 minutes per side. Transfer fish to serving platter and garnish with lemon wedges.

---

6 *POINTS* per serving

Per serving

279 Calories | 5 g Total Fat | 1 g Saturated Fat | 96 mg Cholesterol | 137 mg Sodium
2 g Total Carbohydrate | 0 g Dietary Fiber | 54 g Protein | 90 mg Calcium

chapter 8

shellfish

spicy southern-style shrimp

In the South, shrimp are so plentiful that there seem to be as many shrimp recipes as there are cooks. Leaving the shells on the shrimp as they cook makes the dish a little messier to eat, but lots more flavorful. Serve this dish with slices of crusty bread to sop up the spicy sauce and plenty of napkins.

**makes 12 appetizer
or 6 main-dish servings**

1¹/2 pounds large shrimp

1 teaspoon paprika

Freshly ground pepper

¹/4 teaspoon cayenne

¹/4 teaspoon dried oregano

¹/4 teaspoon dried basil

¹/4 teaspoon salt

2 tablespoons olive oil

1 cup low-sodium chicken broth

2 teaspoons Worcestershire sauce

2 teaspoons hot pepper sauce

2 large garlic cloves, minced

¹/4 cup dry white wine or water

2 tablespoons tomato paste

2 scallions, sliced

1 **With a sharp paring knife** or small scissors, cut through the back of each shrimp just deeply enough to expose the vein; remove the vein, leaving the shell intact. Combine the paprika, pepper, cayenne, oregano, basil, and salt in a large bowl. Add the shrimp and toss to combine. Let stand 15 minutes to blend the flavors.

2 **Heat a large nonstick skillet.** Swirl in the oil, then add the shrimp, ¹/4 cup of the broth, the Worcestershire sauce, pepper sauce, and garlic. Cook until the shrimp shells turn pink, about 2 minutes. Add the remaining ³/4 cup broth, the wine, and tomato paste. Increase the heat to high and cook until the shrimp are just opaque in center, 1–2 minutes longer. With a slotted spoon, transfer the shrimp to a large, deep platter. Bring the sauce to a simmer and cook until slightly thickened, about 1 minute. Stir in the scallions and pour the sauce over the shrimp.

2 *POINTS* per serving

Per appetizer serving

79 Calories | 3 g Total Fat | 1 g Saturated Fat | 70 mg Cholesterol | 146 mg Sodium
2 g Total Carbohydrate | 0 g Dietary Fiber | 10 g Protein | 32 mg Calcium

spicy asian grilled shrimp

Salty and pungent fish sauce, available in Asian markets, contains the liquid from salted, fermented fish. This recipe calls for *nuoc mam*—a Vietnamese fish sauce—but any good fish sauce will enhance the flavor of this dish.

makes 4 servings

1. **Combine the vinegar,** garlic, five-spice powder, ginger, pepper sauce, fish sauce, and oil in a large zip-close bag; add the shrimp. Squeeze out the air and seal the bag; turn to coat the shrimp. Refrigerate one hour.

2. **Spray the grill rack** with nonstick spray and prepare the grill, or spray a nonstick ridged grill pan with nonstick spray and set over medium-high heat.

3. **Drain and discard** the marinade. Grill the shrimp 5 inches from the heat, or on the grill pan (if using) until opaque in the center, about 2 minutes per side.

2 teaspoons rice vinegar

1 garlic clove, minced

3/4 teaspoon five-spice powder

3/4 teaspoon minced peeled fresh ginger

1/2 teaspoon hot pepper sauce

1/2 teaspoon Vietnamese fish sauce (nuoc mam)

1/2 teaspoon sesame oil

1 pound large shrimp, peeled, deveined, and butterflied

Chef's Tips

Five-spice powder—a mixture of cinnamon, cloves, fennel seeds, star anise, and Szechuan peppercorns—is available in most supermarkets. But it is easy enough to mix up a small batch, if you have the spices on hand. Grind equal amounts of the spices to a fine powder in a spice or coffee grinder and store in an airtight container.

To devein and butterfly the shrimp, first peel the shell, tail, and legs from each shrimp. Lay a shrimp on a cutting board with the curved outer edge of the shrimp on the same side as your cutting hand. Using a sharp paring knife, slice along the back of the shrimp from top to tail, cutting the shrimp almost but not entirely in half. Use the knife blade to scrape out the vein, then open the shrimp like a book.

Per serving

123 Calories | 2 g Total Fat | 0 g Saturated Fat | 222 mg Cholesterol | 334 mg Sodium
1 g Total Carbohydrate | 0 g Dietary Fiber | 24 g Protein | 51 mg Calcium

3 *POINTS* per serving

seared scallops with fiery fruit salsa

Searing scallops keeps them plump and tender on the inside, crisp and golden on the outside. When buying scallops, ask to smell them; scallops should have the pleasant, briny scent of the ocean. Keep them refrigerated or on ice until cooking time.

makes 4 servings

1 small papaya, peeled, seeded, and chopped

$1/2$ red bell pepper, seeded and chopped

1 medium red onion, chopped

2 tablespoons fresh lime juice

1 tablespoon chopped fresh cilantro

1 teaspoon minced jalapeño pepper (wear gloves to prevent irritation)

$1/2$ teaspoon salt

2 tablespoons all-purpose flour

Freshly ground pepper

1 pound sea scallops, muscle tabs removed

1 tablespoon olive oil

1 **To make the salsa,** combine the papaya, bell pepper, onion, lime juice, cilantro, jalapeño, and $1/4$ teaspoon of the salt in a bowl.

2 **Combine the flour,** ground pepper, and the remaining $1/4$ teaspoon salt in a large zip-close bag; add the scallops, seal the bag and shake to coat the scallops.

3 **Heat a large nonstick skillet.** Swirl in the oil. Shake the excess flour off the scallops and place them in the skillet. Cook, turning, until the scallops are golden brown on the outside, and just opaque in the center, about 1 minute per side. Serve the scallops over the salsa.

Chef's Tip

Scallops often come with tabs of muscle still attached to them. The muscle is tough and should be removed before cooking. To remove, simply peel the muscle tab away from the scallop and discard.

4 POINTS per serving

Per serving

185 Calories | 4 g Total Fat | 1 g Saturated Fat | 37 mg Cholesterol | 477 mg Sodium
16 g Total Carbohydrate | 2 g Dietary Fiber | 20 g Protein | 51 mg Calcium

seared scallops with fiery fruit salsa

stir-fried scallops

Succulent and sweet, bay scallops measure about a half-inch in diameter, and are usually more expensive than other kinds of scallops. Black sesame seeds, more fragrant and flavorful than the white kind, release a wonderful aroma as they are toasted. Red bean paste is sweetened and often used in desserts; hot bean paste is spicy. Combined with the rich, mellow, and salty oyster sauce, they form a complex flavor base that give this dish its identity. All four ingredients can be found in Asian grocery stores.

makes 4 servings

3/4 cup low-sodium fish broth, vegetable broth, or clam juice

1 tablespoon cornstarch

1 tablespoon oyster sauce

1 1/2 teaspoons red bean paste

1 1/2 teaspoons hot bean paste

4 teaspoons peanut oil

1 pound bay scallops, muscle tabs removed

1 1/2 teaspoons minced peeled fresh ginger

1 garlic clove, minced

1 small zucchini, cut into thin strips

1/3 pound snow peas

1 medium bell pepper, seeded and cut into thin strips

1/2 celery stalk, cut into thin strips

8 small white mushrooms, quartered

4 scallions, thinly sliced

1 tablespoon black sesame seeds, toasted (optional)

2 cups cooked brown rice

1. **Combine the fish broth,** cornstarch, oyster sauce, red bean paste, and hot bean paste in a small bowl.

2. **Heat a nonstick wok** or large nonstick skillet over high heat until a drop of water skitters. Pour in 2 teaspoons of the oil, then add the scallops and cook, turning, until golden brown on the outside and just opaque in the center, about 1 minute per side. Transfer the scallops to a plate, cover, and keep warm.

3. **Return the pan** to the heat. Pour in the remaining 2 teaspoons oil. Then add the ginger and garlic. Stir-fry until fragrant, less than 1 minute. Add the zucchini, snow peas, bell pepper, celery, and mushrooms; stir-fry until the zucchini is tender-crisp, 1–2 minutes. Stir in the broth mixture and bring to a boil. Cook, stirring constantly, until thickened, about 1 minute. Return the scallops to the pan and toss to combine. Sprinkle with the scallions and (if using) sesame seeds and serve with the rice.

Chef's Tip

To toast the sesame seeds, place them in a dry skillet, over medium-low heat. Cook, shaking the pan and stirring constantly, until fragrant, 1–2 minutes. Watch them carefully; sesame seeds can burn quickly. Transfer the seeds to a plate to cool.

6 POINTS per serving

Per serving

318 Calories | 8 g Total Fat | 1 g Saturated Fat | 48 mg Cholesterol | 638 mg Sodium
37 g Total Carbohydrate | 5 g Dietary Fiber | 26 g Protein | 174 mg Calcium

prepping for stir-fry

The key to successful stir-frying is to have all the ingredients ready before beginning.

Stir-frying may be done in stages. In this recipe, the scallops are seared first and then set aside while the vegetables are cooked.

Add the sauce mixture to the vegetables and continue to toss. It will start to thicken almost immediately.

snapper and scallop seviche

Seviche describes a Latin American cold fish preparation, which is "cooked" in a marinade of citrus juice and seasonings. Here, it's served in an edible bowl—the tostada shell. Use only the freshest fish to prepare this delicacy.

makes 4 servings

1/2 pound red snapper fillets, cut into 1 1/4-inch cubes

1/2 pound sea scallops, muscle tabs removed, halved

1/4 cup fresh lime or lemon juice

1/2 teaspoon salt

2 tomatoes, seeded and chopped

1/2 medium red onion, chopped

2 tablespoons minced fresh cilantro

4 teaspoons extra-virgin olive oil

2 teaspoons minced jalapeño pepper (wear gloves to prevent irritation)

1 1/2 teaspoons minced fresh marjoram

4 blue-corn tostada shells

2 cups shredded romaine lettuce

1 **To prepare the seviche,** combine the snapper, scallops, citrus juice, and salt in a large zip-close plastic bag. Squeeze out the air and seal the bag; turn to coat the fish. Refrigerate, turning the bag occasionally, 3–4 hours.

2 **Combine the tomatoes,** onion, cilantro, oil, jalapeño, and marjoram in large bowl; refrigerate, covered, until chilled.

3 **Drain the fish mixture** and discard the marinade. Add to the tomatoes and toss to combine.

4 **Line each tostada shell** with the lettuce; top each with the seviche and serve.

7 POINTS per serving

Per serving

298 Calories | 13 g Total Fat | 1 g Saturated Fat | 40 mg Cholesterol | 210 mg Sodium
23 g Total Carbohydrate | 1 g Dietary Fiber | 25 g Protein | 70 mg Calcium

clams steamed in beer

East Coast littleneck clams are the smallest of the hard-shell clams, also known as "quahogs" (pronounced "ko-hogs"). Only buy clams that are closed; if a clam is open, tap the shell—if it does not snap shut, it is dead and should not be eaten. Live clams can be stored up to 2 days in the refrigerator but, ideally, should be cooked the same day they are purchased.

makes 4 servings

1 cup water

1¼ cups beer (lager or pale ale)

3 dozen littleneck clams, scrubbed

4 teaspoons prepared olivada or sun-dried tomato pesto

1 cup prepared salsa

½ lime, peeled and chopped

2 tablespoons fresh cilantro leaves

4 (½-inch thick) slices French bread, toasted

1 **Bring the water** and beer to a rolling boil in a large pot. Add the clams, cover, and steam until they open, 5–7 minutes, stirring after 3 minutes. Discard any clams that do not open.

2 **Meanwhile, spread each** bread slice with a teaspoon of olivada.

3 **Divide the clams** and broth among 4 large warmed soup bowls. Top with the salsa, chopped lime, and cilantro, and serve with the bread slices.

Chef's Tip

Olivada—an Italian olive spread made of pureed black olives, olive oil, and pepper—packs big olive flavor in tiny amounts. Find it in gourmet grocery stores or better supermarkets.

Per serving

190 Calories | 4 g Total Fat | 1 g Saturated Fat | 29 mg Cholesterol | 760 mg Sodium
20 g Total Carbohydrate | 2 g Dietary Fiber | 17 g Protein | 76 mg Calcium

4 *POINTS* per serving

mussels in saffron and white wine broth

This recipe is fragrant with the aroma of saffron. Hand picked from the purple crocus, saffron threads are typically used to season bouillabaisse, paella, and risotto. Store the costly spice in an airtight container in a cool, dark place.

makes 4 servings

1^1/$_2$ teaspoons unsalted butter

1 garlic clove, chopped

^{1}/$_2$ cup dry white wine

1^1/$_2$ tablespoons half-and-half

^{3}/$_4$ teaspoon saffron threads

1 cup low-sodium fish or vegetable broth, or clam juice

2 scallions, thinly sliced

1 small tomato, peeled, seeded, and chopped

1^1/$_2$ tablespoons fresh lemon juice

40 mussels, scrubbed and debearded

1 tablespoon chopped fresh chives

1 **Melt the butter** in a large pot, then add the garlic. Sauté until the garlic is fragrant, about 1 minute. Add the wine, half-and-half, and saffron; simmer 5 minutes. Add the broth, the scallions, tomato, and lemon juice; simmer 5 minutes.

2 **Add the mussels,** cover, and steam until they open, about 5 minutes. Shake the pot, holding down the lid with a kitchen towel, to redistribute the mussels. Return the pot to the heat for another 2 minutes. Discard any mussels that do not open. Divide the mussels into four warm bowls; stir the chives into the broth, then pour over the mussels.

Chef's Tips

To peel and seed the tomato, bring a large pot of water to a boil. Have ready a bowl of ice water. Cut a shallow "X" into the bottom of the tomato. Submerge the tomato in boiling water for 10–15 seconds. Plunge into ice water, then remove immediately and peel the tomato with a paring knife, starting at the "X." If the tomato does not peel easily, return it to the boiling water briefly, shock it in the ice water again, and peel. Cut the tomato in half horizontally and remove the seeds, then chop.

The hairy filaments that protrude from a mussel are known as a "beard." To remove, pinch the filaments between thumb and forefinger and pull firmly. Wait to debeard mussels until as close to cooking time as possible. Scrub mussels thoroughly under running water before cooking.

3 *POINTS* per serving

Per serving

154 Calories | 5 g Total Fat | 1 g Saturated Fat | 62 mg Cholesterol | 500 mg Sodium
6 g Total Carbohydrate | 0 g Dietary Fiber | 16 g Protein | 121 mg Calcium

classic boiled lobster

Available throughout the year, fresh lobsters should be purchased alive—the tail will curl under the body when picked up—and stored for only a few hours before cooking. Lobster must be cooked live or killed just prior to cooking. Here, the creamy white meat of the lobster is complemented by a fragrant lemon-herb dipping sauce.

makes 4 servings

1 **To make the dipping sauce,** melt the margarine in a skillet; add the lemon juice, parsley, tarragon, watercress, salt, and pepper. Transfer the dipping sauce to a bowl.

2 **Fill a lobster pot** or 12-quart stockpot two-thirds full of water and bring to a rolling boil. Add the lobsters, cooking in batches if necessary, and boil until they are bright red, 10–11 minutes. Use tongs to place the lobsters on a platter. Serve with the lemon-herb dipping sauce and lemon wedges.

$1/4$ cup reduced-calorie tub margarine

1 tablespoon fresh lemon juice

2 teaspoons minced fresh parsley

2 teaspoons minced fresh tarragon or $1/2$ teaspoon dried

2 teaspoons finely chopped watercress

$1/4$ teaspoon salt

Freshly ground pepper

4 ($1 1/2$-pound) lobsters

1 lemon, cut into wedges

Chef's Tip

To kill the lobsters prior to cooking, place a lobster on a cutting board and insert the tip of a large knife into the middle of the base of the head with the blade pointing towards the eyes. Pull the knife all the way down through the shell, splitting the head in half. Repeat with remaining lobsters.

Per serving

224 Calories | 7 g Total Fat | 1 g Saturated Fat | 127 mg Cholesterol | 949 mg Sodium
3 g Total Carbohydrate | 0 g Dietary Fiber | 36 g Protein | 109 mg Calcium

5 *POINTS* per serving

crab, pear, and cheese strudel

Made with light, crisp phyllo dough, this strudel has a delectably rich filling of savory and sweet ingredients. Creamy melted mozzarella cheese and crispy water chestnuts add welcome texture and crunch.

makes 4 servings

2 small pears, peeled, cored, and chopped

1/2 pound cooked jumbo lump crabmeat, picked over

3/4 cup coarsely grated skim-milk mozzarella cheese

1/2 cup finely chopped lean Virginia ham

3/4 cup minced drained water chestnuts

6 scallions, thinly sliced

1 tablespoon fresh lemon juice

1/4 teaspoon crushed red pepper

6 (12 × 17-inch) sheets phyllo dough, room temperature

4 teaspoons vegetable oil

1 teaspoon plain dried bread crumbs

1. **Preheat the oven** to 375°F. Spray a 10 × 15-inch jellyroll pan with nonstick spray.

2. **To prepare the filling,** combine the pears, crabmeat, cheese, ham, water chestnuts, scallions, lemon juice, and crushed red pepper in a bowl.

3. **Cover the sheets** of phyllo with plastic wrap to keep them from drying out. Place 1 phyllo sheet onto a 16-inch sheet of wax paper and brush evenly with 1/2 teaspoon of the oil. Top with the remaining sheets of phyllo dough, brushing each sheet with 1/2 teaspoon oil. Sprinkle the top sheet evenly with the bread crumbs.

4. **Spoon the filling,** lengthwise, about 1 inch from a long side of the phyllo stack. Fold the 1 inch of dough over the filling and then fold in 1 inch of the short edges. Roll up the strudel, using the wax paper to help lift the dough. Transfer the roll to the pan, brush with the remaining 1 teaspoon oil. With a sharp knife, lightly cut the top to indicate 4 portions, being careful not to cut all the way through. Bake the strudel until lightly browned and heated through, 15–20 minutes. Let cool 10 minutes, then cut at the marks and serve.

Chef's Tip

You can usually find phyllo dough in the freezer section of your supermarket, but it must be fully thawed before using. Store unopened phyllo dough in the refrigerator for up to one month. Once the dough has been opened, use it within a few days.

6 POINTS per serving

Per serving
306 Calories | 9 g Total Fat | 2 g Saturated Fat | 66 mg Cholesterol | 604 mg Sodium
32 g Total Carbohydrate | 4 g Dietary Fiber | 23 g Protein | 162 mg Calcium

crab, pear, and cheese strudel

grilled soft-shell crabs

The blue crab is often eaten in its "soft shell" stage, which lasts from April to September in the United States. Ask your fishmonger to clean the crabs and plan to cook them the day they are purchased. Serve these with Green Papaya Salsa (page 274), or try them with a side dish of the black bean preparation from Southwestern Vegetable-Tortilla Bake (page 238).

makes 4 servings

³/₄ cup red wine vinegar

³/₄ cup dry white wine

¹/₄ cup fresh lemon juice

¹/₂ medium red bell pepper, minced

3 tablespoons extra-virgin olive oil

2 scallions, minced

1 roasted jalapeño pepper, peeled, seeded, deveined, and minced (wear gloves to prevent irritation)

3 garlic cloves, minced

1¹/₂ teaspoons chopped fresh basil

1¹/₂ teaspoons chopped fresh tarragon

1¹/₂ tablespoons chopped fresh thyme

4 jumbo soft-shell crabs

1 **Combine the vinegar,** wine, lemon juice, bell pepper, oil, scallions, jalapeño, garlic, basil, tarragon, and thyme in a large zip-close plastic bag; add the crabs. Squeeze out the air and seal the bag; turn to coat the crabs. Refrigerate, turning the bag occasionally, for 2 hours.

2 **Spray the grill rack** with nonstick spray and prepare the grill, or spray a nonstick ridged grill pan with nonstick spray and set over medium-high heat.

3 **Drain the marinade** from the crabs, pressing out the excess, and discard. Grill the crabs 5 inches from the heat, or on the grill pan (if using) until reddish brown, about 2 minutes per side.

Chef's Tip

To roast the jalapeño pepper, spray the broiler rack with nonstick spray; preheat the broiler. Broil the pepper 5 inches from the heat, turning frequently with tongs, until the skin is shriveled and darkened, 5–10 minutes. Place the pepper in a small bowl, cover with plastic wrap, and let steam for 10 minutes. When cool enough to handle, peel and seed.

10 *POINTS* per serving

Per serving

403 Calories | 23 g Total Fat | 5 g Saturated Fat | 45 mg Cholesterol | 1,150 mg Sodium 34 g Total Carbohydrate | 0 g Dietary Fiber | 12 g Protein | 84 mg Calcium

chapter 9

poultry

jerk chicken

Jerk seasoning originated in Jamaica and is used on grilled meats throughout the Caribbean. Jerk seasoning varies from cook to cook, but it usually includes hot chiles, onion, and allspice (which is known as "pimento" in Jamaica). Serve the chicken with black beans and Green Papaya Salsa (page 274) or Tropical Fruit Salsa (page 270).

makes 4 servings

2 tablespoons whole allspice

1/2 cup chopped onion

2 scallions, chopped

1/2 Scotch bonnet, Jamaican hot, or habanero chile, seeded and minced (wear gloves to prevent irritation)

1 1/2 teaspoons dark rum

1/2 teaspoon cinnamon

1/2 teaspoon salt

1/2 teaspoon coarsely ground pepper

1/4 teaspoon ground nutmeg

4 (1/4-pound) skinless boneless chicken breasts

1 **Preheat the oven** to 350°F. Spread the allspice in a small baking pan or ovenproof skillet and toast 5 minutes. Let cool, then coarsely grind in a spice grinder or mini food processor.

2 **Combine the allspice** with the onion, scallions, chile, rum, cinnamon, salt, pepper, and nutmeg in a food processor. Process until the mixture forms a thick paste.

3 **Using a spoon** or rubber-gloved hands, rub the paste on each chicken breast, then place in a zip-close plastic bag. Squeeze out the air and seal the bag. Refrigerate for 30 minutes.

4 **Spray the grill rack** with nonstick spray; prepare the grill. Grill the chicken 5 inches from the heat, turning once, until cooked through, 10–12 minutes.

4 POINTS per serving

Per serving
208 Calories | 4 g Total Fat | 1 g Saturated Fat | 96 mg Cholesterol | 420 mg Sodium
4 g Total Carbohydrate | 1 g Dietary Fiber | 36 g Protein | 43 mg Calcium

jerk chicken, with green papaya salsa (page 274)

poached chicken breast in spicy broth

Moist chicken breasts and shrimp infused with Mediterranean flavor are reminiscent of the French seafood classic, Bouillabaisse. The broth may be prepared ahead and refrigerated in an airtight container for up to 2 days or frozen for up to 2 weeks. On the day of serving, finish the dish by preparing the medley of leek, fennel, okra, and a few shrimp. Accompany this dish with steamed rice.

makes 4 servings

1 teaspoon olive oil

1 garlic clove, minced

1 tablespoon tomato paste

2 tablespoons dry white wine

3 cups low-sodium chicken broth

1 teaspoon chopped fresh tarragon

$1/2$ teaspoon saffron threads

1 (2-inch) piece orange zest

$1/4$ teaspoon salt

1 bay leaf

1 large leek, white part only, cleaned and thinly sliced lengthwise

$1^3/4$ cups thinly sliced fennel

$1/3$ cup chopped okra

4 ($1/4$-pound) skinless boneless chicken breasts

1 cup chopped, seeded, and peeled tomatoes

8 shrimp, peeled and deveined

$1^1/2$ teaspoons fresh lemon juice

$1/8$ teaspoon freshly ground white pepper

1 **Heat the oil** in a soup pot, then add the garlic. Sauté until fragrant, about 30 seconds. Add the tomato paste and cook, stirring constantly, until rust-colored, about $1^1/2$ minutes. Add the white wine; cook, scraping up the browned bits from the bottom of the pot. Add the broth, tarragon, saffron, orange zest, salt, and bay leaf; simmer 15 minutes. Remove and discard the orange zest and bay leaf.

2 **Add the leek,** fennel, and okra; continue to simmer until the vegetables are tender, about 10 minutes. Add the chicken breasts and tomatoes; cook at a gentle simmer until the chicken is cooked through, about 10 minutes. Add the shrimp during the last 3 minutes of cooking. Just before serving, season with the lemon juice and pepper.

Chef's Tips

The zest of the orange is the peel without any of the pith (white membrane). To remove the zest from the orange, use a zester or the fine side of a vegetable peeler.

Leeks often pick up sand between their layers as they grow. To clean a leek, trim the dark green tops (reserve the tops for flavoring soups or stews) and the roots, leaving the root end intact to hold the layers together. Slice the leek lengthwise, fan open the layers, and rinse thoroughly under running water.

6 *POINTS* per serving

Per serving

302 Calories | 8 g Total Fat | 2 g Saturated Fat | 139 mg Cholesterol | 402 mg Sodium
12 g Total Carbohydrate | 3 g Dietary Fiber | 45 g Protein | 95 mg Calcium

herb-breaded chicken with creamy mustard sauce

This chicken is dipped in buttermilk, dredged in an herbed breading, and baked. The result is a crispy, low-fat solution to fried chicken. The creamy, sweet and sour sauce makes a fine contrast of flavor and texture. Excellent accompaniments to this dish are pan-steamed sugar snap peas with morel mushrooms and Country Corn Bread (page 292).

makes 4 servings

1 **Preheat the oven** to 375°F. Spray the rack of a roasting pan with nonstick spray and place it in the pan. Combine the parsley, tarragon, basil, and chives in a small bowl.

2 **Combine the cornmeal** and corn-flake crumbs in a shallow dish; add one-half of the herb mixture. Combine the remaining herbs with the buttermilk in another shallow dish. Dip each chicken breast into the buttermilk mixture. Coat the chicken on both sides with the cornmeal mixture, shaking off the excess (discard the excess cornmeal mixture). Arrange the chicken on the rack and bake until cooked through, 30–35 minutes.

3 **Meanwhile, dissolve the arrowroot** in 2 tablespoons of the broth in a small bowl. Bring the remaining broth to a simmer in a small saucepan; stir in the arrowroot mixture. Return to a simmer, stirring constantly, until thickened, 1–2 minutes. Remove from the heat; stir in the evaporated milk, mustard, honey, and pepper.

4 **Serve the sauce** pooled under the chicken or on the side.

2 tablespoons chopped fresh parsley

2 tablespoons chopped fresh tarragon

2 tablespoons chopped fresh basil

2 tablespoons chopped fresh chives

1/3 cup cornmeal

1/3 cup corn-flake crumbs

1/2 cup low-fat buttermilk

4 (1/4-pound) skinless boneless chicken breasts

2 1/4 teaspoons arrowroot

1 cup low-sodium chicken broth

1/4 cup evaporated fat-free milk

2 tablespoons Dijon mustard

1 1/2 teaspoons honey

1/8 teaspoon freshly ground pepper

Per serving

296 Calories | 6 g Total Fat | 2 g Saturated Fat | 96 mg Cholesterol | 287 mg Sodium
19 g Total Carbohydrate | 2 g Dietary Fiber | 40 g Protein | 130 mg Calcium

6 *POINTS* per serving

chicken breasts with peaches in zinfandel wine sauce

Most people are familiar with white Zinfandel, a blush wine, but Zinfandel grapes are also used to produce red wines that range in character from light and fruity to spicy and robust. This recipe can be doubled, but only if you'll be serving eight, not to make extra for another meal. It's best the day it's made. Serve with a Belgian endive salad, green beans, or Swiss chard.

makes 4 servings

$1/2$ cup apple cider

$2^1/4$ teaspoons cider vinegar

$1^1/2$ teaspoons minced shallot

$1/2$ teaspoon minced garlic

4 ($1/4$-pound) skinless, boneless chicken breasts

$1^1/2$ teaspoons cornstarch

1 cup low-sodium chicken broth

$3/4$ cup sliced, peeled peaches (1 large or 2 small peaches)

$1/4$ cup dry red Zinfandel wine

1 **Combine the cider,** vinegar, shallot, and garlic in a zip-close plastic bag; add the chicken. Squeeze out the air and seal the bag; turn to coat the chicken. Refrigerate, turning the bag occasionally, at least 30 minutes.

2 **Preheat the oven** to 375°F. Spray the rack of a roasting pan with nonstick spray and place in the pan. Shake the excess marinade from the chicken and arrange on the rack. Bake until cooked through, 30–35 minutes.

3 **Meanwhile, dissolve the cornstarch** in 2 tablespoons of the broth in a small bowl. Combine the remaining broth, the peaches, and wine in a small saucepan. Bring the mixture to a boil and stir in the cornstarch mixture. Simmer, stirring, until heated through and slightly thickened, about 2 minutes.

4 **When the chicken is cooked,** slice each breast across the grain. Spoon the warm sauce over and serve.

Chef's Tip

Select freestone peaches, if possible. For easy peeling, immerse the whole peach in boiling water for 15–30 seconds, then into ice water to stop the cooking. Starting at the stem end, use a paring knife to slip the skin from the flesh.

5 _POINTS_ per serving

Per serving

247 Calories | 4 g Total Fat | 1 g Saturated Fat | 96 mg Cholesterol | 180 mg Sodium
9 g Total Carbohydrate | 2 g Dietary Fiber | 36 g Protein | 28 mg Calcium

chicken breasts with artichokes and mustard sauce

This recipe brings together the flavors of two mustards: Dijon and whole-grain. Dijon mustards—ranging from mild to hot—are made from brown or black mustard seeds and usually include white wine. Whole-grain mustards come in many styles, from hot to sweet and mild.

makes 4 servings

1 **Place the chicken breasts,** skinned-side down, between 2 sheets of wax paper and pound to an even thickness with a meat mallet or the bottom of a heavy saucepan. Season the chicken with salt and pepper (if using).

2 **Preheat the oven** to 200°F. Heat 1 teaspoon of the oil in a large nonstick skillet then add the chicken. Sauté, working in batches if necessary, turning once, until the chicken is golden brown and cooked through, 3–4 minutes per side. Transfer the breasts to a platter, cover with foil, and place in the oven to keep warm while you prepare the sauce.

3 **In the same pan,** swirl in the remaining teaspoon of oil, then add the shallots. Sauté until translucent. Dissolve the cornstarch in 2 teaspoons of the broth in a small bowl; add the remaining broth to the pan and bring to a boil. Stir in the cornstarch mixture and continue stirring until thickened, about 1 minute. Stir in the vinegar, whole-grain mustard, and Dijon mustard. Add the artichoke hearts, olives, and tarragon; simmer until heated through, about 3 minutes. Spoon the sauce over the chicken and serve.

4 ($\frac{1}{4}$-pound) skinless boneless chicken breasts

Salt (optional)

Freshly ground pepper (optional)

2 teaspoons vegetable oil

1 tablespoon minced shallot

1 teaspoon cornstarch

1 cup low-sodium chicken broth

1$\frac{1}{2}$ tablespoons balsamic vinegar

3 teaspoons whole-grain mustard

1$\frac{1}{2}$ teaspoons Dijon mustard

4 artichoke hearts, quartered and cooked (or four frozen hearts, thawed and quartered)

6 kalamata olives, pitted and halved

1 tablespoon chopped fresh tarragon

Chef's Tip

To trim fresh artichokes, snap off their outer leaves until you reach the inner leaves, which are pale green at the base and darker green at the tip. Slice off all but about $\frac{1}{2}$ inch of these leaves. Cut off all but about 1 inch of the stems and peel the bottoms and stems with a vegetable peeler. Cut each artichoke into quarters and use a spoon or paring knife to trim away the fuzzy choke and purple leaves. Submerge the artichokes in a bowl of water with a half lemon squeezed into it until ready to cook. To cook the artichokes, simmer in lightly salted water until tender, 15–20 minutes.

Per serving

260 Calories | 8 g Total Fat | 2 g Saturated Fat | 98 mg Cholesterol | 279 mg Sodium
7 g Total Carbohydrate | 2 g Dietary Fiber | 38 g Protein | 54 mg Calcium

5 *POINTS* per serving

moroccan chicken with saffron rice

Fresh orange, dried apricots, and a dash of spice create the Moroccan taste in this one-skillet meal. This chicken is served with saffron rice, but substitute couscous if you like. Prepare it a day ahead if you can; the flavors improve with time.

makes 4 servings

2 cups water

1 cup long-grain rice

Pinch saffron threads

2 teaspoons olive oil

4 (1/4-pound) skinless boneless chicken breasts

1 leek, rinsed and thinly sliced

1/3 cup dried apricots, thinly sliced

1 teaspoon ground cumin

1/4 teaspoon cinnamon

1/4 teaspoon crushed red pepper

2 cups coarsely chopped tomatoes

1 cup low-sodium chicken broth

1 orange, peeled and cut into sections

1 **Bring the water** to a boil in a saucepan; stir in the rice and saffron. Reduce the heat to low; cook, covered, until all the water is absorbed and rice is tender, 20 minutes. Remove from the heat; keep warm.

2 **Meanwhile, heat a large** nonstick skillet. Swirl in the oil, then add the chicken. Cook, turning occasionally, until the chicken is browned and cooked through, about 4 minutes per side. Transfer to a plate.

3 **In the same skillet,** combine the leek, apricots, cumin, cinnamon, and crushed red pepper; sauté until the leek is softened, about 5 minutes. Add the tomatoes and broth; bring to a boil. Reduce the heat; simmer, covered, until the mixture is heated through, about 3 minutes.

4 **Return the chicken** to the skillet; stir in the orange sections. Cook, turning, until the chicken is heated through, 3 minutes. Serve the chicken and vegetables over the warm rice.

Chef's Tip

We like using Turkish apricots, which are sold whole and are smaller than other varieties (you'll need about 12 for this recipe).

8 POINTS per serving

Per serving
395 Calories | 5 g Total Fat | 1 g Saturated Fat | 67 mg Cholesterol | 123 mg Sodium
54 g Total Carbohydrate | 4 g Dietary Fiber | 32 g Protein | 71 mg Calcium

grilled chicken burritos

For an easy summer weeknight meal, roll flour tortillas into burritos with this cilantro-lime marinated chicken. Serve these with our Tomatillo Salsa (page 12) or your favorite bottled salsa, rice, and beans. The chicken can be grilled one day ahead and refrigerated (reheat the chicken before making the burritos). This recipe can be doubled, but don't roll up the tortillas until ready to serve.

makes 4 servings

2 teaspoons chopped fresh cilantro

1½ teaspoons fresh lime juice

1 garlic clove, minced

1 teaspoon minced shallot

Freshly ground pepper

4 (¼-pound) skinless boneless chicken breasts

4 (12-inch) flour tortillas

½ cup prepared guacamole

1 cup Tomatillo Salsa (page 12) or bottled chunky tomato salsa

1 **Combine the cilantro,** lime juice, garlic, shallot, and pepper in a zip-close plastic bag; add the chicken. Squeeze out the air and seal the bag; turn to coat the chicken. Refrigerate, turning the bag once, for at least 30 minutes.

2 **Spray the grill** or broiler rack with nonstick spray; prepare the grill or preheat the broiler. Shake any excess marinade from the chicken and grill or broil 5 inches from the heat, turning frequently, until cooked through, about 12 minutes.

3 **Meanwhile, loosely wrap** the tortillas in foil and place in a preheated 250°F oven until warmed through, 8–10 minutes, or stack the tortillas between 2 damp paper towels and microwave on High for 30–45 seconds.

4 **Thinly slice** the chicken across the grain. Spread each warmed tortilla with the guacamole and fill with a sliced chicken breast. Roll the tortillas into cones and serve with the salsa.

Per serving

362 Calories | 10 g Total Fat | 5 g Saturated Fat | 96 mg Cholesterol | 616 mg Sodium

24 g Total Carbohydrate | 2 g Dietary Fiber | 39 g Protein | 69 mg Calcium

8 *POINTS* per serving

gremolata-stuffed chicken breasts with tomato relish

Gremolata is a classic Italian garnish, usually consisting of parsley, garlic, and lemon zest, for rich dishes such as osso buco. Here, it makes a delicious complement to chicken. This savory entrée can be doubled to serve eight and will store well overnight if you're planning a luncheon. Try serving it over hot rice or orzo pasta.

makes 4 servings

4 large plum tomatoes, seeded and chopped

2 teaspoons olive oil

2 teaspoons balsamic vinegar

1/4 teaspoon salt

Freshly ground pepper

1 cup packed fresh flat-leaf parsley leaves, finely chopped

1 garlic clove, minced

1/2 teaspoon grated lemon zest

1/4 teaspoon salt

1/4 teaspoon pepper

4 (1/4-pound) skinless boneless chicken breasts

1 **To prepare the relish,** combine the tomatoes, oil, vinegar, salt, and pepper in a bowl; cover and let stand at room temperature.

2 **Preheat the oven** to 450°F. Spray a baking sheet with nonstick spray. Combine the parsley, garlic, lemon zest, salt, and pepper in a small bowl.

3 **Place the chicken breasts,** skinned-side down, between 2 sheets of wax paper. Pound the chicken to 1/4-inch thickness, using a meat mallet or the bottom of a heavy saucepan. Remove and discard the top sheet of wax paper; spread the chicken with the parsley mixture. Start with the narrower ends and roll each chicken breast around the filling; remove and discard the remaining wax paper.

4 **Place the chicken,** seam-side down, on the baking sheet. Bake until the chicken is cooked through, 10–12 minutes. Let stand 5 minutes. Slice each breast on the diagonal into four pieces. Serve with the relish.

Chef's Tip

The zest of the lemon is the peel without any of the pith (white membrane). To remove the zest from the lemon for this recipe, use a zester or the fine side of a vegetable grater; wrap the lemon in plastic wrap and refrigerate for use at another time.

4 POINTS per serving

Per serving

182 Calories | 6 g Total Fat | 1 g Saturated Fat | 72 mg Cholesterol | 368 mg Sodium
5 g Total Carbohydrate | 1 g Dietary Fiber | 27 g Protein | 39 mg Calcium

gremolata-stuffed chicken breasts with tomato relish, and orzo

spicy szechuan chicken

This complex, spicy dish is perfect with Asian-style noodles or brown rice. The chicken will need 2 hours to take on the flavor of the spicy seasoning blend—a homemade interpretation of the classic Asian seasoning known as five-spice powder.

makes 4 servings

$1/2$ teaspoon Szechuan peppercorns

1 teaspoon cinnamon

$1/2$ teaspoon anise seeds

1 teaspoon sugar

4 ($1/4$-pound) skinless boneless chicken breasts, cut into thin strips

2 teaspoons peanut oil

4 scallions, thinly sliced

1 ($1/2$-inch) piece fresh ginger

2 cups thinly sliced mushrooms

4 cups thinly sliced bok choy

$3/4$ cup water chestnuts, coarsely chopped

1 tablespoon reduced-sodium soy sauce

1 **Toast the peppercorns** in a dry large nonstick skillet, shaking the pan, until they begin to smoke, about 1 minute. Crush the toasted peppercorns in a mortar and pestle or grind them in a spice or coffee grinder. Sift the ground pepper through a fine sieve.

2 **Return the skillet** to the heat; combine the cinnamon and anise seeds, stirring constantly, until fragrant and lightly browned, 45–60 seconds. Transfer to a plate and let cool.

3 **Combine the peppercorn powder,** cinnamon, anise seeds, and sugar in a zip-close plastic bag; add the chicken. Squeeze out the air and seal the bag; turn to coat the chicken. Refrigerate, turning the bag occasionally, at least 2 hours.

4 **Heat a nonstick wok** or skillet over high heat until a drop of water skitters. Pour in 1 teaspoon of the oil and swirl to coat the pan, then add the chicken. Stir-fry until the chicken is cooked through, 1–5 minutes. Transfer to a plate.

5 *POINTS* per serving

Per serving

194 Calories | 29 g Total Fat | 1 g Saturated Fat | 66 mg Cholesterol | 263 mg Sodium
10 g Total Carbohydrate | 4 g Dietary Fiber | 29 g Protein | 109 mg Calcium

5 **Return the skillet** to the heat. Pour in the remaining 1 teaspoon oil and swirl to coat the pan, then add the scallions and ginger. Stir-fry until the scallions are softened, about 2 minutes. Add the mushrooms and stir-fry until their juices have been released and evaporated, 3–4 minutes. Add the bok choy and stir-fry until wilted, 3–4 minutes. Add the chicken, water chestnuts, and soy sauce. Cook, stirring gently, until heated through, 3–4 minutes.

Chef's Tips

Reddish-brown Szechuan peppercorns, a medium hot spice, can be purchased in Asian markets and specialty stores. The peppercorn berries come from the prickly ash tree and are usually toasted to bring out their distinctive aroma and flavor.

Small greenish brown anise seeds bring a sweet licorice flavor to this dish. Find them in some supermarkets and health food stores.

If you like, you can substitute an equal amount of pork loin for the chicken.

walnut chicken

Here, chicken is cooked along with a pilaf of bulgur wheat and walnuts. Bulgur—wheat kernels that have been steamed, hulled, dried, and cracked— is available in most supermarkets. Most Americans know it best as the base for the classic Middle Eastern salad, Tabbouleh (page 215), but it also makes a nutritious and unique pilaf.

makes 4 servings

1 teaspoon vegetable oil

3/4 pound skinless boneless chicken breasts, cut into chunks

1 medium onion, chopped

2 medium carrots, peeled and chopped

2 tablespoons chopped walnuts

1/2 teaspoon caraway seeds

1/2 teaspoon cumin seeds

1 1/2 cups bulgur

2 cups low-sodium chicken broth

2 tablespoons golden raisins

1/8 teaspoon cinnamon

Pinch salt

1 **Heat the oil** in a large nonstick skillet, then add the chicken, onions, carrots, walnuts, caraway seeds, and cumin seeds. Sauté until the onions are golden brown, 4–5 minutes. Add the bulgur and sauté 1–2 minutes.

2 **Add the broth,** raisins, cinnamon, and salt; bring to a boil. Reduce the heat to low; simmer, covered, until the chicken is cooked through and the bulgur is tender, about 15 minutes.

8 *POINTS* per serving

Per serving

402 Calories | 7 g Total Fat | 1 g Saturated Fat | 68 mg Cholesterol | 200 mg Sodium
52 g Total Carbohydrate | 12 g Dietary Fiber | 37 g Protein | 63 mg Calcium

lemon-ginger grilled chicken

Inspired by Lemon Chicken—the Chinese restaurant favorite—this heavenly, slightly tart dish can be served hot or cold.

makes 4 servings

1 **Combine the lemon zest,** lemon juice, ginger, brown sugar, oil, and chiles in a zip-close plastic bag; add the chicken. Squeeze out the air and seal the bag; turn to coat the chicken. Refrigerate, turning the bag occasionally, at least 1 hour.

2 **Spray the broiler** or grill rack with nonstick spray; preheat the broiler or prepare the grill.

3 **Pour the marinade** into a small saucepan and boil, stirring constantly, 3 minutes, adding a tablespoon of water if needed. Remove from the heat.

4 **Broil or grill the chicken** 5 inches from the heat, turning occasionally and brushing with the marinade until cooked through, 10–12 minutes.

Grated zest of 1 lemon
(about 2 tablespoons)

$1/3$ cup fresh lemon juice

2 teaspoons minced peeled
fresh ginger

2 teaspoons packed
dark brown sugar

1 teaspoon peanut oil

2 small dried red hot chiles
(such as Thai or bird), seeded

4 ($1/4$-pound) skinless boneless
chicken thighs

Chef's Tips

To seed the chiles, simply pull off their stems and shake out the seeds. Find dried hot chiles in Asian markets; they'll last up to one year in an airtight container in a cool, dry place.

Select a plump lemon with smooth, yellow skin that feels heavy for its size. If the lemon is greenish, it is probably not ripe. The zest of the lemon is the peel without any of the pith (white membrane). When using both the zest and juice of a lemon: roll the lemon with the heel of your hand, remove the zest from the lemon, using a zester or the fine side of a vegetable grater. Pierce the lemon with a paring knife and squeeze out the juice; the pits will stay behind.

Per serving

203 Calories | 10 g Total Fat | 3 g Saturated Fat | 81 mg Cholesterol | 76 mg Sodium
4 g Total Carbohydrate | 0 g Dietary Fiber | 22 g Protein | 15 mg Calcium

5 *POINTS* per serving

balsamic braised chicken thighs

The rich, dark meat in chicken thighs is a perfect match for assertive flavorings like fennel, orange, and balsamic vinegar. This one-pot recipe can be easily doubled; just freeze the leftovers in an airtight container for up to 2 weeks, then thaw in the refrigerator or microwave.

makes 4 servings

3 tablespoons all-purpose flour

3 tablespoons grated Parmesan cheese

4 (1/4-pound) chicken thighs, skinned

1 tablespoon olive oil

1 fennel bulb, thinly sliced

1 red bell pepper, sliced

1 medium onion, thinly sliced

1/2 cup orange juice

1/3 cup balsamic vinegar

1 **Combine the flour** and cheese in a zip-close plastic bag; add the chicken. Shake to coat the chicken with the flour mixture, shaking off the excess (reserve the remaining flour mixture).

2 **Heat a nonstick skillet.** Swirl in the oil, then add the chicken. Cook, turning occasionally, until browned, 4–5 minutes per side. Transfer to a plate.

3 **Reduce the heat.** Add the fennel, bell pepper, onion, and the reserved flour mixture; sauté until the vegetables are very soft, about 10 minutes. Increase the heat to high, add the orange juice and vinegar; cook, stirring, until slightly thickened, about 2 minutes. Add the chicken and stir to coat. Reduce the heat and simmer, covered, until the chicken is cooked through, about 15 minutes.

6 *POINTS* per serving

Per serving
270 Calories | 9 g Total Fat | 2 g Saturated Fat | 97 mg Cholesterol | 200 mg Sodium
20 g Total Carbohydrate | 3 g Dietary Fiber | 26 g Protein | 105 mg Calcium

chicken and shrimp pot pie with an herb-cracker crust

This healthy interpretation of a pot pie features a hearty chicken and shrimp stew topped with a crisp crackerlike crust. This recipe can be doubled, but only if you'll be serving eight, not to make ahead for another meal. It's best the day it's made.

makes 4 servings

1 **Prepare crust.** Then, bring the broth to a boil in a soup pot; reduce the heat and simmer, then add the chicken. Simmer, covered, 4 minutes. Add the shrimp and continue simmering 1 minute. Skim the surface of the broth with a ladle to remove any fat or foam. Remove the chicken and shrimp with a slotted spoon; transfer to a plate. Return the broth to a simmer.

2 **Dissolve the arrowroot** in the water in a small bowl. Stir the arrowroot mixture into the broth; bring to a simmer, and stir until thickened, about 2 minutes. Add the potato and cook until tender, about 15 minutes.

3 **Combine the evaporated milk** and mustard in a small bowl, then stir into the simmering mixture. Return to a simmer.

4 **Meanwhile, heat the butter** in a skillet, then add the onion, celery, carrot, and bell pepper. Sauté until the vegetables are tender, about 8 minutes. Stir into the potato mixture, along with the chicken, shrimp, and peas. Add the Worcestershire sauce, thyme, rosemary, pepper, and pepper sauce. Cook, stirring as needed, until the stew returns to a simmer, about 5 minutes.

5 **Divide the stew** into bowls and top each with an Herb-Cracker Crust.

1 recipe Herb-Cracker Crust (page 295), warm or room temperature

3 cups low-sodium chicken broth

1/2 pound skinless boneless chicken breasts, cut into 1-inch cubes

8 extra-large shrimp, peeled, deveined, and cut into 1-inch pieces

2 tablespoons water

1 tablespoon arrowroot

1 large all-purpose potato, peeled and cut into 1-inch cubes

1 cup evaporated fat-free milk

1 tablespoon Dijon mustard

1 tablespoon unsalted butter

1/2 medium onion, finely chopped

1 celery stalk, finely chopped

1 medium carrot, peeled and finely chopped

1/2 green bell pepper, finely chopped

3/4 cup thawed frozen peas

1 tablespoon Worcestershire sauce

1 1/2 tablespoons chopped fresh thyme

2 1/4 teaspoons chopped fresh rosemary

Freshly ground pepper

1/4 teaspoon hot pepper sauce

Per serving

509 Calories | 12 g Total Fat | 6 g Saturated Fat | 147 mg Cholesterol | 632 mg Sodium
57 g Total Carbohydrate | 5 g Dietary Fiber | 43 g Protein | 322 mg Calcium

10 *POINTS* per serving

paella valenciana

Paella is named after the two-handled shallow pan used to prepare the dish. This traditional Spanish favorite varies according to the cook, but paella usually includes rice, saffron, chicken, shellfish, and peas. This recipe can be doubled, but don't make it ahead; it should be served fresh from the pan.

makes 4 servings

4 chicken legs, skinned

1 teaspoon olive oil

$1/3$ medium onion, chopped

1 red or green bell pepper, chopped

$1^1/2$ teaspoons minced jalapeño pepper (wear gloves to prevent irritation)

1 garlic clove, minced

$1/2$ cup sliced mushrooms

$1/8$ teaspoon saffron threads

$1^1/4$ cups long-grain white rice

$2^1/4$ cups low-sodium chicken broth

8 clams, scrubbed

8 mussels, scrubbed and debearded

8 extra-large shrimp, peeled and deveined

$2/3$ cup fresh or thawed frozen peas

1 **Preheat the oven** to 350°F. Spray the rack of a roasting pan with nonstick spray and place in the pan. Arrange the chicken legs on the rack and roast until browned and an instant-read thermometer inserted in the thigh registers 160°F, about 50 minutes. Transfer the chicken to a plate, leaving the oven on.

2 **Heat the oil** in a paella pan or large ovenproof pot with a lid, then add the onion. Sauté until the onion is browned, about 7 minutes. Add the bell pepper, jalapeño, and garlic; sauté until slightly softened, 2–3 minutes. Add the mushrooms and sauté until they begin to release their juices. Add the saffron and rice; sauté briefly, then add the broth and bring to a simmer. Cover and bake 12 minutes.

3 **Carefully add the chicken legs** with their juices, the clams, mussels, shrimp, and peas. Cover and continue baking until the clams and mussels have opened and the shrimp and rice are cooked, about 8 minutes. Discard any clams or mussels that don't open. Serve at once.

Chef's Tip

The hairy filaments that protrude from a mussel are known as a "beard." To remove, pinch the filaments between thumb and forefinger and pull firmly. Wait to debeard mussels until as close to cooking time as possible. Scrub mussels thoroughly under running water before cooking.

12 _POINTS_ per serving

Per serving

558 Calories | 13 g Total Fat | 3 g Saturated Fat | 191 mg Cholesterol | 451 mg Sodium
57 g Total Carbohydrate | 3 g Dietary Fiber | 50 g Protein | 91 mg Calcium

mexican-style roast chicken

This roast chicken is flavored by the distinctive chile poblano, a staple in the Mexican kitchen. Poblanos can be found in produce sections of good super-markets or in specialty markets. Look for those with shiny blackish-green skin; this is when their flavor—from piquant to mild—is richest. This chile is mild enough to chop up and toss into salads or to cut into strips, and serve with vegetables.

makes 8 servings

3 poblano chiles, seeded, deveined and cut into chunks

2 onions, halved

$1/2$ cup packed fresh cilantro

$1/4$ cup fresh lime juice

$1/2$ teaspoon salt

Freshly ground pepper

1 ($4^1/2$-pound) roasting chicken

1 **Preheat the oven** to 350°F. Spray the rack of a roasting pan with nonstick spray and place in the pan.

2 **Combine the chiles** and 3 of the onion halves in a food processor; add the cilantro, lime juice, $1/4$ teaspoon of the salt, and a grinding of the pepper; process until finely chopped.

3 **Gently loosen the skin** from the breast and leg portions of the chicken; stuff the chile mixture evenly under the skin.

4 **Sprinkle the inside** of the chicken with the remaining $1/4$ teaspoon salt and another grinding of the pepper; add the remaining onion half and truss the chicken. Place the chicken, breast-side up, in the roasting pan. Roast until an instant-read thermometer inserted in the inner thigh registers 180°F, 2–$2^1/2$ hours. Let stand 10 minutes before carving. Remove and discard the onion and skin. Scrape off and discard the chile mixture before eating, if desired. Serve warm.

Chef's Tip

Trussing the chicken gives it a neater appearance when it comes out of the oven. To truss, cut a 30-inch length of kitchen twine. Tie the legs together at the ankles with the center of the twine, then loop each end around its corresponding wing at the elbow joint. Pull the ends of the twine over the lower third of the breast to join them; tie them as tightly as possible.

Per serving

248 Calories | 10 g Total Fat | 3 g Saturated Fat | 116 mg Cholesterol | 257 mg Sodium
0 g Total Carbohydrate | 0 g Dietary Fiber | 38 g Protein | 20 mg Calcium

6 *POINTS* per serving

plum-glazed hens

Cornish game hens—each a perfect dinner for two—are a nice change from chicken. You may only be able to find frozen Cornish hens in your supermarket; just thaw them in your refrigerator a day ahead.

makes 4 servings

2 (1-pound) Cornish game hens, skinned and halved

3 tablespoons reduced-sodium soy sauce

3 tablespoons honey

1 1/2 tablespoons plum sauce

1 teaspoon five-spice powder

1 **Preheat the oven** to 400°F. Line a roasting pan with foil; spray the rack with nonstick spray, and place in the pan. Place the hens, skinned-side down, on the rack.

2 **Combine the soy sauce,** honey, plum sauce, and five-spice powder in a bowl. Brush the hens with one-fourth of the soy sauce mixture. Roast about 10 minutes; turn the hens over and brush with another one-fourth of the mixture. Roast, brushing the hens every 5 minutes, using all the remaining soy sauce mixture, until an instant-read thermometer inserted in the inner thigh registers 180°F, 15–20 minutes. Serve warm or at room temperature.

Chef's Tips

Find bottled plum sauce in the Asian section of your supermarket.

Five-spice powder, a staple in many Chinese dishes, is a heady blend of Szechuan peppercorns, star anise, fennel or anise seeds, cloves, and cinnamon. If you can't find it in your supermarket, look for it in Asian markets.

3 *POINTS* per serving

Per serving

161 Calories | 3 g Total Fat | 1 g Saturated Fat | 75 mg Cholesterol | 524 mg Sodium
16 g Total Carbohydrate | 0 g Dietary Fiber | 17 g Protein | 16 mg Calcium

whiskey-glazed smoked turkey breast with orange herb conserve

In this elegant dish, store-bought smoked turkey is accentuated with a whiskey-honey glaze and an herbal citrus conserve, which is a mixture of fruit, sugar, and seasonings cooked until thick. The recipe actually calls for more turkey than you will need to serve four, so you can double or triple the conserve, or you can save the leftover turkey for sandwiches.

1 **Combine the whiskey,** brown sugar, and honey in a saucepan. Cook, stirring, until the sugar dissolves and the mixture comes to a simmer. Remove from the heat and set aside.

2 **Preheat the oven** to 350°F. Place the turkey in a roasting pan and brush it with half of the whiskey glaze. Add $1/2$ cup of the water to the bottom of the pan. Roast the turkey breast, basting again with the remaining glaze after 15 minutes, until it is heated through and the outside glaze caramelizes, about 35 minutes total.

3 **Meanwhile, to prepare the conserve:** Combine the remaining $1/4$ cup water, the orange, lemon, sugar, and sherry in a saucepan. Simmer until the citrus rinds are very soft, adding more water as needed, about 20 minutes. Transfer the mixture to a nonreactive bowl; add the vinegar, tarragon, sage, parsley, and thyme. Set aside to cool.

4 **Thinly slice the turkey** and serve with the conserve.

makes 4 servings

$1/4$ cup southern-style whiskey, such as Jack Daniel's

$1/4$ cup packed dark brown sugar

2 tablespoons honey

1 skinless smoked turkey breast half (about 3 pounds)

$3/4$ cup water

1 orange, thinly sliced

$1/2$ lemon, thinly sliced

$1/2$ cup sugar

$1 1/2$ tablespoons dry sherry

$2 1/4$ teaspoons champagne vinegar or white wine vinegar

$1/2$ teaspoon chopped fresh tarragon

$1/2$ teaspoon chopped fresh sage

$1/2$ teaspoon chopped fresh parsley

$1/4$ teaspoon chopped fresh thyme

Chef's Tip

This dish is equally good served hot or cold. The conserve can be made up to 2 days ahead and refrigerated.

Per serving (four 1-ounce slices of turkey with $1/2$ of the conserve)

317 Calories | 4 g Total Fat | 2 g Saturated Fat | 61 mg Cholesterol | 976 mg Sodium
48 g Total Carbohydrate | 2 g Dietary Fiber | 21 g Protein | 41 mg Calcium

6 POINTS per serving

duck breasts with roasted onion vinaigrette

Boned duck breasts, sold with the skin intact, are called magrets. In this recipe the skin is removed to reduce the fat. Fresh duck is usually available from late spring until winter. If purchasing frozen duck, look for grade A.

makes 4 servings

3$^1/_2$ tablespoons cider vinegar

2 cups prepared demi-glace sauce

12 shallots, peeled

1 medium onion, chopped

1 cup chopped leek

2 tablespoons chopped garlic cloves

2 tablespoons olive oil

1 pound skinless boneless duck breasts

2 ounces curly endive (frisée) or chicory

2 tablespoons chopped fresh chives

1 **Preheat the oven** to 400°F. Combine 1$^1/_2$ tablespoons of the vinegar, 1$^1/_3$ cups of the demi-glace, and the shallots in a small baking dish. Roast the shallots until tender, stirring occasionally, about 1 hour. Set aside to cool.

2 **Meanwhile, to prepare the vinaigrette,** place the onion, leek, and garlic in a medium baking dish and toss with 1 tablespoon of the oil. Roast until golden brown, 35 minutes. Add the remaining $^2/_3$ cup demi-glace, scraping up the browned bits from the bottom of the pan. Add the remaining 2 tablespoons vinegar; transfer the onion mixture to a small bowl, and cool completely. Stir in the remaining 1 tablespoon of oil.

3 **Reduce the oven temperature** to 375°F. Spray a nonstick ovenproof skillet with nonstick spray and set over medium-high heat. Add the duck breast and cook, turning once, until golden brown, about 3 minutes per side. Bake until an instant-read thermometer inserted in the center of a breast registers 165°F, about 10 minutes. Let stand for 12–15 minutes, then carve into thin slices.

4 **Divide the frisée** onto plates and top each with the sliced duck. Drizzle with the vinaigrette, sprinkle with the chives, and serve with the roasted shallots.

Chef's Tip

Demi-glace is an intensely flavored, classical French brown veal sauce. It takes many hours to make demi-glace from scratch, but today's home cooks are fortunate in that well-stocked supermarkets and gourmet groceries now carry prepared demi-glace. It can be purchased frozen or as a shelf-stable concentrate.

5 *POINTS* per serving

Per serving

275 Calories | 7 g Total Fat | 2 g Saturated Fat | 90 mg Cholesterol | 169 mg Sodium 26 g Total Carbohydrate | 3 g Dietary Fiber | 30 g Protein | 111 mg Calcium

duck breasts with roasted onion vinaigrette

duck and sausage gumbo

Like many gumbos, this hearty stew is thickened with okra and served over rice. If you have the time, prepare it a day or two ahead and let the flavors meld for a more complex taste. Duck breasts are now sold in supermarkets, but if you like, substitute chicken breasts.

makes 6 servings

¹/₂ teaspoon vegetable oil

2 (¹/₂-pound) skinned duck breasts

¹/₂ pound turkey kielbasa, sliced

3 celery stalks, chopped

1 large onion, chopped

1 green bell pepper, chopped

4 large garlic cloves, minced

2 tablespoons all-purpose flour

1 teaspoon dried thyme

¹/₂ teaspoon salt

¹/₄ teaspoon cayenne

Freshly ground pepper

1 (28-ounce) can diced tomatoes in juice

3 cups low-sodium chicken broth

2 bay leaves

1 (10-ounce) box frozen sliced okra

2 scallions, sliced

2 tablespoons chopped fresh parsley

3 cups hot cooked white-and-wild rice blend

1 **Heat a soup pot.** Swirl in the oil, then add the duck breasts. Cook, turning, until the duck is browned, about 4 minutes per side. Transfer the duck to a plate. Add the kielbasa to the pot and sauté until browned, about 8 minutes. Transfer to a plate.

2 **Add the celery,** onion, bell pepper, and garlic to the pot. Sauté until the vegetables are softened, about 5 minutes. Stir in the flour, thyme, salt, cayenne, and pepper; sauté 2 minutes. Stir in the tomatoes, broth, and bay leaves; bring to a boil. Reduce the heat, cover, and simmer 20 minutes. Stir in the kielbasa and okra. Simmer until the okra is tender, about 15 minutes. Discard the bay leaves.

3 **Thinly slice the duck,** then add it to the pot with the scallions and parsley; simmer 1 minute. Serve over the rice.

7 POINTS per serving

Per serving

346 Calories | 9 g Total Fat | 3 g Saturated Fat | 84 mg Cholesterol | 879 mg Sodium
38 g Total Carbohydrate | 5 g Dietary Fiber | 28 g Protein | 132 mg Calcium

chapter 10

meat and game

tenderloin of beef with blue cheese and herb crust

A savory oven-browned blue cheese-and-herb bread crumb topping is a delicious accent to beef tenderloin medallions. The beauty of this impressive dish is that it is incredibly simple to make. Serve with pan-steamed vegetables, potatoes, and a bottle of good red wine.

makes 4 servings

2 slices white bread, crusts removed, toasted

3 tablespoons crumbled blue cheese

2 tablespoons chopped fresh parsley

2 tablespoons chopped fresh chives

Freshly ground pepper

1/2 cup prepared demi-glace sauce

2 tablespoons Madeira

1 teaspoon vegetable oil

4 (3-ounce) center-cut beef tenderloin medallions

1 **Preheat the oven** to 400°F. Crumble the toast into a bowl and blend to a coarse paste with the blue cheese, parsley, chives, and pepper.

2 **To prepare the Madeira sauce,** combine the demi-glace and Madeira in a small saucepan. Bring the sauce to a boil, reduce the heat to low, and keep hot.

3 **Spray the rack** of a roasting pan with nonstick spray and place in the pan. Heat a large nonstick skillet over high heat, add the oil, then wipe the pan with a wadded paper towel to absorb the excess. Dry-sear the medallions until just browned, about 1 minute per side.

4 **Arrange the medallions** on the roasting rack. Coat the top side of each medallion with the blue cheese mixture. Roast until the crust is golden brown and the meat is done to taste, 3–4 minutes for medium-rare. Serve the medallions on a pool of warm Madeira sauce.

Chef's Tip

Dry-searing and dry-sautéing are similar techniques in which food is cooked in a sauté pan or other cooking vessel coated with a very thin film of oil to help with heat transfer and to protect the food from burning in the moments before the food releases its own fat. To dry-sear or dry-sauté, heat a skillet over high heat. Pour 1 teaspoon of oil into the skillet, then wipe the pan with a wadded paper towel to distribute a thin coat of oil and absorb the excess (be careful not to burn yourself). Add the foods to the pan and cook as directed. The major difference between the two techniques is that dry-seared foods are browned on the stovetop and finished in the oven, whereas dry-sautéed foods are fully cooked on the stovetop. Cooking spray is not recommended for these techniques as the high heat may cause the spray to burn and become sticky.

6 POINTS per serving

Per serving (1 medallion with 1/4 of the sauce)

254 Calories | 13 g Total Fat | 5 g Saturated Fat | 77 mg Cholesterol | 291 mg Sodium 7 g Total Carbohydrate | 0 g Dietary Fiber | 26 g Protein | 60 mg Calcium

tenderloin of beef with blue cheese and herb crust, and rösti potatoes (page 260)

tenderloin of beef with wild mushrooms

Select an assortment of specialty mushrooms to use in this dish. Oyster, chanterelle, morel, and shiitake mushrooms are all good choices. Though less desirable, cremini, portobello, and white mushrooms can also be used.

makes 4 servings

¹/₄ cup low-sodium chicken broth

¹/₄ medium leek, rinsed and thinly sliced

¹/₂ cup prepared demi-glace sauce

4 cups wild mushrooms, sliced

¹/₄ cup Madeira

1 teaspoon chopped fresh thyme

¹/₂ teaspoon chopped fresh sage

Freshly ground pepper

1 teaspoon vegetable oil

4 (3-ounce) center-cut beef tenderloin medallions

1 **Heat the broth** in a saucepan, then add the leek. Bring just to a simmer; reduce the heat, cover, and simmer until the leek is tender, about 3 minutes; drain and set aside.

2 **Combine the demi-glace** and mushrooms in a saucepan and bring to a boil. Reduce the heat; add the Madeira, thyme, sage, and pepper. Simmer until the liquid is reduced by one-third, about 5 minutes. Add the leek; keep warm.

3 **Heat a large nonstick skillet** over high heat. Add the oil, then wipe the pan with a wadded paper towel to absorb the excess. Dry-sauté the medallions until browned and done to taste, about 2 minutes per side for medium-rare. Transfer to a plate; keep warm.

4 **Add the mushroom-leek mixture** to the skillet; cook, scraping up the browned bits from the bottom of the pan, until the liquid comes to a boil. Serve over the medallions.

Chef's Tips

For information on dry-sautéing and demi-glace sauce, see the Chef's Tip accompanying Tenderloin of Beef with Blue Cheese and Herb Crust (page 180).

Leeks often pick up sand between their layers as they grow. To clean a leek, trim the dark green tops (reserve the tops for flavoring soups or stews) and the roots, leaving the root end intact to hold the layers together. Slice the leek lengthwise, fan open the layers, and rinse thoroughly under running water.

5 *POINTS* per serving

Per serving
202 Calories | 8 g Total Fat | 3 g Saturated Fat | 71 mg Cholesterol | 162 mg Sodium
2 g Total Carbohydrate | 0 g Dietary Fiber | 25 g Protein | 16 mg Calcium

provençal beef tenderloin

This beef tenderloin is excellent served hot or cold. It is flavored with a delightful mixture of fresh herbs that recall the flavors of Provence, France.

makes 12 servings

1 (3-pound) beef tenderloin, trimmed

3/4 cup minced fresh parsley

3 tablespoons minced fresh rosemary

3 tablespoons Dijon mustard

6–8 garlic cloves, minced

1 tablespoon minced fresh oregano

1 tablespoon minced fresh thyme

1 tablespoon olive oil

Freshly ground pepper

1 **Place the tenderloin** on a sheet of plastic wrap. Combine the parsley, rosemary, mustard, garlic, oregano, thyme, oil and pepper in a small bowl and blend to a paste. Rub the tenderloin with the herb paste, wrap it in plastic, and refrigerate 1 hour to blend the flavors.

2 **Preheat the oven** to 425°F. Spray a 9 × 13-inch baking dish or shallow roasting pan with nonstick spray. Remove the tenderloin from the plastic wrap and place in the pan. Roast until the beef reaches an internal temperature of 130°F for rare, 30–40 minutes. Let stand 10 minutes before slicing.

Chef's Tips

Beef tenderloin is best when cooked and served rare to medium-rare; if a lean cut of meat is overcooked it becomes tough and dry. Test for doneness with an instant-read thermometer: Insert the thermometer into the middle of the tenderloin for the most accurate reading, and wait for the temperature indicator to come to a full stop before reading it.

It's important to realize that meats will continue to cook after coming out of the oven (this is called "carryover cooking"), so it's best to remove the meat at a temperature slightly lower than actually desired. For instance, if you prefer your meat medium-rare but continue to roast to 145°F you will have well-done meat by the time you carve. Meat should be removed from the oven—for medium rare—between 130°–135°F (this accounts for carryover cooking).

Per serving

209 Calories | 11 g Total Fat | 4 g Saturated Fat | 71 mg Cholesterol | 76 mg Sodium
2 g Total Carbohydrate | 0 g Dietary Fiber | 24 g Protein | 24 mg Calcium

5 *POINTS* per serving

tournedos of beef, hunter's style

"Hunter's style" refers to a quick, classic sauce made with wild mushrooms, shallots, and wine—the kind of ingredients a hunter might gather in the wild, along with a few items carried from home. If you decide to use fresh thyme, you'll need about 8 sprigs, along with a few extra for garnish.

makes 4 servings

1 ounce lean boiled ham, cut into 4 (6 × ³/₄-inch) strips

4 (3-ounce) beef tournedos

1 garlic clove

4 (1-ounce) slices French bread, crusts removed, toasted

4 teaspoons unsalted butter

3 cups sliced mushrooms

4 medium shallots, chopped

1 teaspoon chopped fresh thyme, or ¹/₂ teaspoon dried

¹/₂ cup dry red wine

¹/₂ cup low-sodium beef or vegetable broth

Freshly ground pepper

Thyme sprigs (optional)

1 **Wrap 1 ham strip** around the circumference of each tournedos and secure with a toothpick. Slice the garlic in half and rub the toast on both sides with the cut section of the clove. Set aside.

2 **Heat 2 teaspoons** of the butter in a skillet, then add the mushrooms, shallots, and thyme. Sauté until the vegetables are tender, 5–8 minutes. Transfer to a plate.

3 **Return the pan** to the heat; add the tournedos. Cook, turning, until browned, 2–4 minutes per side. Transfer to the same plate.

4 **Combine the wine** and broth in the skillet and cook, scraping up the browned bits from the bottom of the pan, until the liquid has reduced to ¹/₂ cup. Swirl in the remaining 2 teaspoons butter to thicken the sauce.

5 **Return the mushroom mixture** and the tournedos to the skillet. Cook, turning the tournedos occasionally, until done to taste, 5–9 minutes. Remove the toothpicks. Serve each tournedos on a toast slice, topped with the mushroom mixture, a grinding of pepper, and garnished (if using) with a thyme sprig.

Chef's Tip

Tournedos are small steaks cut from the narrow end of the tenderloin; they should be about 1–1¹/₂ inches thick.

7 *POINTS* per serving

Per serving
320 Calories | 12 g Total Fat | 5 g Saturated Fat | 67 mg Cholesterol | 394 mg Sodium
26 g Total Carbohydrate | 2 g Dietary Fiber | 25 g Protein | 51 mg Calcium

grilled flank steak with pineapple and roasted shallots

The key to grilling flank steaks (or any other food) is a thoroughly preheated grill. Scrub the grill before you begin, to remove any debris that might cause the steak to stick. Steamed asparagus or green beans and grilled sweet potatoes or yams make excellent accompaniments to this dish. Skirt or sirloin steaks would also be suitable for this recipe, as would chicken parts or pork chops.

makes 6 servings

1 **Combine the pineapple,** pineapple juice, onion, lime, cilantro, chili powder, soy sauce, vinegar, garlic, oil, jalapeño (if using), and hot pepper sauce in a zip-close plastic bag; add the steak. Squeeze out the air and seal the bag; turn to coat the steak. Refrigerate, turning the bag occasionally, at least 2 hours or overnight.

2 **Spray the grill rack** with nonstick spray; prepare the grill.

3 **Remove the steak** from the marinade, scraping off any excess. Grill the steak 5 inches from the heat about 5 minutes per side or until done to taste. Let stand 10 minutes.

4 **Meanwhile, transfer the marinade** to a saucepan and bring it to a boil. Add the broth and simmer 5 minutes more. Taste the sauce and add more lime juice, pepper sauce, or cilantro to taste.

5 **Slice the steak** thinly on an angle across the grain. Serve, topped with the sauce and sprinkled with the shallots.

$1^1/_2$ cups finely chopped fresh or drained canned crushed pineapple

1 cup unsweetened pineapple juice

$1/_2$ medium red onion, sliced

1 lime, thinly sliced

3 tablespoons chopped fresh cilantro

1 tablespoon chili powder

1 tablespoon reduced-sodium soy sauce

1 tablespoon red wine vinegar

2 garlic cloves, minced

2 teaspoons olive oil

2 teaspoons minced jalapeño pepper (optional; wear gloves to prevent irritation)

A few drops hot pepper sauce

1 ($1^1/_2$-pound) flank steak, trimmed

$1/_2$ cup reduced-sodium beef broth

6–8 shallots, roasted and torn into small pieces

Chef's Tip

To roast the shallots, preheat the oven to 425°F. Peel and place the shallots in a small roasting pan or ovenproof skillet. Spray with nonstick spray and roast until golden brown, about 30 minutes. When cool enough to handle, use your hands to tear the shallots into small pieces.

Per serving

270 Calories | 10 g Total Fat | 4 g Saturated Fat | 46 mg Cholesterol | 292 mg Sodium
18 g Total Carbohydrate | 2 g Dietary Fiber | 27 g Protein | 47 mg Calcium

6 *POINTS* per serving

bolivian beef stew

There are many variations of this spicy, slow-cooking, one-pot meal. Serve it with warm Country Corn Bread (page 292) and salad greens dressed with lemon juice. Adjust the amount of jalapeño pepper to suit your family and friends. This is a good recipe to double. It will also freeze well; cool the stew to room temperature, store in an airtight container, and freeze for up to 2 weeks. Thaw in the refrigerator or microwave.

makes 4 servings

1 teaspoon vegetable oil

1 medium onions, chopped

1/2 red or green bell pepper, chopped

1 jalapeño pepper, seeded and chopped (optional; wear gloves to prevent irritation)

1 pound boneless lean beef round, cut into 2-inch cubes

2 cups canned stewed chopped tomatoes

1 cup low-sodium beef broth

1/4 teaspoon salt

2 cups cubed peeled acorn or winter squash

2 medium red potatoes, cubed

2 small ears of corn, cut into 1-inch rounds

2 tablespoons minced fresh cilantro

1 **Heat the oil** in a large nonstick skillet, then add the onions, bell pepper, and (if using) the jalapeño. Sauté until the onions are lightly browned, 6–7 minutes. Transfer to a plate.

2 **Return the skillet** to the heat; add the beef. Sauté until browned and cooked through, 8–10 minutes. Add the tomatoes, broth, and salt. Return the onion mixture to the pan, bring to a boil, and reduce the heat to low. Simmer, covered, stirring occasionally, until the beef is tender, 1–1 1/2 hours.

3 **Add the squash,** potatoes, and corn. Simmer, covered, until the vegetables are tender, about 20 minutes. Serve, sprinkled with the cilantro.

8 *POINTS* per serving

Per serving
390 Calories | 9 g Total Fat | 3 g Saturated Fat | 67 mg Cholesterol | 602 mg Sodium
48 g Total Carbohydrate | 8 g Dietary Fiber | 32 g Protein | 93 mg Calcium

"carpaccio" with caper sauce

Carpaccio—thinly sliced raw beef fillet—is an Italian appetizer best done in restaurants where a skilled chef can slice the beef paper-thin. A great alternative for the home cook is to have rare roast beef sliced as thin as possible at the deli. Arrange and garnish the beef like carpaccio.

makes 4 servings

1 **To prepare the caper sauce,** combine the parsley, lemon juice, and oil in a food processor. Add 1 teaspoon of the capers, the pepper, red pepper (if using), and the salt. Pulse until well blended and thick. By hand, stir in the remaining 1 teaspoon capers.

2 **Arrange the roast beef** evenly among 4 chilled plates. Drizzle each portion with an equal amount of the caper sauce; season with freshly ground pepper.

1 cup packed fresh flat-leaf parsley leaves, rinsed and dried

1 tablespoon fresh lemon juice

1 tablespoon extra-virgin olive oil

2 teaspoons capers, drained and rinsed

Freshly ground pepper

$1/8$ teaspoon crushed red pepper (optional)

Pinch salt

6 ounces rare roast beef, thinly sliced

Chef's Tip

Capers come in several varieties; the finest are the petite nonpareil from France. There are larger capers from Italy and Spain, and California produces excellent capers, as well. Drain the brine from the capers before using.

Per serving
138 Calories | 9 g Total Fat | 3 g Saturated Fat | 34 mg Cholesterol | 117 mg Sodium
1 g Total Carbohydrate | 1 g Dietary Fiber | 12 g Protein | 25 mg Calcium

3 *POINTS* per serving

veal scaloppine with lemon and capers

If possible, have the butcher cut scaloppine from the top round. This is the most desirable part of the round, as the meat is lean and perfect for quick sautéing. Serve this elegant dish with pan-steamed broccoli rabe and a crisp Italian wine.

makes 4 servings

1/4 cup seasoned dried bread crumbs

1 pound thinly sliced veal scaloppine, pounded flat

1/4 cup water

2 teaspoons cornstarch

1/2 cup low-sodium chicken broth

1 tablespoon fresh lemon juice

1 tablespoon capers, drained and chopped

1 lemon, thinly sliced

1 **Place the bread crumbs** on a piece of wax paper. Spray a large nonstick skillet with nonstick spray and set over medium-high heat. Coat the veal on both sides in the bread crumbs, shaking off and discarding the excess. Working in batches, if necessary, place the veal in the skillet and cook until golden brown, about 1 minute per side. Transfer the scaloppine to a warm platter; keep warm.

2 **Whisk together the water** and cornstarch in a bowl; whisk in the broth and lemon juice. Pour into the skillet and cook, scraping up the browned bits from the bottom of the pan, until thickened, 1–2 minutes. Stir in the capers and pour over the scaloppine. Serve topped with the lemon slices.

---

3 *POINTS* per serving

Per serving
162 Calories | 3 g Total Fat | 1 g Saturated Fat | 89 mg Cholesterol | 224 mg Sodium
8 g Total Carbohydrate | 0 g Dietary Fiber | 25 g Protein | 28 mg Calcium

sautéed veal with wild mushrooms and leeks

Try serving this elegant dish with barley and sautéed spinach. Chanterelle, oyster, morel, and shiitake are a few of the mushroom varieties that work well in this recipe, but select what is freshest.

makes 4 servings

1 tablespoon coarsely ground pepper

2 teaspoons chopped fresh thyme

$1/2$ teaspoon minced garlic

1 pound veal scaloppine

$1/4$ cup low-sodium vegetable broth or water

1 small leek, rinsed and chopped

3 cups wild mushrooms, sliced

1 cup prepared demi-glace sauce

1 teaspoon vegetable oil

1 **Combine the pepper,** 1 teaspoon of the thyme, and the garlic in a bowl. Place the veal on a plate and sprinkle on both sides with the pepper mixture. Cover and refrigerate at least 30 minutes.

2 **Heat the broth** in a saucepan, then add the leek. Cook until the leek is tender, about 3 minutes. Add the mushrooms and cook until tender, about 5 minutes. Add the demi-glace and bring to a simmer; reduce the heat and keep hot.

3 **Heat a large nonstick skillet** over high heat; add the oil, then wipe the pan with a wadded paper towel to absorb the excess. Working in batches, dry-sauté the scaloppine until browned and done to taste, about $1^1/2$ minutes on the first side and 1 minute on the second side for medium-rare. Transfer the scaloppine to a plate.

4 **Add the mushroom-leek mixture** to the skillet; cook, scraping up the browned bits from the bottom of the pan, until the liquid comes to a simmer. Return the scaloppine to the pan to reheat briefly. Serve the veal topped with the mushroom-leek mixture and sprinkled with the remaining thyme.

Chef's Tips

Select leeks that are bright green, smooth, and white toward the root end. Small leeks tend to be more tender than large ones. Store leeks in the refrigerator in a plastic bag for up to 5 days.

For information on dry-sautéing, see the feature on the following page and the Chef's Tip accompanying Tenderloin of Beef with Blue Cheese and Herb Crust (page 180).

Store mushrooms in a paper bag or in their cardboard container (replace the plastic wrap with a barely damp paper towel) for 3–4 days. Avoid storing mushrooms in plastic—it traps moisture making them turn slimy.

Per serving

281 Calories | 8 g Total Fat | 3 g Saturated Fat | 155 mg Cholesterol | 118 mg Sodium
7 g Total Carbohydrate | 1 g Dietary Fiber | 46 g Protein | 37 mg Calcium

6 *POINTS* per serving

dry sautéing

When dry-sautéing, whatever kind of meat you use, the thickness should be as even as possible. Here, boneless, skinless chicken breasts are pounded lightly between plastic wrap.

To give the pan just the thinnest coating of oil, wipe out excess with a paper towel.

Allow the first side to brown well before turning. The meat is ready to turn when the edges start to look opaque.

roast pork loin with applesauce

Although pork once had a somewhat unhealthy image, today's pork is bred to be leaner. Pork and applesauce are a traditional pairing. The applesauce in this recipe is made in the microwave and takes only minutes.

makes 8 servings

1 **Preheat the oven** to 350°F. Spray the rack of a roasting pan with nonstick spray and place in the pan. Season the pork with the salt and pepper. Roast for 45 minutes. Sprinkle the pork with the rosemary and continue roasting the pork until an instant-read thermometer inserted in the center registers 160°F, about 15 minutes more.

2 **Meanwhile, place the apples** in a microwavable bowl, cover with plastic wrap or a plate, and microwave on High 12 minutes. Transfer the apples to a food processor and puree. Stir in the sugar and cinnamon.

3 **Remove the pork** from the oven and let stand 10 minutes. Slice and arrange on a serving platter. Serve with the applesauce.

1 (2 pound) boneless pork loin, trimmed

1/4 teaspoon salt

Freshly ground pepper

1 teaspoon crumbled dried rosemary

6 Granny Smith apples, cored, peeled and quartered

1/4 cup sugar

1 teaspoon cinnamon

Per serving

309 Calories | 11 g Total Fat | 4 g Saturated Fat | 91 mg Cholesterol | 149 mg Sodium
21 g Total Carbohydrate | 2 g Dietary Fiber | 32 g Protein | 38 mg Calcium

7 POINTS per serving

roast pork loin with honey-mustard sauce

Pork that has been properly roasted is moist and delicious, even as leftovers. If you would like to have enough roasted pork left over for sandwiches or a salad, double the recipe. The cooking time will remain about the same.

makes 4 servings

1 teaspoon vegetable oil

1 pound boneless pork loin, trimmed

1/3 cup water

2 tablespoons minced shallot

1 garlic clove, minced

1/3 cup low-sodium chicken broth

2 tablespoons whole-grain mustard

1 tablespoon tomato paste

1 1/2 teaspoons chopped fresh thyme

1 teaspoon crushed black peppercorns

1 cup prepared demi-glace sauce

2 tablespoons honey

2 1/2 tablespoons red wine vinegar

1/2 teaspoon salt

1 **Preheat the oven** to 325°F. Spray the rack of a roasting pan with nonstick spray and place in the pan. Heat a large nonstick skillet over high heat; add the oil, then wipe the pan with a wadded paper towel to absorb the excess. Dry-sear the pork until golden brown on all sides, about 8 minutes. Place the pork on the roasting rack. Pour the water into the roasting pan and roast 25 minutes. Baste with the pan juices and continue roasting until the pork reaches an internal temperature of 160°F, about 25 minutes more.

2 **Meanwhile, add the shallots** and garlic to the skillet; cook until fragrant, about 30 seconds. Add the broth and cook, scraping up the browned bits from the bottom of the pan, until the broth is slightly reduced, about 5 minutes. Add the mustard, tomato paste, thyme, and pepper; cook, stirring, until the tomato paste has browned. Stir in the demi-glace , honey, vinegar, and salt. Simmer, stirring occasionally, until the mixture thickens to a sauce consistency, about 10 minutes. Keep warm.

3 **Transfer the pork** to a carving board; let stand 10 minutes before slicing. Carefully skim and discard the fat from the juices in the pan, then pour the degreased pan juices into the sauce.

4 **Thinly slice the roast** and serve with the warm sauce.

5 _POINTS_ per serving

Per serving (with 3 tablespoons sauce)
235 Calories | 8 g Total Fat | 3 g Saturated Fat | 63 mg Cholesterol | 479 mg Sodium
12 g Total Carbohydrate | 0 g Dietary Fiber | 27 g Protein | 22 mg Calcium

variation

Roast Pork Loin with Southwestern-Style Sauce: Use spicy Creole mustard in place of whole-grain mustard, maple syrup or molasses instead of honey, and chile-flavored vinegar instead of red wine vinegar. Replace the thyme with an equal amount of chopped cilantro added just before serving, and garnish the sauce with a fine dice of jalapeño peppers.

Chef's Tips

For information on dry-searing and demi-glace sauce, see the Chef's Tip accompanying Tenderloin of Beef with Blue Cheese and Herb Crust (page 180).

The honey-mustard sauce is created using a classical cooking technique known as deglazing. In this technique, liquid is added to the pan used to sear the meat. As it cooks, the liquid releases any food particles stuck to the bottom of the pan, ensuring that every last bit of flavor from the meat is captured in the sauce.

apricot-and-prune-stuffed pork tenderloin with armagnac sauce

Armagnac, an aged brandy from Gascony, France, gives this festive roast extra finesse and depth of flavor. Cognac or another brandy can be used as well. When sliced, the roast reveals a jewel-like center of brandied fruit. Serve it with Brussels sprouts and chestnuts.

makes 4 servings

1/2 cup minced mixed dried fruit

1/2 cup Armagnac, Cognac, or brandy

1 teaspoon vegetable oil

1/2 medium onion, minced

1/2 teaspoon crumbled dried sage leaves

Freshly ground pepper

1 (1-pound) pork boneless tenderloin, trimmed

3/4 teaspoon salt

1 1/4 cups low-sodium chicken broth

1 teaspoon Worcestershire sauce

1 teaspoon cornstarch, dissolved in 1 tablespoon cold water

1 **Preheat the oven** to 375°F. Lightly spray a shallow roasting pan with nonstick spray. Combine the dried fruit and 1/4 cup of the Armagnac in a small bowl.

2 **Heat 1/2 teaspoon** of the oil in a nonstick skillet, then add the onion. Sauté until lightly browned, 6–7 minutes. Transfer to a bowl. Stir in the brandied fruit, the sage, and pepper.

3 **Butterfly the pork** by slicing along the length of the loin, cutting nearly but not completely through. Open the meat and flatten it with your hands. Sprinkle both sides of the pork with 1/2 teaspoon of the salt. Spread the brandied fruit lengthwise over the meat, roll up, and tie with kitchen twine.

4 **Return the skillet** to the heat; add the remaining 1/2 teaspoon oil, then add the stuffed pork loin. Cook the loin, turning, until golden brown on all sides, 6–8 minutes. Place in the roasting pan. Roast until the pork reaches an internal temperature of 160°F, about 30 minutes. Let stand 10 minutes before slicing.

5 **Meanwhile, to make the Armagnac sauce,** combine the broth, the remaining 1/4 cup Armagnac, the Worcestershire sauce, and the remaining 1/4 teaspoon salt in a saucepan. Bring the mixture to a boil and cook, stirring constantly, until the liquid is reduced to about 1 cup. Reduce the heat to low. Stir in the cornstarch mixture. Simmer, stirring constantly, until the liquid is slightly thickened, about 1 minute.

6 **Cut the roast** into 12 slices and serve with the warm Armagnac sauce.

5 *POINTS* per serving

Per serving

254 Calories | 6 g Total Fat | 2 g Saturated Fat | 68 mg Cholesterol | 90 mg Sodium
16 g Total Carbohydrate | 2 g Dietary Fiber | 25 g Protein | 23 mg Calcium

apricot-and-prune-stuffed pork tenderloin with armagnac sauce

cider-braised pork medallions

"Medallions" are small round pieces of meat usually cut from the tenderloin. Look for freshly pressed cider during apple-picking season in the autumn months or in the refrigerator section of a natural food store. Cider has a period before fermentation when it is called sweet cider. Later, as it ferments, cider becomes a little fizzy as its sugar converts to alcohol. It is then called hard cider. Fresh ciders vary widely in their taste and level of fermentation, so be sure to taste the cider before buying a large quantity.

makes 4 servings

$^1/_3$ cup + 2 teaspoons all-purpose flour

$^1/_4$ teaspoon salt

Freshly ground pepper

1 pound boneless pork tenderloin, trimmed and cut into 12 medallions

2 tablespoons vegetable oil

$^1/_2$ cup sweet apple cider

1 tablespoon cider vinegar

1 teaspoon grated lemon zest

1   **Combine the flour** with the salt and a grinding of the pepper in a zip-close plastic bag; add the pork medallions, a few at a time. Seal the bag and shake to coat the medallions; shake off and discard the excess flour.

2   **Heat the oil** in a nonstick skillet, then add the medallions. Cook, turning, until lightly browned, 1–2 minutes per side. Reduce the heat and add the cider. Simmer, covered, until the medallions are cooked through, 1–2 minutes. Transfer the medallions to a warm serving platter; keep warm.

3   **Add the vinegar** and lemon zest to the pan juices; bring to a boil. Cook, stirring occasionally, until slightly thickened, about 5 minutes. Season with another grinding of pepper. Spoon the sauce over the medallions and serve.

6 *POINTS* per serving

Per serving
240 Calories | 11 g Total Fat | 2 g Saturated Fat | 74 mg Cholesterol | 208 mg Sodium
9 g Total Carbohydrate | 0 g Dietary Fiber | 25 g Protein | 9 mg Calcium

lamb shish kebab

Shish kebabs are perfect for an outdoor grill party, but are just as delicious when done in the broiler. Serve these with couscous and Chickpea Flatbread (page 296).

makes 4 servings

1/2 cup fresh lemon juice

1/2 cup dry white wine

1 1/2 tablespoons minced garlic

1 tablespoon chopped fresh parsley

2 teaspoons chopped fresh mint

1 1/2 teaspoons crushed pepper

3/4 teaspoons coriander seeds

1 pound trimmed lamb leg meat, cut into 1-inch cubes

1 small red bell pepper, cut into 1-inch pieces

1 small green bell pepper, cut into 1-inch pieces

1 small yellow bell pepper, cut into 1-inch pieces

1 medium onion, cut into 1-inch pieces

1 **Combine the lemon juice,** wine, garlic, parsley, mint, pepper, and coriander in a 9 × 13-inch glass baking dish.

2 **Alternately thread the lamb** and vegetables onto 8 (8-inch) metal skewers. Lay the kebabs in the pan, turning to coat with the marinade. Cover with plastic wrap, and refrigerate for at least 30 minutes and up to 2 hours.

3 **Spray the grill** or broiler rack with nonstick spray; prepare the grill or preheat the broiler.

4 **Remove the kebabs** from the marinade; discard the marinade. Grill or broil the kebabs 5 inches from the heat until the vegetables are tender and the lamb is done to taste, about 2 minutes per side for medium-rare. Use tongs or hot pads to transfer the skewers to plates (the skewer handles become extremely hot).

Per serving

252 Calories | 9 g Total Fat | 3 g Saturated Fat | 102 mg Cholesterol | 90 mg Sodium
7 g Total Carbohydrate | 2 g Dietary Fiber | 33 g Protein | 37 mg Calcium

5 *POINTS* per serving

broiled lamb chops with white bean–rosemary sauce

"Frenched" lamb chops have been trimmed of all extra fat around the bones; a good butcher or full-service meat counter will do it for you. Serve this elegant dish at a special dinner party, with roasted root vegetables on the side.

makes 4 servings

3 tablespoons reduced-sodium soy sauce

1 tablespoon Worcestershire sauce

1 tablespoon Dijon mustard

1 tablespoon vegetable oil

4 teaspoons chopped fresh rosemary

2 teaspoons chopped fresh thyme

2 teaspoons chopped fresh sage

Freshly ground pepper

8 (3-ounce) Frenched lamb rib chops

2 cups prepared demi-glace sauce

1 1/4 cups cooked cannellini (white kidney) beans

1/2 teaspoon salt

1 **Combine the soy sauce,** Worcestershire sauce, mustard, oil, 2 teaspoons of the rosemary, the thyme, sage, and a grinding of the pepper in a zip-close bag; add the lamb. Squeeze out the air and seal the bag; turn to coat the lamb. Refrigerate 30 minutes.

2 **Combine the demi-glace,** beans, 1/4 teaspoon of the salt, and another grinding of the pepper in a medium saucepan. Bring to a simmer; reduce the heat, cover, and cook 15 minutes. Keep hot.

3 **Spray the broiler rack** with nonstick spray; preheat the broiler.

4 **Remove the lamb chops** from the marinade and season with the remaining 1/4 teaspoon of the salt and another grinding of the pepper. Discard the marinade. Broil the lamb chops 5 inches from the heat until done to taste, about 2 minutes per side for medium-rare.

5 **Divide the sauce** and beans between 4 deep plates or soup plates. Serve the chops over the sauce and beans, sprinkled with the remaining 2 teaspoons rosemary.

Chef's Tip

Demi-glace is an intensely flavored, classical French brown veal sauce. It takes many hours to make demi-glace from scratch, but today's home cooks are fortunate in that well-stocked supermarkets and gourmet groceries now carry prepared demi-glace. It can be purchased frozen or as a shelf-stable concentrate. Follow package directions to reconstitute concentrated demi-glace.

Per serving (with 3/4 cup sauce and beans)

11 *POINTS* per serving

525 Calories | 21 g Total Fat | 7 g Saturated Fat | 162 mg Cholesterol | 841 mg Sodium
20 g Total Carbohydrate | 4 g Dietary Fiber | 61 g Protein | 110 mg Calcium

broiled lamb chops with white bean–rosemary sauce

braised lamb shanks

Braising is simple one-pot cooking done in a heavy casserole with a fitted lid. Braising is often used for cooking leaner, tougher cuts of meat such as lamb shanks. There is a lot of flavor in these cuts and as the meat slowly cooks, the connective tissues dissolve, the meat becomes tender, and the juices develop into a rich sauce. The sauce should be skimmed of fat as it cooks. Serve with couscous or rice pilaf to soak up every drop of the flavorful sauce.

makes 4 servings

2 teaspoons curry powder

$^1/_2$ teaspoon salt

$^1/_2$ teaspoon caraway seeds, crushed

$^1/_2$ teaspoon ground coriander

$^1/_2$ teaspoon cinnamon

$^1/_4$ teaspoon ground cayenne

Pinch ground allspice

Freshly ground pepper

4 ($^1/_2$-pound) lamb shanks, trimmed

1 teaspoon vegetable oil

4 medium onions, thinly sliced

1 green bell pepper, chopped

1 red bell pepper, chopped

1 garlic clove, minced

2 cups low-sodium chicken broth

2 tablespoons raisins, chopped

6 dried apricot halves, thinly sliced

1 tablespoon tomato paste (no salt added), dissolved in $^1/_2$ cup hot water

1 **Preheat the oven** to 300°F. Combine the curry powder, salt, caraway, coriander, cinnamon, cayenne, allspice, and pepper in a small bowl. Rub 1 tablespoon of the seasoning mixture on the lamb shanks.

2 **Heat a flameproof** 2-quart casserole or Dutch oven over high heat, add the oil, then wipe the pan with a wadded paper towel to absorb the excess. Dry-sear the shanks until just browned, about 2 minutes per side. Transfer to a plate; keep warm.

3 **Reduce the heat** to medium. Add the onions, bell peppers, garlic, and the remaining seasoning mixture to the casserole. Cook, stirring frequently, until softened, about 5 minutes.

4 **Stir in the broth,** raisins, apricots, and the tomato paste mixture. Return the lamb to the casserole and spoon some of the vegetables over the shanks. Bring the mixture just to a boil. Cover, the casserole and place it in the oven. Braise until the lamb is fork tender, about $1^1/_2$ hours. Serve each lamb shank topped with the sauce.

Chef's Tips

Purchase lamb hindshanks rather than foreshanks. Hindshanks may be slightly more expensive, but they are meatier than foreshanks.

For information on dry-searing, see the Chef's Tip accompanying Tenderloin of Beef with Blue Cheese and Herb Crust (page 180).

Per serving

243 Calories | 6 g Total Fat | 2 g Saturated Fat | 70 mg Cholesterol | 419 mg Sodium
25 g Total Carbohydrate | 5 g Dietary Fiber | 25 g Protein | 71 mg Calcium

5 *POINTS* per serving

lamb curry with dried fruit

The spice combination of paprika, cinnamon, crystallized ginger, and coriander produces a delicate curry flavor as the lamb cooks. Serve the curry with rice pilaf or couscous. This is a good recipe to double. It will also freeze well; cool the curry to room temperature, store in an airtight container, and freeze for up to 2 weeks. Thaw in the refrigerator or microwave.

makes 4 servings

1 **Cook the lamb** in a large nonstick skillet, breaking it apart with a spoon, until no longer pink, 4–5 minutes. Drain the excess fat and transfer to a medium bowl.

2 **Return the pan** to the heat; swirl in the oil, then add the onions. Sauté until softened, 3–5 minutes. Add the garlic, jalapeño (if using), the paprika, and cinnamon. Cook, stirring frequently, until fragrant, 1–2 minutes.

3 **Add the broth,** apricots, figs, raisins, and ginger; stir in the lamb. Bring to a boil; reduce the heat and simmer, uncovered, stirring occasionally, until the fruit is tender, 15 minutes. Stir in the coriander and pepper.

1 pound lean ground lamb (10% or less fat)

2 teaspoons vegetable oil

2 medium onions, chopped

4 garlic cloves, minced

1 1/2 teaspoons seeded and minced jalapeño pepper (optional; wear gloves to prevent irritation)

1 teaspoon sweet paprika

1/2 teaspoon cinnamon

1 1/2 cups low-sodium beef broth

6 dried apricot halves, coarsely chopped

2 large dried figs, halved

2 tablespoons golden raisins

1 tablespoon chopped crystallized ginger

1 teaspoon ground coriander

Freshly ground pepper

Per serving

297 Calories | 9 g Total Fat | 3 g Saturated Fat | 74 mg Cholesterol | 109 mg Sodium
28 g Total Carbohydrate | 3 g Dietary Fiber | 27 g Protein | 62 mg Calcium

6 *POINTS* per serving

sautéed venison with roasted onion sauce

Depending on what's at your farmers' market, you may be able to find unusual vegetables, such as Italian cipollini onions or beets in a rainbow of colors (pick the smallest you can find). Save time by roasting all the vegetables at once, but use separate roasting pans, as the beets will color everything. The shallots, beets, and the roasted onion can be prepared a day ahead; refrigerate them in separate airtight containers.

makes 4 servings

^{1}/3 cup chopped onion

^{1}/4 medium leek, rinsed and chopped (about ^{1}/2 cup)

7 garlic cloves, peeled

1 tablespoon + 1 teaspoon olive oil

^{3}/4 teaspoon salt

3 tablespoons malt vinegar

1 cup prepared demi-glace sauce

Freshly ground pepper

12 shallots or cipollini onions, peeled

12 baby golden or Chioggia beets

4 (3^1/2 ounce) boneless venison loin chops

2 tablespoons snipped fresh chives (1-inch lengths)

1 **Preheat the oven** to 425°F.

2 **To prepare the roasted onion sauce,** toss the onion, leek, garlic, ^{1}/2 tablespoon of the oil, and ^{1}/4 teaspoon of the salt in a small roasting pan or baking dish. Roast, stirring occasionally, until golden brown, about 25 minutes. Stir the vinegar into the hot pan, scraping up the browned bits from the bottom of the pan. Pour the contents of the roasting pan into a large saucepan and add the demi-glace. Partially cover, bring to a simmer, and cook for 30 minutes. Strain the sauce through a fine sieve, pressing down on the solids to recover as much sauce as possible, then discard the solids. Add a grinding of the pepper; cover and keep warm.

3 **Toss the shallots** with ^{3}/4 teaspoon of the oil in a small roasting pan; season with ^{1}/4 teaspoon of the salt, and a grinding of the pepper. Combine the beets with ^{3}/4 teaspoon of the oil in another small roasting pan; season with ^{1}/4 teaspoon of the salt, and another grinding of the pepper. Roast until the shallots are golden brown, about 30 minutes, and the beets are cooked through, about 40 minutes. When cool enough to handle, peel the beets. Keep the shallots and beets warm.

4 **Season the venison** with the remaining ^{1}/4 teaspoon salt and a grinding of the pepper. Heat a large ovenproof skillet over high heat; add the remaining 1 teaspoon oil, then wipe the pan with a wadded paper towel to absorb the excess. Dry-sauté the venison until it is browned and done to taste, about 2 minutes per side for medium-rare. Transfer to a plate and let stand 5 minutes.

5 POINTS per serving

Per serving

235 Calories | 7 g Total Fat | 2 g Saturated Fat | 84 mg Cholesterol | 556 mg Sodium
18 g Total Carbohydrate | 2 g Dietary Fiber | 27 g Protein | 52 mg Calcium

5 **To serve,** place each venison chop on a pool of the sauce, then arrange 3 roasted shallots and 3 roasted beets in an alternating pattern around each portion. Sprinkle with the chives.

Chef's Tips

For information on dry-sautéing and demi-glace, see the Chef's Tip accompanying Tenderloin of Beef with Blue Cheese and Herb Crust (page 180).

Venison is available at specialty butchers and some supermarkets; try to order it in advance. The quality of meat—whether purchased from a good butcher or obtained from a hunter—depends on how the meat was handled in the field. Meat from wild animals tends to be leaner and less tender than meat from domestic animals.

Select plump citrus fruits with smooth, brightly colored skin. If the skin is greenish it is probably not ripe. The zest of the citrus fruit is the peel without any of the pith (white membrane). When using both the zest and juice of a citrus fruit, first roll the fruit with the heel of hand, then remove the zest, using a zester or the fine side of a vegetable grater. Next, pierce the fruit with a paring knife and squeeze out the juice; the pits will stay behind.

venison steaks with cumberland sauce

Cumberland sauce, excellent with game meat, usually includes a combination of red currant jelly, citrus zest, port wine, mustard, and other seasonings. You can make the sauce up to 2 days ahead and store it in the refrigerator; the flavors will develop even further. You may need to thin it with a little water as you reheat it; it will thicken when it cools.

makes 4 servings

1 teaspoon olive oil

1 fennel bulb, thinly sliced (about 2 cups)

1 small head radicchio, shredded (about 2 cups)

3 tablespoons red currant jelly

1 tablespoon orange zest

2 teaspoons lemon zest

$1/3$ cup fresh orange juice

3 tablespoons fresh lemon juice

$1/3$ cup ruby port wine

1 teaspoon cornstarch dissolved in 1 tablespoon water

1 teaspoon minced shallot

$1/2$ teaspoon dry mustard

Pinch ground ginger

Pinch cayenne

2 (6-ounce) venison steaks

$1/2$ teaspoon salt

$1/2$ teaspoon freshly ground pepper

1 **Heat the oil** in a large nonstick skillet, then add the fennel and radicchio. Cook, stirring occasionally, until very soft, 30 minutes.

2 **To prepare the Cumberland sauce,** melt the red currant jelly in a saucepan. Add the orange zest, lemon zest, orange juice, lemon juice, port, the dissolved cornstarch, the shallot, mustard, ginger, and cayenne. Bring to a boil, reduce the heat and simmer for 3 minutes. Keep warm.

3 **Spray the broiler** or grill rack with nonstick spray and preheat the broiler or prepare the grill.

4 **Sprinkle both sides** of the steaks with the salt and pepper. Broil or grill the steaks 5 inches from the heat until done to taste, about $1 1/2$ minutes per side for medium-rare.

5 **Thinly slice the steaks** and serve them over the vegetable mixture; drizzle with the Cumberland sauce.

---

5 *POINTS* per serving

Per serving

224 Calories | 7 g Total Fat | 2 g Saturated Fat | 68 mg Cholesterol | 338 mg Sodium
19 g Total Carbohydrate | 2 g Dietary Fiber | 20 g Protein | 47 mg Calcium

indian grilled buffalo kebabs

Commercially raised buffalo meat is tender and juicy; it has all the good flavor of prime beef but is much leaner. If buffalo is not available in the market, try beef or pork. The meat should marinate 24 hours for best results.

makes 4 servings

1 **Combine the onion,** yogurt, garlic, ginger, cumin, pepper, and nutmeg in a 9 × 13-inch glass dish.

2 **Thread the buffalo** onto 8 (8-inch) metal skewers. Place the skewers in the marinade, turning to coat, cover with plastic wrap, and refrigerate for 24 hours.

3 **Spray the grill** or broiler rack with nonstick spray; prepare the grill or preheat the broiler.

4 **Remove the skewers** from the marinade; discard the marinade. Grill or broil the skewers 5 inches from the heat until the buffalo is done to taste, about 3 minutes per side for medium-rare. Use tongs or hot pads to transfer the skewers to plates (the skewer handles become extremely hot).

¹/₃ cup chopped onion

¹/₄ cup plain light yogurt

1¹/₂ tablespoons minced garlic

2 teaspoons minced peeled fresh ginger

¹/₄ teaspoon ground cumin

¹/₂ teaspoon crushed black peppercorns

¹/₄ teaspoon ground nutmeg

1 pound trimmed buffalo top round, cut into 1-inch cubes

Per serving

135 Calories | 2 g Total Fat | 1 g Saturated Fat | 53 mg Cholesterol | 72 mg Sodium
4 g Total Carbohydrate | 0 g Dietary Fiber | 24 g Protein | 54 mg Calcium

3 *POINTS* per serving

buffalo chili

Using buffalo meat—which is much leaner than beef—results in a chili with rich flavor but less fat than beef chili. Here, the meat gets dry-seared on the stove, then simmered in the oven in the chili mixture, until it is meltingly tender. This recipe can be doubled and leftovers will freeze well. Cool the chili to room temperature, store in an airtight container and freeze for up to 2 weeks. Thaw in the refrigerator or microwave.

makes 4 servings

1 teaspoon vegetable oil

1 1/2 pounds buffalo top round, trimmed and cut into 1-inch cubes

1 medium onion, chopped

2 1/2 tablespoons minced garlic

3 tablespoons chili powder

2 tablespoons tomato paste

1 cup low-sodium beef broth

4 large tomatoes, seeded and chopped (about 3 1/2 cups)

1/2 teaspoon cayenne

1/4 teaspoon salt

1/4 teaspoon crushed black peppercorns

1 **Preheat the oven** to 350°F.

2 **Heat a large ovenproof pot** over high heat; add the oil, then wipe the pan with a wadded paper towel to absorb the excess. Dry-sear the buffalo until browned, 5 minutes. Add the onion and garlic; sauté until the onion is translucent, 3–5 minutes. Stir in the chili powder and tomato paste; cook, stirring, until the tomato paste has browned.

3 **Add the broth;** cook, scraping up the browned bits from the bottom of the pan. Stir in the tomatoes, cayenne, salt, and pepper. Bring the chili to a boil, cover, and place in the oven. Bake until the meat is tender, about 1 hour.

Chef's Tip

For information on dry-searing, see the Chef's Tip accompanying Tenderloin of Beef with Blue Cheese and Herb Crust (page 180).

5 *POINTS* per serving

Per serving

245 Calories | 4 g Total Fat | 1 g Saturated Fat | 78 mg Cholesterol | 291 mg Sodium
15 g Total Carbohydrate | 3 g Dietary Fiber | 38 g Protein | 56 mg Calcium

chapter 11

grains

herbed basmati rice

Aromatic varieties of long-grain rice—such as basmati, jasmine, wild pecan, Texmati, Wehani, and popcorn rice, some of which you'll find in your supermarket, others in specialty or health food stores—can be delicious on their own or combined with just a few ingredients. Here, celery, garlic, and herbs help highlight the nutty accents of basmati rice in this surprisingly refreshing rice dish.

makes 4 servings

1 cup basmati rice

1 teaspoon vegetable oil

1/2 celery stalk, minced

1 garlic clove, minced

1/2 cup minced fresh flat-leaf parsley

1/2 teaspoon dried thyme

1 **Cook the rice** according to package directions.

2 **Meanwhile, heat the oil** in a nonstick skillet, then add the celery and garlic. Sauté until the celery just begins to soften, 1–2 minutes. Stir in the parsley and thyme; cook, stirring constantly, until the celery is softened, about 2 minutes. Transfer the celery to a large bowl, add the rice and toss to combine.

3 POINTS per serving

Per serving
165 Calories | 2 g Total Fat | 0 g Saturated Fat | 0 mg Cholesterol | 9 mg Sodium
34 g Total Carbohydrate | 2 g Dietary Fiber | 3 g Protein | 37 mg Calcium

lemon-dill rice

This rice dish is the perfect accompaniment to fish or shellfish. Drizzle poached sea scallops with a teaspoon of extra-virgin olive oil, then sprinkle them with a mixture of minced dill, garlic, and lemon zest and serve with this brightly flavored side dish.

makes 4 servings

1 **Preheat the oven** to 350°F. Heat 2 tablespoons of the broth in a large ovenproof saucepan or skillet with a lid, then add the onion. Cook until the onion is softened, about 5 minutes. Add the remaining broth, the rice, wine, lemon juice, bay leaf, and zest; bring to a boil. Cover the pan tightly, transfer to the oven, and bake until the rice is tender and the liquid is absorbed, about 18 minutes.

2 **Remove the pan** from the oven, discard the bay leaf, and gently stir in the dill.

$1^3/4$ cups low-sodium chicken broth

1 small onion, finely chopped

1 cup long-grain white rice

2 tablespoons dry white wine

2 tablespoons fresh lemon juice

1 bay leaf

$1/2$ teaspoon grated lemon zest

$1^1/2$ teaspoons chopped fresh dill

Per serving

201 calories | 1 g Total Fat | 1 g Saturated Fat | 2 mg Cholesterol | 65 mg Sodium
40 g Total Carbohydrate | 1 g Dietary Fiber | 5 g Protein | 27 mg Calcium

4 *POINTS* per serving

hazelnut wild rice

Toasted hazelnuts give this blend of wild and brown rice extra richness, crunch, and depth of flavor. Using the gentle, surrounding heat of an oven allows the rice to cook evenly.

makes 4 servings

$^1/_4$ cup skinned hazelnuts

$^1/_2$ cup wild rice, rinsed

$2^1/_2$ cups low-sodium chicken broth

1 small onion, finely chopped

$^1/_2$ cup brown rice

2 scallions, chopped

1 **Preheat the oven** to 350°F. Place the hazelnuts in an ovenproof skillet or jellyroll pan and toast in the oven, stirring frequently, until fragrant, about 5 minutes. Coarsely chop the nuts and set aside.

2 **Combine the wild rice** with $1^1/_2$ cups of the broth in an ovenproof saucepan; bring the broth to a boil. Cover tightly and bake until the rice is tender, about 45 minutes. Remove the pan from the oven; let stand, covered, 5 minutes.

3 **Meanwhile, heat 2 tablespoons** of the remaining broth in another ovenproof saucepan, then add the onion. Cook until the onion is softened, about 5 minutes. Add the remaining broth and the brown rice; bring to a boil. Cover tightly and bake until the rice is tender and the liquid is absorbed, about 40 minutes. Remove the pan from the oven.

4 **Gently toss both rices** with the hazelnuts and scallions in a large bowl.

Chef's Tip

The brown skin surrounding hazelnuts is bitter and should be removed. You can either purchase skinned hazelnuts, or skin them yourself by first baking them in a 350°F oven until the skins begin to flake, 10–15 minutes. Working in batches, place a handful of nuts in a clean kitchen towel and rub them together until most of the skin has been removed.

5 *POINTS* per serving

Per serving

239 Calories | 7 g Total Fat | 1 g Saturated Fat | 3 mg Cholesterol | 92 mg Sodium
37 g Total Carbohydrate | 4 g Dietary Fiber | 9 g Protein | 40 mg Calcium

dicing an onion

Trim the onion stem and root ends (keep root intact). Halve lengthwise through the root and peel each half. Lay the cut side down and make a series of evenly spaced, parallel, lengthwise cuts with the tip of a chef's knife, cutting just to the root.

Make two or three horizontal cuts parallel to the work surface, from the onion's stem end toward the root end, but do not cut all the way through.

To complete the dice, make even, crosswise cuts with a chef's knife, all the way through, from stem to root end. The closer the cuts in step one and in this step, the finer the dice will be.

wild and brown rice pilaf with cranberries

Tart-sweet apple and cranberry flavors contrast the nuttiness of wild and brown rice in this vibrant pilaf. If you like, substitute orange or apple juice for the white wine when soaking the cranberries.

makes 4 servings

1/4 cup dried cranberries

3 tablespoons dry white wine

2 cups low-sodium chicken broth

1/2 cup apple cider

1/2 teaspoon salt

1/2 cup wild rice, rinsed

1 small onion, finely chopped

1/2 cup brown rice

1 **Preheat the oven** to 350°F. Combine the cranberries with the wine in a nonreactive bowl; let stand 20 minutes. Drain the cranberries, reserving the liquid.

2 **Combine 1 cup** of the broth, the cider, 1/4 teaspoon of the salt, and the wild rice in a ovenproof saucepan; bring the broth to a boil. Cover tightly and bake until the rice is tender, about 45 minutes. Remove the pan from the oven; let stand, covered, 5 minutes.

3 **Meanwhile, heat the cranberry liquid** in another ovenproof saucepan, then add the onion. Cook, stirring frequently, until softened, about 5 minutes. Add the remaining broth, the remaining salt, and the brown rice; bring the liquid to a boil. Cover tightly and bake until the rice is tender and the liquid is absorbed, about 40 minutes.

4 **Gently toss both rices** with the cranberries in a large bowl.

Chef's Tip

Pilaf is a Middle Eastern grain dish that always begins with sautéing the grain and any vegetables in fat prior to adding the cooking liquid. To cut down on fat calories in this version, we forgo the fat entirely and use the cranberry-soaking liquid instead as a medium to soften the onion.

Per serving

4 POINTS per serving

215 Calories | 2 g Total Fat | 1 g Saturated Fat | 3 mg Cholesterol | 365 mg Sodium | 37 g Total Carbohydrate | 3 g Dietary Fiber | 7 g Protein | 26 mg Calcium

orange-millet pilaf

You might know millet as the tiny yellow pelletlike grains in bird-seed mixes, but the kind sold for cooking has the hard shells removed. Tasty, light, and versatile, it looks like couscous when cooked. Toasting it enhances its nutty flavor, and cooking it in orange juice gives it a refreshing and subtle fruitiness.

makes 4 servings

2 medium oranges

3/4 cup millet

1/4 teaspoon salt

2 teaspoons vegetable oil

1 garlic clove, minced

2 tablespoons chopped fresh flat-leaf parsley

1 **Grate the zest** from one of the oranges; juice them both. Add enough water to the juice to make 1 1/4 cups liquid.

2 **Toast the millet** in a saucepan, stirring until golden and fragrant, about 6–8 minutes. Add the orange juice and salt; bring the mixture to a boil. Reduce the heat and simmer, covered, until the millet has popped and the liquid is absorbed, 25–30 minutes.

3 **Heat the oil** in a small, nonstick skillet, then add the garlic. Sauté the garlic until fragrant, about 1 minute. Stir in the orange zest; cook 10 seconds. Scrape the garlic-zest mixture over the millet, add the parsley, and fluff with a fork.

Chef's Tip

Millet may be coated with a bitter white substance that should be washed away before cooking. Rinse the millet in several changes of cool water, using your hands to scrub the grains together. Drain and spread the grain out in a thin layer on a baking sheet to air dry before toasting.

Per serving

194 Calories | 4 g Total Fat | 0 g Saturated Fat | 0 mg Cholesterol | 148 mg Sodium
35 g Total Carbohydrate | 5 g Dietary Fiber | 5 g Protein | 33 mg Calcium

3 POINTS per serving

kasha with walnuts and apples

Kasha is roasted buckwheat groat, a grain with a nutty, toasted flavor. Cooking the kasha briefly with a beaten egg white prevents clumping and coats the grains, making them less mushy when cooked. In this dish, kasha perfectly compliments the sweet-tart taste of the apple.

makes 4 Servings

1 egg white

1 cup kasha

2 teaspoons vegetable oil

1 Granny Smith apple, cored and chopped

2 celery stalks, chopped

1 onion, chopped

1 cup apple juice

3/4 cup water

1/4 teaspoon salt

Freshly ground pepper

1/4 cup toasted walnuts, chopped

1 **Lightly beat the egg white** in a medium bowl; stir in the kasha. Transfer to a small skillet and cook, stirring to separate the grains, until dry, 4–5 minutes.

2 **Heat the oil** in a saucepan, then add the apple, celery, and onion. Cook, stirring as needed until the apple is softened, 8–10 minutes. Add the kasha; cook, stirring to coat, about 1 minute.

3 **Stir in the apple juice,** water, salt, and pepper; bring to a boil. Reduce the heat and simmer, covered, until the kasha is tender, about 15 minutes. Fluff the Kasha with a fork and serve, sprinkled with the walnuts.

Chef's Tip

To toast the walnuts, place them in a small skillet over medium low heat; shake the pan and stir constantly until lightly browned and fragrant, 3–5 minutes. Watch them carefully when toasting; walnuts can burn quickly. Transfer the nuts to a plate to cool.

3 POINTS per serving

Per serving
173 Calories | 7 g Total Fat | 1 g Saturated Fat | 0 mg Cholesterol | 181 mg Sodium
25 g Total Carbohydrate | 3 g Dietary Fiber | 5 g Protein | 28 mg Calcium

tabbouleh

Bulgur, the star of this traditional Middle Eastern cold salad, is formed when wheat berries are steamed, hulled, dried, and cracked. This traditional salad is terrific when served with toasted pita triangles spread with hummus or baba ghanoush.

makes 4 servings

1 Bring the water to a boil in a saucepan. Stir in the bulgur. Remove from the heat; cover and let stand until the water is absorbed, 20–25 minutes.

2 Combine the tomatoes, parsley, lemon juice, onion, scallions, garlic, oil, salt, and pepper in a large bowl. Add the bulgur; toss to combine. Refrigerate the tabbouleh, covered, until well chilled, at least 3 hours. Serve, garnished with the lemon slices.

1 cup water

$^2/_3$ cup bulgur

2 medium tomatoes, chopped

$^2/_3$ cup chopped flat-leaf parsley

$^1/_3$ cup fresh lemon juice

1 small red onion, chopped

2 scallions, sliced (green part only)

1 garlic clove, minced

2 teaspoons olive oil

$^1/_4$ teaspoon salt

Freshly ground pepper

Lemon slices

Chef's Tip

Add an extra layer of flavor by substituting chopped mint for half of the chopped parsley.

Per serving

132 Calories | 3 g Total Fat | 0 g Saturated Fat | 0 mg Cholesterol | 163 mg Sodium
25 g Total Carbohydrate | 6 g Dietary Fiber | 4 g Protein | 39 mg Calcium

2 *POINTS* per serving

minted wheat berries with oranges

You can find wheat berries, also known as whole-grain wheat, at health-food stores or Middle Eastern markets. High in protein, wheat berries will keep for up to 1 year stored airtight in a cool, dark place. (If you can't locate them, substitute bulgur or brown rice and follow the cooking times according to package directions.)

makes 4 servings

2^1/$_4$ cups water

1 cup wheat berries, rinsed

2 navel oranges, peeled and sectioned

^{1}/$_2$ carrot, peeled and finely chopped

^{1}/$_2$ red onion, minced

^{1}/$_2$ cup chopped fresh mint

3 tablespoons fresh lemon juice

2 teaspoons olive oil

^{1}/$_4$ teaspoon salt

Freshly ground pepper

1 **Bring the water** to a boil in a saucepan. Stir in the wheat berries; reduce the heat and simmer, covered, until the berries are tender and the water is absorbed, 1^1/$_2$–2 hours. Fluff the wheat berries with a fork, then let stand 5 minutes.

2 **Combine the wheat berries** with the orange sections, carrot, onion, mint, lemon juice, oil, salt, and pepper in a large bowl; toss to combine. Refrigerate the salad, covered, for 1 hour before serving.

4 POINTS per serving

Per serving
227 Calories | 3 g Total Fat | 0 g Saturated Fat | 0 mg Cholesterol | 154 mg Sodium
45 g Total Carbohydrate | 9 g Dietary Fiber | 9 g Protein | 69 mg Calcium

quinoa pilaf with red peppers

Quick-cooking and nutritionally superior to all other grains, quinoa (pronounced KEEN-wah) pairs well with most foods, including lamb, poultry, and fish. The germ, which completely surrounds the rest of the grain, falls away during cooking and remains slightly crunchy, while the grain itself becomes meltingly soft. Before cooking, quinoa must be washed very well to remove its natural bitter coating.

makes 4 servings

1 **Pour the quinoa** into a bowl of cold water and wash it by rubbing it between your hands. Drain and repeat until the water is clear, one to two more times.

2 **Heat 2 tablespoons** of the broth in a medium saucepan, then add the shallot and garlic. Cook, stirring frequently, until the shallot is softened, about 1 minute. Add the remaining broth, the quinoa, bay leaf, thyme, salt, and white pepper; bring to a boil. Reduce the heat and simmer, covered, until the quinoa is translucent and the liquid is absorbed, about 15 minutes.

3 **Remove the pan** from the heat. Let stand, 5 minutes, then fluff the pilaf with a fork, and discard the bay leaf and thyme sprig. Stir in the bell pepper.

1 cup quinoa

2 cups low-sodium chicken broth

1 tablespoon minced shallot

3 garlic cloves, minced

1 bay leaf

1 thyme sprig

$1/4$ teaspoon salt

$1/8$ teaspoon freshly ground white pepper

3 tablespoons chopped roasted red bell pepper

Chef's Tip

Use bottled roasted pepper, or roast your own. To roast a bell pepper, spray the broiler rack with nonstick spray; preheat the broiler. Broil the pepper 5 inches from the heat, turning frequently with tongs, until the skin is shriveled and darkened, 10–20 minutes. Place the pepper in a small bowl, cover with plastic wrap, and let steam for 10 minutes. When cool enough to handle, peel and seed. Or, to save time, use bottled roasted peppers.

Per serving

186 Calories | 4 g Total Fat | 1 g Saturated Fat | 3 mg Cholesterol | 225 mg Sodium
32 g Total Carbohydrate | 3 g Dietary Fiber | 8 g Protein | 40 mg Calcium

3 *POINTS* per serving

couscous with wild mushrooms and walnuts

Quick-cooking couscous can be made in the same amount of time as "instant" rice. Couscous is not exactly a grain (it's actually a grain product made from wheat, like pasta), but it is included in this chapter because it is usually treated more like grain than a pasta. This dish makes a wonderful base for savory vegetable stews or curries, or as a side dish with grilled lamb or pan-seared fish.

makes 4 servings

2 cups low-sodium chicken broth or water

1 cup couscous

1/2 cup sliced wild mushrooms (try shiitake or porcini)

1 teaspoon grated orange zest

1/4 teaspoon salt

2 tablespoons coarsely chopped toasted walnuts

1 **Bring the broth** to a boil in a saucepan. Add the couscous, stirring to remove any lumps. Bring the mixture to a boil, stirring constantly, then remove from the heat. Gently stir in the mushrooms, orange zest, and salt. Cover the couscous and let stand 5 minutes.

2 **Using two forks,** gently fluff the couscous, taking care to break up the lumps. Serve, sprinkled with the walnuts.

Chef's Tips

Dried mushrooms may be substituted for fresh. Use 1/4 cup dried mushrooms and reconstitute them by pouring enough boiling water over them to cover completely. Let soak for about 15 minutes and drain. To give the couscous cooking liquid more robust flavor, strain the mushroom soaking liquid through a coffee filter and use it in place of part of the broth or water. If you can't find fresh or dried wild mushrooms, sliced domestic mushrooms are an acceptable substitute.

To toast the walnuts, place them in a small skillet over medium low heat; shake the pan and stir constantly until lightly browned and fragrant, 3–5 minutes. Watch them carefully when toasting; walnuts can burn quickly. Transfer the nuts to a plate to cool.

4 POINTS per serving

Per serving

220 Calories | 4 g Total Fat | 1 g Saturated Fat | 3 mg Cholesterol | 221 mg Sodium 38 g Total Carbohydrate | 3 g Dietary Fiber | 9 g Protein | 23 mg Calcium

goat cheese polenta

Cooled cooked polenta is thick enough to slice. When the slices are browned on the stovetop, they become golden on the outside, creamy and savory on the inside. Rewarm leftovers (if you have any) on a grill or in a broiler and use as a base for delicious open-faced roasted red pepper and sautéed mushroom sandwiches.

makes 4 servings

1 cup instant polenta

Freshly ground pepper

$1/4$ teaspoon salt

3 cups low-sodium chicken broth

3 garlic cloves, minced

$1/3$ cup crumbled goat cheese

$1/2$ teaspoon chopped fresh chives

$1/2$ teaspoon chopped fresh thyme

1 **Combine the polenta,** pepper, and salt in a bowl.

2 **Heat 2 tablespoons** of the broth in a medium saucepan, then add the garlic. Cook, stirring frequently, until the garlic is softened, about 1 minute. Add the remaining broth; bring to a boil. Slowly pour in the polenta mixture in a thin, steady stream whisking constantly, reduce the heat continue whisking, and cook 5 minutes. Remove the pan from the heat and stir in the cheese, chives, and thyme.

3 **Brush a 1-quart square baking dish** with water; spread the polenta evenly in the dish. Refrigerate, covered, until firm and chilled, about 1 hour. Unmold the polenta; cut into 8 rectangles.

4 **Spray a nonstick skillet** with nonstick spray and set over medium-high heat then, then add the polenta. Cook, turning the polenta once, until heated through and lightly browned, 2–3 minutes per side.

Chef's Tip

Polenta is the Italian word for coarsely ground yellow cornmeal. This recipe uses instant polenta, which has undergone special processing to make it cook faster. Regular polenta may be substituted, but the cooking time will increase to about 30 minutes. Polenta is properly cooked when it begins to pull away from the sides of the pan as it is stirred.

Per serving

206 Calories | 6 g Total Fat | 3 g Saturated Fat | 14 mg Cholesterol | 316 mg Sodium
30 g Total Carbohydrate | 3 g Dietary Fiber | 9 g Protein | 59 mg Calcium

4 *POINTS* per serving

farro with parsley and toasted almond salsa

Discover the hearty, nutty flavor of farro, a grain widely enjoyed in the Tuscany region of Italy. Farro can be purchased as either whole or cracked grain from many health food stores. Although either will work in this recipe, you should adjust the cooking time as noted. Serve this dish with a variety of steamed vegetables on the side.

makes 6 servings

2 cups water

1/2 carrot, peeled

1/2 medium onion

Pinch dried thyme

Pinch dried oregano

1/4 bay leaf

1/4 pound farro, rinsed and drained (about 3/4 cup)

1/4 teaspoon salt

1 tablespoon minced shallot

1 tablespoon red wine vinegar

1/4 cup chopped toasted almonds

1/2 cup chopped fresh parsley

1 tablespoon chopped fresh basil

1 tablespoon extra-virgin olive oil

2 teaspoons chopped fresh tarragon

1 1/2 teaspoons capers, drained and chopped

1 **Combine the water,** carrot, onion, thyme, oregano, and bay leaf in a saucepan. Bring the mixture to a boil; stir in the farro and the salt. Reduce the heat and simmer, covered, until the farro kernels are soft and chewy, 45–50 minutes for whole-grain farro, 20–25 minutes for cracked farro. Drain the farro if any liquid remains. Discard the carrot, onion, and bay leaf.

2 **Meanwhile, combine the shallot** and vinegar in a nonreactive bowl; let stand 20 minutes. Add the almonds, parsley, basil, oil, tarragon, and capers. Spoon the herb-almond mixture over the farro and serve.

Chef's Tip

To toast the almonds, place them in a small skillet over medium low heat; shake the pan and stir constantly until fragrant, 3–5 minutes.

2 POINTS per serving

Per serving
130 Calories | 7 g Total Fat | 0.5 g Saturated Fat | 0 mg Cholesterol | 140 mg Sodium
16 g Total Carbohydrate | 4 g Dietary Fiber | 4 g Protein | 25 mg Calcium

farro with parsley and toasted almond salsa

native grain cakes of corn, wild rice, and quinoa

These grain cakes combine the mellow, nutty flavor of wild rice with corn meal and quinoa (pronounced KEEN-wah), the little ivory-colored grain that packs a big protein punch. Delicious with a zesty tomato sauce and steamed vegetables, these cakes can be made up to a day ahead and baked just before mealtime.

makes 4 servings

$1/4$ cup wild rice

$3^1/2$ cups low-sodium vegetable broth

$1/8$ teaspoon salt

Freshly ground pepper

$1/3$ cup quinoa

$3/4$ cup yellow cornmeal

$1/4$ teaspoon ground cumin

Pinch cayenne

$1/4$ cup corn-flake crumbs

1 **Rinse the wild rice** in cold water and drain. Bring the rice and $3/4$ cup of the broth to a boil in a saucepan; reduce the heat and simmer, covered, until tender, about 40 minutes. Season with a pinch of salt and a grinding of the pepper; fluff with a fork, and spread in a shallow dish to cool.

2 **Meanwhile, rinse the quinoa** several times in cold water and drain. Bring the quinoa and $3/4$ cup of the broth to a boil in a saucepan; reduce the heat and simmer, covered, until tender, about 15 minutes. Season with a pinch of salt and a grinding of the pepper; fluff with a fork, and spread in a shallow dish to cool.

3 **Bring the remaining 2 cups broth** to a boil in a saucepan. Slowly whisk in $1/3$ cup plus 2 teaspoons of the cornmeal. Reduce the heat and simmer, stirring constantly, until the cornmeal is thick and porridge-like, about 10 minutes. Remove from the heat, stir in the wild rice, quinoa, cumin, and cayenne. Transfer to a shallow dish and let cool slightly.

4 POINTS per serving

Per serving
220 Calories | 3 g Total Fat | 1 g Saturated Fat | 0 mg Cholesterol | 151 mg Sodium
40 g Total Carbohydrate | 4 g Dietary Fiber | 9 g Protein | 21 mg Calcium

4 **Preheat the oven** to 375°F.

5 **Shape the grain mixture** into eight 3-inch cakes. Combine the remaining cornmeal with the corn-flake crumbs. Dredge the cakes in the cornmeal mixture, pressing the mixture onto the cakes as necessary to coat both sides. Place the cakes on a nonstick baking sheet and spray the cakes lightly on both sides with nonstick spray. Bake until the cakes are lightly browned and heated through, 15–20 minutes.

Chef's Tip

You can find quinoa in health-food stores and some supermarkets. The germ, which completely surrounds the rest of the grain, falls away during cooking and remains slightly crunchy, while the grain itself becomes meltingly soft. Before cooking, quinoa must be washed very well to remove its natural bitter coating.

risotto with scallops and asparagus

Short-grain rices like Italy's Arborio variety pack slightly more nutritional value into each grain than their long- and medium-grain counterparts. But the real draw of this elegant seafood main dish is its flavor! If bay scallops are unavailable, use sea scallops cut into quarters.

makes 4 servings

3 cups water

1¼ cups low-sodium chicken broth

2 teaspoons olive oil

½ medium red onion, finely chopped

1⅓ cup Arborio or other short-grain rice

12 thin asparagus spears, cut diagonally into 1-inch pieces

1¼ pounds bay scallops, muscle tabs removed

1 tablespoon fresh lemon juice

½ teaspoon grated lemon zest

¾ teaspoon salt

Freshly ground pepper

¼ cup grated Asiago cheese

1 **Bring the water** and broth to a boil in a saucepan. Reduce the heat and keep at a simmer.

2 **Heat the oil** in a nonstick saucepan, then add the onion. Reduce the heat and sauté 1 minute. Add the rice; cook, stirring to coat, about 2 minutes. Add 1 cup of the broth mixture; cook, stirring, until the liquid is absorbed.

3 **Add ½ cup of the broth** and the asparagus; cook, stirring, until the liquid is absorbed. Continue to add the broth, ½ cup at a time, stirring until it is absorbed before adding more, until the rice is just tender. The cooking time, from the first addition of broth, should be 25–30 minutes. Stir in the scallops, lemon juice, lemon zest, salt, and pepper. Cook until the scallops are opaque, the rice tender, and the liquid absorbed, about 2 minutes. Stir in the cheese and serve.

Chef's Tip

Scallops often come with tabs of muscle still attached to them. The muscle is tough and should be removed before cooking. To remove, simply peel the muscle tab away from the scallop and discard.

9 POINTS per serving

Per serving
440 Calories | 6 g Total Fat | 2 g Saturated Fat | 54 mg Cholesterol | 717 mg Sodium
61 g Total Carbohydrate | 3 g Dietary Fiber | 32 g Protein | 121 mg Calcium

risotto with scallops and asparagus

risotto with peas and scallions

Serve this slow-cooked Italian favorite with slices of lean pork tenderloin. Or substitute reduced-sodium vegetable broth for the chicken broth to create a satisfying vegetarian side or main dish.

makes 4 servings

3$\frac{1}{2}$ cups low-sodium chicken broth

1 tablespoon + 1 teaspoon vegetable oil

1 medium onion, finely chopped

1$\frac{1}{3}$ cups Arborio rice

1 cup dry white wine

1 cup thawed frozen small green peas

4 scallions, sliced (about $\frac{3}{4}$ cup)

Freshly ground pepper

1 **Bring the broth** to a boil in a saucepan. Reduce the heat and keep at a simmer.

2 **Heat the oil** in a nonstick saucepan, then add the onion. Reduce the heat and sauté 1 minute. Add the rice; cook, stirring to coat, about 2 minutes. Add the wine and 1 cup of the broth; cook, stirring, until the liquid is absorbed.

3 **Add 1 cup of the broth,** the peas, and $\frac{1}{2}$ cup of the scallions; cook, stirring, until the liquid is absorbed. Continue to add the broth, $\frac{1}{2}$ cup at a time, stirring until it is absorbed before adding more, until the rice is just tender. The cooking time, from the first addition of broth, should be 25–30 minutes. Stir in the pepper and serve the rice, sprinkled with the remaining scallions.

Chef's Tip

If you prefer, substitute an equal amount of broth for the wine.

8 *POINTS* per serving

Per serving

416 Calories | 6 g Total Fat | 1 g Saturated Fat | 4 mg Cholesterol | 165 mg Sodium
72 g Total Carbohydrate | 4 g Dietary Fiber | 12 g Protein | 65 mg Calcium

chapter 12

eggs, beans, cheese, and tofu

cheese soufflé

The classic, puffy soufflé begins with a béchamel (white sauce) base to which cheese, seasonings, and egg yolks are added. Stiffly beaten egg whites are folded into the base to make a light and fluffy concoction. Have the table set and guests ready as the soufflé bakes. That way, you can bring it right from the oven to the table and dig in when it's at its puffiest and most glorious.

makes 4 servings

3 tablespoons all-purpose flour

1 cup low-fat (1%) milk

1 1/2 cups shredded reduced-fat cheddar cheese

1/2 teaspoon salt

1/8 teaspoon cayenne

2 eggs, separated

2 egg whites

1 **In a small bowl,** stir the flour into 3 tablespoons of the milk until smooth. Whisk the milk-flour mixture and the remaining milk together in a heavy-bottomed saucepan and place over low heat. Cook, stirring, until the mixture thickens, about 5 minutes. Remove from the heat; stir in the cheese, 1/4 teaspoon of the salt, and the cayenne. Transfer to a bowl and let cool slightly.

2 **Preheat the oven** to 350°F. Stir a small amount of the cheese mixture into the egg yolks, then add all the egg yolk mixture into the cheese mixture and whisk to combine.

3 **Beat all 4 egg whites** until foamy; add the remaining 1/4 teaspoon salt, and beat until stiff but not grainy. Stir one-fourth of the egg whites into the cheese mixture. Fold in the remaining egg whites with a rubber spatula. Scrape the mixture into a 3-quart ungreased soufflé dish. Bake until puffed and cooked through, 35 minutes. Serve immediately.

Chef's Tips

Allow the egg whites to come to room temperature. Make sure the bowl and beaters are squeaky clean and dry, and that the egg whites are free of any yolk. Add a small pinch of salt or cream of tartar to the whites to help keep them stable. Start slowly and when the whites become quite foamy, increase the speed of the mixer and beat to stiff peaks. When the beater is lifted out of the egg whites, they will stand up in stiff, stable peaks.

To fold egg whites, use a rubber spatula; cut down to the bottom of the bowl, lift and turn the whites over, turn the bowl and repeat.

Per serving

5 *POINTS* per serving

198 Calories | 9 g Total Fat | 6 g Saturated Fat | 131 mg Cholesterol | 636 mg Sodium
9 g Total Carbohydrate | 0 g Dietary Fiber | 20 g Protein | 464 mg Calcium

cheese soufflé

vegetarian refried beans

The brown-and-pink pinto bean is the standard bean used in *frijoles refritos,* or refried beans. Refried beans are typically made with lard; this vegetarian version uses corn oil and plenty of spices for flavor. As they cook, some of the beans will break down to a puree and some of the beans will remain whole, giving this dish a creamy yet slightly chunky texture. Serve refried beans with Mexican or Southwestern dishes, garnished with shredded lettuce and sliced radishes.

makes 4 servings

$^1/_2$ teaspoon corn oil

$^1/_3$ cup chopped onion

2 garlic cloves, minced

$^1/_2$ teaspoon ground cumin

$^1/_2$ teaspoon chili powder

1 (15-ounce) can pinto beans, drained and rinsed

1 cup vegetable broth

1 sun-dried tomato half, minced (not oil-packed)

$^1/_4$ teaspoon salt

Hot pepper sauce (optional)

Heat a large nonstick skillet. Swirl in the oil, then add the onion, garlic, cumin, and chili powder. Sauté until the onion is translucent, 3–4 minutes. Add the beans, broth, tomato, and salt. Simmer over low heat, stirring constantly, until the beans begin to pull away from the edge of the pan, 15–20 minutes. Season with the pepper sauce (if using).

---

2 *POINTS* per serving

Per serving

111 Calories | 2 g Total Fat | 0 g Saturated Fat | 0 mg Cholesterol | 450 mg Sodium
19 g Total Carbohydrate | 5 g Dietary Fiber | 6 g Protein | 52 mg Calcium

lima bean and roasted corn succotash

This recipe can be made year-round using frozen lima beans, but the fresh beans have a creamy texture and appealing flavor that is unmistakably better. You are most likely to find fresh lima beans at your local farmers' market in the early summer.

makes 4 servings

1 **Bring the lima beans** and 1 inch of water to a boil in a saucepan. Reduce the heat and simmer, covered, until tender, about 15 minutes for fresh beans, or 5 minutes for frozen beans. Drain and set aside.

2 **Cook the corn** in a large, dry cast-iron skillet, stirring occasionally, until golden brown, about 6 minutes. Stir in the lima beans, chives, tarragon, butter, salt, and pepper. Cook, stirring occasionally, until the flavors are blended, about 5 minutes. Serve at once.

2 pounds fresh lima beans, shelled (about 2 cups), or one 10-ounce box frozen lima beans, thawed

2 cups fresh corn (from about 4 ears), or 1 (9-ounce) box frozen corn, thawed

$1/4$ cup minced fresh chives

$1^1/_2$ teaspoons chopped fresh tarragon

$1^1/_2$ teaspoons unsalted butter

$1/_8$ teaspoons salt

Freshly ground pepper

Chef's Tip

Because it retains heat so well, a cast-iron skillet is essential for pan-roasting the corn. The hot pan helps the sugars in the corn to caramelize, creating a deep, roasted flavor in minutes.

Per serving

208 Calories | 3 g Total Fat | 1 g Saturated Fat | 4 mg Cholesterol | 117 mg Sodium
41 g Total Carbohydrate | 7 g Dietary Fiber | 9 g Protein | 33 mg Calcium

4 *POINTS* per serving

chickpea and vegetable tagine

Tagine, a Moroccan stew, is usually gently simmered in an earthenware vessel and served with couscous. This tagine of vegetables has the exotic fragrance of cumin, pepper, and cinnamon.

makes 4 servings

1 tablespoon olive oil

2 medium onions, chopped

3 garlic cloves, minced

1¹/₂ teaspoons ground cumin

Freshly ground pepper

¹/₄ teaspoon cinnamon

1 cup water

1 (2-pound) butternut squash, peeled, seeded, and cut into chunks

3 carrots, peeled and cut into chunks

1 (15-ounce) can chickpeas, rinsed and drained

1 (14-ounce) can diced tomatoes in juice (no salt added)

1 sweet potato, peeled and cut into chunks (about 1 cup)

3 parsnips, peeled and cut into chunks

1 bay leaf

¹/₄ cup chopped fresh flat-leaf parsley

1 **Heat a large saucepan.** Swirl in the oil, then add the onions. Sauté until the onions are softened, about 5 minutes. Add the garlic; sauté until golden, about 1 minute. Add the cumin, pepper, and cinnamon; cook, stirring, 1 minute.

2 **Stir in the water,** squash, carrots, chickpeas, tomatoes, sweet potato, parsnips, and the bay leaf; bring to a boil. Reduce the heat and simmer, partially covered, until the vegetables are tender, 45–55 minutes. Discard the bay leaf and sprinkle with the parsley.

Chef's Tip

To peel the squash, cut the top and bottom off the squash, then cut in half cross-wise, separating the narrow top part of the squash from the round bottom part. This step makes it easier to handle the squash. Remove the seeds. Use a very sharp, sturdy vegetable peeler or a sharp knife to cut the skin away from the squash.

7 *POINTS* per serving

Per serving
380 Calories | 6 g Total Fat | 1 g Saturated Fat | 0 mg Cholesterol | 307 mg Sodium
73 g Total Carbohydrate | 19 g Dietary Fiber | 12 g Protein | 187 mg Calcium

braised black-eyed peas

Black-eyed peas originated in Asia and were introduced to the United States through the African slave trade. Also known as cowpeas, they are round white beans with a black "eye" in the curved portion of the bean. Serve this dish with pork or ham.

makes 4 servings

1 bacon slice, chopped

2 tablespoons chopped onion

2 cups frozen black-eyed peas

1 1/4 cups low-sodium chicken broth

2 tablespoons finely chopped sun-dried tomatoes (not oil-packed)

1 small bay leaf

1 small fresh thyme sprig

1 **Preheat the oven** to 350°F.

2 **Cook the bacon** in an ovenproof pot with a fitted lid, stirring frequently, until crisp. Add the onion and sauté until lightly browned, about 4 minutes. Add the black-eyed peas, broth, tomatoes, bay leaf, and thyme.

3 **Bring to a simmer,** then cover, and bake until the peas have absorbed the broth, about 25 minutes. Discard the bay leaf and thyme sprig before serving.

Chef's Tip

Black-eyed peas are available canned, frozen, and dried year-round, and fresh at certain times of the year. If available, fresh black-eyed peas may be substituted for frozen. Dried peas may also be substituted in this recipe, but they must be cooked first according to package directions until they are almost tender, but not quite fully cooked. Do not use canned black-eyed peas in this recipe; they are already fully cooked and therefore do not work well with this cooking method, because they become too soft.

Per serving

154 Calories | 3 g Total Fat | 1 g Saturated Fat | 1 mg Cholesterol | 47 mg Sodium
24 g Total Carbohydrate | 4 g Dietary Fiber | 9 g Protein | 31 mg Calcium

3 POINTS per serving

hoppin' john

In the Southeastern United States, Hoppin' John is a traditional New Year's Day dish said to bring good luck in the coming year. For a Southern feast, pair this dish with grilled ham steaks or baked catfish, sautéed or braised greens, such as Southern-Style Kale (page 249), and Country Corn Bread (page 292). Add a dash of vinegar to the greens just before serving, or pass it on the side.

makes 4 servings

1/2 cup fresh or dried black-eyed peas

1 bacon slice, chopped

1/2 cup chopped onion

2 garlic cloves, finely minced

1/4 crushed red pepper (or to taste)

3/4 cup long-grain white rice

1 red or green bell pepper, seeded and chopped

1 1/4 cups low-sodium chicken broth

1 bay leaf

1 fresh thyme sprig, or 1/2 teaspoon dried

1/4 teaspoon salt

Freshly ground pepper

Hot pepper sauce

1 **Place the black-eyed peas** in a pot and add enough cold water to cover by about 2 inches. Bring the water to a simmer and cook until the peas are just tender, about 12 minutes for fresh black-eyed peas, or 1 hour for dried peas. Add more water as necessary to keep the peas submerged during cooking. Drain the peas and reserve.

2 **Cook the bacon** in a separate saucepan, stirring frequently, until crisp. Remove the bacon with a slotted spoon and transfer it to a paper towel-lined plate.

3 **Pour off all but enough bacon fat** to lightly coat the pan. Add the onion, garlic, and crushed red pepper. Sauté until the onion turns golden brown, about 5 minutes. Add the rice and bell pepper to the pan and sauté for another 2 minutes. Add the broth and bring to a boil. Add the black-eyed peas, bay leaf, and thyme. Cover tightly and cook over low heat until the rice is tender and has absorbed all the liquid, 18–20 minutes.

4 **Discard the bay leaf** and thyme sprig, fluff with a fork, and gently fold in the bacon. Season, if necessary, with the salt and pepper. Serve with the pepper sauce.

Chef's Tips

You can also use canned black-eyed peas, but it is not necessary to cook them separately in advance. Just drain and rinse them first, then add the peas to the rice during the last 10 minutes of cooking time.

To make this dish vegetarian, replace the bacon with 1–2 teaspoons of olive or peanut oil, increase the garlic to 3 cloves, and use vegetable broth or water to replace the chicken broth.

Per serving

4 POINTS per serving

238 Calories | 2 g Total Fat | 1 g Saturated Fat | 3 mg Cholesterol | 221 mg Sodium
45 g Total Carbohydrate | 4 g Dietary Fiber | 10 g Protein | 51 mg Calcium

roasted corn and black beans

Roasting fresh corn on the cob lends a special depth of flavor to the corn.
In this dish, roasted corn and black beans combine with Southwestern flavors
for a fresh tasting, brightly flavored vegetable combination.

makes 4 servings

2 medium ears of corn

$1/2$ teaspoon olive oil

$1/4$ cup chopped red onion

1 garlic clove, minced

$1/2$ teaspoon minced
jalapeño pepper (wear gloves
to prevent irritation)

$1/2$ cup rinsed canned black beans

1 small plum tomato, chopped

2 teaspoons fresh lime juice

$1/8$ teaspoon salt

2 teaspoons chopped fresh cilantro

1 **Preheat oven** to 400°F. Loosen, but do not remove the husks from the corn. Remove the corn silk. Tie the husk closed again around each ear of corn with a strip of husk and dampen with water. Place the corn on a baking sheet and roast until tender, about 30 minutes. Let cool slightly, then remove the husks and cut the corn from the cobs.

2 **Heat a large skillet.** Swirl in the oil, then add the onion, garlic, and jalapeño. Sauté until the onion is translucent, about 3 minutes. Add the corn, beans, tomato, lime juice, and salt. Cook, stirring, until heated through, about 5 minutes. Stir in the cilantro.

Per serving

80 Calories | 1 g Total Fat | 0 g Saturated Fat | 0 mg Cholesterol | 209 mg Sodium
18 g Total Carbohydrate | 3 g Dietary Fiber | 3 g Protein | 17 mg Calcium

1 *POINT* per serving

black bean cakes

Packed with the traditional Southwestern flavors of cumin, chili powder, lime, and cilantro, these cakes make a satisfying yet light meal when served with tossed baby greens. The small amount of chorizo adds a big flavor kick; buy the smallest package of chorizo you can find and freeze the leftovers for use in other recipes.

makes 4 servings

1 (15-ounce) can black beans, drained and rinsed

2 tablespoons low-sodium chicken both, vegetable broth, or water

1 tablespoon chopped chorizo sausage

1/3 cup chopped onion

2 garlic cloves, minced

1/2 teaspoon minced jalapeño pepper (wear gloves to prevent irritation)

1/4 teaspoon ground cumin

1/4 teaspoon chili powder

1 egg white, lightly beaten

1/4 cup + 2 tablespoons cornmeal

1 1/2 teaspoons fresh lime juice

2 teaspoons chopped fresh cilantro

1/4 teaspoon salt

1 1/2 tablespoons plain nonfat yogurt

1 1/2 tablespoons light sour cream

1/2 cup prepared tomato salsa

1 **Puree half the beans** with the broth in a food processor, adding more broth or water if necessary, until they form a paste. Combine the pureed beans with the remaining beans.

2 **Sauté the chorizo** in a nonstick skillet until browned, about 3 minutes. Add the onion, garlic, and jalapeño; sauté until the onion is translucent, about 4 minutes. Add the cumin and chili powder and sauté until fragrant, about 1 minute. Transfer the mixture to a bowl and let cool.

3 **Combine the chorizo mixture** with the beans; stir in the egg white, 2 tablespoons of the cornmeal, the lime juice, cilantro, and salt. Let stand 5 minutes; form into eight 2-inch cakes. Lightly dust both sides of the cakes with the remaining cornmeal, shaking off the excess.

4 **Spray a large nonstick skillet** with nonstick spray and set over medium-high heat. Add the cakes and cook, in batches if necessary, until browned on each side and hot in the center, about 1 minute on each side.

5 **Combine the yogurt** and sour cream in a small bowl. Serve the cakes with a small dollop of the yogurt mixture and the salsa.

Chef's Tips

Chorizo is a spicy pork sausage widely used in Spanish and Mexican cooking. Find it in well-stocked supermarkets and specialty food stores.

To make a vegetarian version of this dish, use vegetable broth or water to puree the beans, omit the chorizo, and use 1/2 teaspoon of vegetable oil to sauté the onion, garlic, and jalapeño in Step 2.

3 POINTS per serving

Per serving (2 cakes with 2 teaspoons yogurt sauce)
165 Calories | 3 g Total Fat | 2 g Saturated Fat | 7 mg Cholesterol | 651 mg Sodium
25 g Total Carbohydrate | 7 g Dietary Fiber | 10 g Protein | 65 mg Calcium

black bean and cornmeal loaf

This hearty vegetarian loaf, colorfully studded with vegetables and black beans, is cut into triangles, sautéed, and served warm. Make the loaf a day ahead, but wait to sauté the triangles until right before serving. Serve the crispy, golden brown triangles with a steaming cup of tomato soup on a chilly day.

makes 6 servings

1 Heat a large nonstick skillet. Swirl in the oil, then add the onion, bell peppers, and garlic. Sauté until the onion is translucent, about 3 minutes. Remove from the heat and stir in the beans, tomatoes, cilantro, and hot pepper sauce.

2 Bring the broth to a boil in a saucepan; add the salt and pepper. Slowly whisk in the cornmeal. Reduce the heat and simmer, stirring constantly, until the mixture pulls away from the sides of the pot, about 10 minutes. Remove the pan from the heat and fold in the bean mixture.

3 Spray a 1-quart ($4 \times 8^1/_2$-inch) loaf pan with nonstick spray. Transfer the cornmeal-bean mixture to the pan, gently pressing with a rubber spatula and smoothing the top. Cover and refrigerate until firm, 8–10 hours.

4 Unmold the loaf and slice into 6 equal pieces; slice each piece on the diagonal to make a total of 12 triangles.

5 Spray a nonstick skillet with nonstick spray and place over medium-high heat. Lightly dust the triangles with the flour, shaking off the excess; cook, turning, until lightly browned, about $1^1/_2$–2 minutes per side. Arrange 2 triangles on each plate and top each with the salsa (if using).

1 tablespoon vegetable oil

$^1/_2$ cup finely chopped red onion

$^1/_2$ cup finely chopped
red bell pepper

$^1/_2$ cup finely chopped
green bell pepper

3 garlic cloves, minced

1 (15-ounce) can black beans,
drained and rinsed

3 tablespoons finely chopped
sun-dried tomatoes
(not oil-packed)

1 tablespoon chopped
fresh cilantro

Dash hot pepper sauce

2 cups low-sodium vegetable broth

$^1/_2$ teaspoon salt

$^1/_4$ teaspoon crushed
black peppercorns

$^2/_3$ cup cornmeal

2 tablespoons all-purpose flour

$^1/_2$ cup prepared salsa (optional)

Per serving

149 Calories | 3 g Total Fat | 1 g Saturated Fat | 2 mg Cholesterol | 475 mg Sodium
25 g Total Carbohydrate | 5 g Dietary Fiber | 6 g Protein | 34 mg Calcium

2 POINTS per serving

southwestern vegetable-tortilla bake

Give this spicy casserole a try next time you have company—with two kinds of beans, bell and jalapeño peppers, onions, cheese between the tortillas, and salsa on top—it's a surefire crowd pleaser. If you want to prepare the dish ahead, do not bake it. Simply assemble, cover, and refrigerate overnight. Let the casserole stand at room temperature one hour, then bake as directed. Serve with salsa and light sour cream, if you like.

makes 6 servings

1 (15-ounce) can black beans, rinsed and drained

1 cup + 2 tablespoons low-sodium vegetable broth

1 tablespoon dark rum

1 tablespoon red wine vinegar

1 large garlic clove, minced

1 1/2 teaspoons minced jalapeño pepper (wear gloves to prevent irritations)

1/2 teaspoon coarsely ground pepper

1/4 teaspoon salt

1/4 teaspoon hot pepper sauce

1 red bell pepper, seeded and thinly sliced

2 onions, thinly sliced

8 (6-inch) corn tortillas, halved

1 (16-ounce) can fat-free refried beans (spicy or regular), heated

1/2 cup shredded extra-sharp cheddar cheese

1/2 cup shredded jalapeño-flavored Monterey Jack cheese

1 **Bring the black beans,** 1 cup of the broth, the rum, vinegar, garlic, jalapeño, pepper, salt, and pepper sauce to a boil in a saucepan. Reduce the heat and simmer 15 minutes; drain and set aside.

2 **Bring the remaining** 2 tablespoons broth to a boil in a nonstick skillet, then add the bell pepper and onions. Reduce the heat and simmer, covered, stirring occasionally, until the vegetables are tender, about 10 minutes; set aside.

3 **Preheat the oven** to 350°F. Spray a 7 × 11-inch baking dish with nonstick spray. Arrange 5 tortilla halves in an overlapping layer on the bottom of the pan and spread the refried beans over the top; sprinkle with the cheddar cheese. Top with 5 more tortilla halves. Scatter the onion-pepper mixture over the tortillas; top with the black beans. Top with the remaining 6 tortilla halves; sprinkle with the Jack cheese.

4 **Cover loosely with aluminum foil** and bake 20 minutes. Remove the foil and bake until lightly browned, 10 minutes longer.

6 *POINTS* per serving

Per serving

315 Calories | 8 g Total Fat | 4 g Saturated Fat | 20 mg Cholesterol | 1,023 mg Sodium

45 g Total Carbohydrate | 11 g Dietary Fiber | 16 g Protein | 247 mg Calcium

stir-fried garden vegetables with marinated tofu

Marinated tofu lends a meatlike quality to this colorful, slightly spicy vegetable stir-fry. Select a variety of your favorite seasonal vegetables that need little advance preparation, such as sugar snap peas, summer squashes, broccoli and cauliflower florets, and bean sprouts. If you're short on time, pick up a bag of pre-cut vegetables in the produce section at the market.

1 **To marinate the tofu,** combine the tofu, soy sauce, ginger, and garlic in a zip-close plastic bag. Squeeze out the air and seal the bag; turn to coat the tofu. Refrigerate, turning the bag occasionally, about 20 minutes.

2 **Drain the tofu** and discard the marinade. Dry the tofu with paper towels and dust with the flour, shaking off the excess.

3 **Heat a nonstick wok** or skillet over high heat until a drop of water skitters. Pour in the oil and swirl to coat the pan, then add the tofu and stir-fry until lightly browned, about 2 minutes. Transfer the tofu to a plate.

4 **Add the scallion,** ginger, and garlic to the pan and toss briefly. Add the mixed vegetables, in batches if necessary, and stir-fry until tender-crisp, about 4 minutes, depending on the vegetables. Return all the vegetables to the pan (if cooking in batches). Add the tofu, soy sauce, and hot bean paste; toss to combine. Stir in the five-spice powder and sesame oil. Serve over the brown rice, sprinkled with the toasted sesame seeds.

Chef's Tips

Depending on the vegetables you choose for this dish, you may need to add them to the wok at different times. Longer-cooking vegetables, such as broccoli, cauliflower, and carrots should be added first and allowed to cook for a couple of minutes before adding shorter-cooking vegetables, such as summer squash and bean sprouts.

Hot bean paste, also known as bean paste with chiles, can be purchased in Asian groceries and some supermarkets.

makes 4 servings

MARINATED TOFU

8 ounces firm tofu, drained and cubed

2¼ teaspoons reduced-sodium soy sauce

1½ teaspoons minced peeled fresh ginger

1 garlic clove, minced

2 tablespoons all-purpose flour

2½ teaspoons peanut oil

STIR-FRIED VEGETABLES

1 scallion, thinly sliced

1½ teaspoons minced peeled fresh ginger

1 garlic clove, minced

1¼ pounds mixed vegetables, cut into bite-size pieces

3 tablespoons reduced-sodium soy sauce

1½ teaspoons hot bean paste

½ teaspoon five-spice powder

¼ teaspoon Asian (dark) sesame oil

1½ cups cooked brown rice

1 tablespoon sesame seeds, toasted

Per serving

308 Calories | 13 g Total Fat | 2 g Saturated Fat | 0 mg Cholesterol | 718 mg Sodium
35 g Total Carbohydrate | 7 g Dietary Fiber | 11 g Protein | 185 mg Calcium

6 *POINTS* per serving

tofu provençal

Tofu, high in protein, low in calories, is made from curdled soy milk, and is available in several textures. Tofu can be refrigerated for up to a week. Store tofu in water and change the water daily. This flavorful stew is delicious with pasta, rice, or steamed new potatoes.

makes 4 servings

1 tablespoon olive oil

2 medium onions, thinly sliced

1 red bell pepper, thinly sliced

2 garlic cloves, minced

1 medium zucchini, thinly sliced

2 teaspoons finely chopped fresh thyme, or 1 teaspoon dried

1 (14^1/$_2$-ounce) can diced tomatoes

1^1/$_2$ pounds firm tofu, cut into 1-inch cubes

Pinch salt

Freshly ground pepper

^{1}/$_4$ cup chopped fresh basil

1 **Heat the oil** in a nonstick skillet, then add the onions. Sauté until lightly browned, about 5 minutes. Add the bell pepper and sauté until it begins to soften, 2–3 minutes. Add the garlic and sauté until fragrant, about 30 seconds. Stir in the zucchini and thyme and sauté until lightly browned, 4–5 minutes.

2 **Stir in the tomatoes;** reduce the heat and simmer, partially covered, stirring occasionally, for 10 minutes. Stir in the tofu, salt, and pepper; simmer, uncovered, until heated through, about 5 minutes longer. Stir in the basil just before serving.

5 *POINTS* per serving

Per serving

222 Calories | 11 g Total Fat | 2 g Saturated Fat | 0 mg Cholesterol | 458 mg Sodium
18 g Total Carbohydrate | 4 g Dietary Fiber | 16 g Protein | 308 mg Calcium

chapter 13

vegetables

parmesan-roasted asparagus

This dish is elegant and surprisingly easy. Roasting asparagus produces an unexpected and surprisingly delicious alternative to steaming.

makes 4 servings

2 bunches asparagus, trimmed

1 tablespoon olive oil

1 tablespoon grated Parmesan cheese

1/2 teaspoon chopped fresh thyme

1/4 teaspoon salt

Freshly ground pepper

Fresh lemon juice

1 **Preheat the oven** to 425°F.

2 **Combine the asparagus,** oil, Parmesan cheese, thyme, salt, and pepper on a baking sheet. Spread the asparagus in a single layer on a baking sheet.

3 **Roast, tossing once,** until tender, 10–15 minutes. Sprinkle with lemon juice just before serving, warm or at room temperature.

Chef's Tip

Roasting adds wonderful depth of flavor to almost any vegetable. Try substituting Brussels sprouts, broccoli, or cauliflower in this dish, but wait to add the Parmesan until 5 minutes before the end of cooking. Cooking times may vary, depending on the size and cut of your vegetables; cook until they can be easily pierced with a fork.

Per serving

1 *POINT* per serving

57 Calories | 4 g Total Fat | 1 g Saturated Fat | 1 mg Cholesterol | 181 mg Sodium
2 g Total Carbohydrate | 1 g Dietary Fiber | 3 g Protein | 29 mg Calcium

haricots verts with walnuts

Haricots verts is French for extra thin, delicate green beans. Tossed with toasted walnuts, shallot, and garlic, they make an elegant side dish for roast beef and chicken dishes. Regular green beans may be substituted if haricots verts are unavailable.

makes 4 servings

1 **Cook the haricots verts** in a large saucepan of boiling water until tender, 5–6 minutes. Transfer the beans to a serving bowl, reserving 3 tablespoons of the cooking liquid separately.

2 **Heat a small nonstick skillet.** Swirl in the oil, then add the shallot and garlic. Sauté until the shallots are translucent, about 3 minutes. Add to the haricots verts along with the reserved cooking liquid, the walnuts, salt, and pepper. Toss and serve at once.

1 pound haricots verts, trimmed

1 teaspoon olive oil

1 small shallot, minced

1 garlic clove, minced

1 tablespoon chopped toasted walnuts

$1/8$ teaspoon salt

Pinch crushed black peppercorns

Chef's Tip

To toast the walnuts, place them in a small skillet over medium-low heat; cook, shaking the pan and stirring constantly, until lightly browned and fragrant, 3–5 minutes. Watch them carefully when toasting; walnuts can burn quickly. Transfer the nuts to a plate to cool.

Per serving

64 Calories | 2 g Total Fat | 0 g Saturated Fat | 0 mg Cholesterol | 81 mg Sodium
10 g Total Carbohydrate | 4 g Dietary Fiber | 3 g Protein | 48 mg Calcium

1 *POINT* per serving

sautéed spinach in balsamic dressing

Balsamic vinegar, made from the juice of ripened Trebbiano grapes, is dark brown with a mellow sweetness. Aged in wooden barrels, its flavor is affected both by the wood, and by the aging period. Though expensive, it is well worth having a good, aged balsamic vinegar on hand for sprinkling over salads and vegetables, even over frozen vanilla yogurt or ice milk.

makes 4 servings

1 (10-ounce) bag triple-washed spinach, rinsed and chopped

2 teaspoons olive oil

6 shallots, finely chopped

1/4 cup water

1 tablespoon balsamic vinegar

1/2 teaspoon Dijon mustard

1/8 teaspoon salt

Freshly ground pepper

1 **Place the spinach** in a steamer basket and set in a saucepan over 1 inch of boiling water. Cover and steam until just wilted, about 5 minutes; drain.

2 **Heat a large nonstick skillet.** Swirl in the oil, then add the shallots. Sauté until the shallots are translucent, about 5 minutes. Add the water, vinegar, and mustard. Bring the mixture to a boil; cook, stirring constantly, until thickened, 1 minute. Stir in the spinach and toss to coat. Sprinkle with the salt and pepper and serve at once.

1 *POINT* per serving

Per serving

59 Calories | 2 g Total Fat | 0 g Saturated Fat | 0 mg Cholesterol | 105 mg Sodium
8 g Total Carbohydrate | 1 g Dietary Fiber | 2 g Protein | 45 mg Calcium

brussels sprouts with mustard glaze

This dish makes a nice accompaniment to roast turkey and pork. The pungent mustard glaze eliminates the need to season with salt.

makes 4 servings

1 pound Brussels sprouts, trimmed (about 3 cups)

1/2 teaspoon cornstarch

3/4 cup low-sodium vegetable broth

2 teaspoons whole-grain mustard

1 **Cook the Brussels sprouts** in a large pot of boiling water until tender, 6–8 minutes. Drain.

2 **Dissolve the cornstarch** in 1 teaspoon of the broth in a small bowl. Combine the remaining broth with the mustard in a large skillet and bring to a simmer. Stir in the cornstarch mixture and simmer just until thickened, about 1 minute. Add the Brussels sprouts and toss to coat. Serve at once.

Chef's Tip

Brussels sprouts, a member of the cabbage family, are usually available fresh from late summer to late winter. Select small, bright-green sprouts with closed leaves. The smaller sprouts are more tender than the larger ones. Trim the excess stem and outer leaves from the sprouts, and cut a shallow "X" into the base of each sprout to speed the cooking time.

Per serving

60 Calories | 1 g Total Fat | 0 g Saturated Fat | 0 mg Cholesterol | 86 mg Sodium
11 g Total Carbohydrate | 5 g Dietary Fiber | 4 g Protein | 52 mg Calcium

0 POINTS per serving

sweet-and-sour green beans

Cook green beans with care; they lose their color if over-cooked. When buying beans, select crisp, brightly colored pods. Beans are fresh if when snapped in two beads of moisture form at the break point.

makes 4 servings

1 pound green beans, trimmed and cut into 2-inch lengths

2 tablespoons reduced-sodium soy sauce

2 tablespoons ketchup

1 teaspoon red wine vinegar

1 teaspoon cornstarch, dissolved in 3 tablespoons water

1/2 teaspoon hot pepper sauce

1 garlic clove, minced

1 (8-ounce) can bamboo shoots or sliced water chestnuts, drained

1 teaspoon Asian (dark) sesame oil

1 **Place the green beans** in a steamer basket and set in a saucepan over 1 inch of boiling water. Cover and steam until tender-crisp, about 5 minutes; drain.

2 **Combine the soy sauce,** ketchup, vinegar, the cornstarch mixture, and the hot pepper sauce in a small bowl.

3 **Spray a nonstick wok** or skillet with nonstick spray and set over high heat. Add the green beans and garlic. Stir-fry the beans 2 minutes; add the soy sauce mixture and cook, stirring, until thickened, about 2 minutes. Stir in the bamboo shoots and drizzle with the sesame oil. Serve at once.

1 POINT per serving

Per serving
68 Calories | 1 g Total Fat | 0 g Saturated Fat | 0 mg Cholesterol | 383 mg Sodium
12 g Total Carbohydrate | 4 g Dietary Fiber | 3 g Protein | 44 mg Calcium

broccoli with orange-sesame sauce

This tangy citrus sauce, with its hint of ginger and sesame, makes just about any steamed vegetable taste wonderful. Try it on cauliflower, kohlrabi, or carrots, too.

makes 4 servings

1 pound broccoli florets (about 2 1/2 cups)

3/4 cup orange juice

1 tablespoon honey

1 1/2 teaspoons minced peeled fresh ginger

2 teaspoons cornstarch, dissolved in 4 teaspoons water

2 teaspoons fresh lemon juice

1 teaspoon Asian (dark) sesame oil

2 teaspoons sesame seeds, toasted

1 **Place the broccoli** in a steamer basket and set in a saucepan over 1 inch of boiling water. Cover and steam until just tender, 8–10 minutes; drain.

2 **To prepare the sauce,** combine the orange juice, honey, and ginger in a small nonstick saucepan and bring to a boil. Add the cornstarch mixture and return to a boil, stirring. Cook the sauce until thickened, about 1 minute. Remove the pan from the heat; stir in the lemon juice and sesame oil.

3 **Arrange the broccoli** in a serving bowl; top with the sauce, sprinkle with the sesame seeds.

Chef's Tip

To toast the sesame seeds, place them in a dry skillet, over medium-low heat. Cook, shaking the pan and stirring constantly, until the seeds begin to brown lightly, 1–2 minutes. Watch them carefully; sesame seeds can burn quickly. Transfer the seeds to a plate to cool.

Per serving

77 Calories | 2 g Total Fat | 0 g Saturated Fat | 0 mg Cholesterol | 16 mg Sodium
14 g Total Carbohydrate | 2 g Dietary Fiber | 2 g Protein | 47 mg Calcium

1 *POINT* per serving

pan-roasted tomatoes and watercress

Meaty plum tomatoes, also called Roma tomatoes, are the best choice for this deliciously different recipe. Because their water content is lower than other types of tomatoes, they'll brown, not steam, in the skillet. (Their low water content makes plum tomatoes the best choice for tomato sauce, too.)

makes 4 servings

1 tablespoon olive oil

3 large plum tomatoes, cut into 1/2-inch slices

1 large garlic clove, minced

2 tablespoons balsamic vinegar

Pinch salt

Freshly ground pepper

3 cups watercress leaves, rinsed

1 **Heat the oil** in a medium nonstick skillet. Add the tomatoes and sauté until browned on both sides. Transfer to a large salad bowl.

2 **Return the skillet** to the heat; add the garlic and sauté until golden brown, 20–30 seconds. Remove from the heat and stir in the vinegar. Drizzle over the tomatoes; add the salt and pepper and toss to combine. Add the watercress and toss gently. Serve at once.

---

1 *POINT* per serving

Per serving

56 Calories | 4 g Total Fat | 0 g Saturated Fat | 0 mg Cholesterol | 53 mg Sodium
5 g Total Carbohydrate | 1 g Dietary Fiber | 1 g Protein | 36 mg Calcium

southern-style kale

Simmered with smoky bacon, onions, and garlic, kale becomes a delicious and healthy side dish for chicken and pork dishes.

makes 4 servings

6 cups rinsed, stemmed, and chopped kale (about 1^1/$_2$ pounds)

2 bacon slices, chopped

^{1}/$_2$ cup chopped onion

1 garlic clove, minced

^{1}/$_2$ cup low-sodium chicken broth

^{1}/$_4$ teaspoon salt

^{1}/$_8$ teaspoon freshly ground pepper

1 **Cook the kale** in large pot of boiling water until the color brightens, 15–30 seconds. Drain the kale in a colander.

2 **Heat a large nonstick skillet,** then add the bacon. Cook, stirring, until the bacon is browned, about 3 minutes. Add the onion and garlic and sauté until the onion is translucent, 3–5 minutes. Add the kale, broth, salt, and pepper. Cook, uncovered, stirring occasionally, until the kale is tender and most of the liquid has evaporated, about 15 minutes. Serve at once.

Chef's Tip

Select crisp small bunches of green kale without any signs of yellowing on the leaves. If the center stems of the kale are tough, remove them before chopping the leaves.

Per serving

82 Calories | 3 g Total Fat | 1 g Saturated Fat | 3 mg Cholesterol | 257 mg Sodium
12 g Total Carbohydrate | 2 g Dietary Fiber | 5 g Protein | 144 mg Calcium

1 *POINT* per serving

artichokes and mushrooms in white wine sauce

This slightly sweet-and-sour dish gets some of its delicious flavor from a seasoning called a *sachet d'épices*. Serve it with roasted, baked, or sautéed chicken.

makes 4 servings

4 medium artichokes

¹/₂ lemon

3–4 parsley stems

¹/₂ teaspoon dried thyme

¹/₂ teaspoon cracked black peppercorns

2 bay leaves

¹/₂ teaspoon coriander seeds

1 tablespoon olive oil

¹/₂ pound mushrooms, halved

1 garlic clove, minced

³/₄ cup water

¹/₂ cup dry white wine

1 tablespoon fresh lemon juice

1¹/₂ teaspoons tomato paste

¹/₄ teaspoon salt

1 tablespoon chopped fresh parsley

1 **To trim the artichokes,** snap off the outer leaves of the artichokes until you reach the inner leaves, which are pale green at the base and darker green at the tip. Slice off all but about ¹/₂ inch of these leaves. Cut off all but about 1 inch of the stems and peel the bottoms and stems with a vegetable peeler. Cut each artichoke into quarters and use a spoon or paring knife to trim away the fuzzy choke and purple leaves. Submerge the artichokes in a bowl of water with the half lemon squeezed into it until ready to cook.

2 **To make the sachet d'épices,** tie the parsley stems, thyme, pepper, bay leaves, and coriander seeds in a small cheesecloth bag or place in a tea ball (also see Chef's Tip).

3 **Drain the artichokes.** Heat a large nonstick skillet. Swirl in the oil, then add the mushrooms. Sauté until tender and browned, about 5 minutes. Add the garlic and sauté until fragrant, about 30 seconds. Stir in the artichoke bottoms, water, wine, lemon juice, tomato paste, salt, and the sachet d'épices. Reduce the heat and simmer, covered, until the artichokes are tender, about 15–20 minutes.

4 **Discard the sachet d'épices** and transfer the artichokes and mushrooms to a serving plate. Sprinkle with the parsley and serve at once.

Chef's Tip

The purpose of a *sachet d'épices* (pronounced sa-SHAY DAY-peace), literally "bag of spices," is to allow for easy removal of aromatic ingredients after their flavor has been infused into the dish. To make a sachet, cut a square of cheesecloth large enough to encase the aromatic ingredients. Place the ingredients in the center of the square, gather up the edges, and tie with a piece of kitchen twine to make a pouch.

3 *POINTS* per serving

Per serving

131 Calories | 5 g Total Fat | 1 g Saturated Fat | 0 mg Cholesterol | 271 mg Sodium 16 g Total Carbohydrate | 2 g Dietary Fiber | 6 g Protein | 63 mg Calcium

saffron cauliflower and onions

Saffron-scented, golden-yellow cauliflower and tiny pearl onions make a lovely addition to an antipasto plate. Or, serve as a side dish with chicken or fish. A delicate way to season any dish, such as this one, is with a *sachet d'epices,* a seasoning pouch that you remove before serving.

makes 4 servings

1 **To make the sachet d'épices,** tie the parsley stems, thyme, pepper, bay leaves, and coriander seeds in a small cheesecloth bag or place in a tea ball (see the Chef's Tip accompanying Artichokes and Mushrooms in White Wine Sauce, page 250).

2 **Heat a medium nonstick skillet.** Swirl in the oil, then add the onions. Sauté until lightly browned, 6–7 minutes. Add the garlic and sauté until fragrant, about 30 seconds. Stir in the cauliflower, water, wine, lemon juice, saffron, salt, pepper, and the sachet d'épices. Reduce the heat and simmer, covered, until the vegetables are tender, 12–15 minutes. Discard the sachet. Serve at once or cool to room temperature and serve as part of an antipasto selection.

3–4 parsley stems

$1/2$ teaspoon dried thyme

$1/2$ teaspoon cracked black peppercorns

2 bay leaves

$1/2$ teaspoon coriander seeds

1 tablespoon olive oil

$1/2$ pound small pearl onions, peeled

1 garlic clove, minced

$1 1/2$ cups cauliflower florets

1 cup water

$1/4$ cup dry white wine

2 tablespoons fresh lemon juice

$1/2$ teaspoon saffron threads

$1/2$ teaspoon salt

Freshly ground pepper

Chef's Tips

To peel pearl onions, plunge them into boiling water for 1 minute. Drain the onions and rinse then with cold water. The skins will slip off easily. Trim off the roots.

Saffron, the stigma of a particular type of crocus flower, is the world's most expensive spice. Each flower yields only 3 stigmas, which must be handpicked and dried. There are over 14,000 stigmas in each ounce of saffron. A little goes a long way, though, so it's worth the price. Choose saffron threads rather than powdered saffron, which loses its flavor quickly. Store saffron in an airtight container in a cool, dry, dark place.

Per serving

77 Calories | 4 g Total Fat | 0.5 g Saturated Fat | 0 mg Cholesterol | 306 mg Sodium
0 g Total Carbohydrate | 2 g Dietary Fiber | 3 g Protein | 48 mg Calcium

1 *POINT* per serving

baked red cabbage with raisins

Baking red cabbage brings out its natural sweetness, which is complemented beautifully by the sweet-sour flavorings in this side dish. It's also one of the easiest ways to prepare cabbage; you can assemble the rest of the meal while it bakes. Try it with roasted chicken or turkey, or with pork chops.

makes 4 servings

1/4 cup cider vinegar

3 tablespoons packed light brown sugar

3 cups finely shredded red cabbage

1/2 medium red onion, thinly sliced

1/4 cup raisins

Preheat the oven to 450°F. Combine the vinegar and sugar in a 2-quart shallow baking dish and stir until the sugar is dissolved. Add the cabbage, onion, and raisins; toss gently to combine. Cover and bake, stirring after 10 minutes, until wilted, 30–40 minutes. Serve warm.

1 *POINT* per serving

Per serving

88 Calories | 0 g Total Fat | 0 g Saturated Fat | 0 mg Cholesterol | 11 mg Sodium
23 g Total Carbohydrate | 2 g Dietary Fiber | 1 g Protein | 44 mg Calcium

wild rice succotash

Wild rice and mushrooms bring an earthy flavor to the classic succotash of cooked corn and lima beans. Leave out the wild rice for a more traditional succotash. Organize the ingredients ahead of time, and the dish can be cooked and ready to serve in minutes.

makes 4 servings

1 **Combine the water** and wild rice in a saucepan and bring to a boil. Reduce the heat, simmer, covered, until the rice is just tender and the grains are beginning to split open, 35–45 minutes. Drain off any remaining liquid.

2 **Heat the oil** in a large nonstick skillet, then add the corn and mushrooms. Sauté until the mushrooms are tender, about 5 minutes. Stir in the wild rice, lima beans, tomatoes, scallions, and salt; heat through. Remove from the heat and stir in the tarragon and pepper. Serve at once.

1 cup water

1/3 cup wild rice, rinsed

2 teaspoons extra-virgin olive oil

1/2 cup corn kernels

1 cup chopped assorted wild mushrooms (oyster, cremini, and shiitake)

1/3 cup thawed frozen baby lima beans

2 plum tomatoes, chopped

2 scallions, thinly sliced

1/4 teaspoon salt

2 teaspoons chopped fresh tarragon

1/4 teaspoon crushed black peppercorns

Per serving

127 Calories | 3 g Total Fat | 1 g Saturated Fat | 0 mg Cholesterol | 163 mg Sodium
20 g Total Carbohydrate | 3 g Dietary Fiber | 4 g Protein | 16 mg Calcium

2 *POINTS* per serving

spicy vegetable sauté with saffron rice

This zesty vegetable medley is beautifully colorful against a backdrop of brilliant yellow, saffron-flavored basmati rice. Black onion seeds, available in health food stores that sell spices in bulk, add a unique flavor. Prepare the steamed vegetables ahead and store them in the refrigerator so this dish will come together easily.

makes 4 servings

1 cup basmati rice, rinsed

1¼ cups low-sodium vegetable broth or water

1 teaspoon saffron threads

1 turnip, peeled and cut into cubes

½ cauliflower head, cut into florets

1 carrot, peeled and sliced into ¼-inch rounds

1 large bunch broccoli, cut into florets

½ teaspoon salt

2 teaspoons vegetable oil

1 tablespoon mustard seeds

1½ teaspoons black onion seeds

½ teaspoon cumin seeds

½ onion, chopped

1 tablespoon minced peeled fresh ginger

1 jalapeño pepper, seeded and minced (wear gloves to prevent irritation)

3 garlic cloves, minced

4 dried small hot red chiles

1 **Place the rice** in a large bowl with enough cold water to cover, and let soak 30 minutes. Bring the broth to a boil in a saucepan. Remove from the heat and crumble in the saffron threads. Set aside to steep while the rice soaks.

2 **Meanwhile, place the turnip** in a steamer basket and set in a saucepan over 1 inch of boiling water. Cover and steam 2 minutes. Add the cauliflower and carrot; steam 3 minutes. Add the broccoli and steam until the vegetables are tender-crisp, about 5 minutes more. Drain.

3 **Drain the rice** and add it to the saffron broth with the salt. Bring the rice to a gentle simmer and cook, partially covered, until most of the liquid has been absorbed, about 8 minutes. Cover the pan tightly, reduce the heat to low or place in a 250°F oven, and let the rice steam 10 minutes. Remove the pan from the heat and let stand, covered, 5 minutes. Fluff with a fork.

4 **Meanwhile, heat the oil** in a large nonstick skillet, then add the mustard seeds, black onion seeds, and cumin seeds. When they begin to pop, add the steamed vegetables and the onion; sauté until heated through, 2 minutes. Lower the heat, and add the ginger, jalapeño, garlic, and chiles. Sauté until the flavors are blended, about 5 minutes. Discard the chiles. Serve the vegetables over the warm saffron rice.

Chef's Tip

Soaking the basmati rice before cooking allows each grain to lengthen, resulting in exceptionally fine long grains.

5 *POINTS* per serving

Per serving

283 Calories | 4 g Total Fat | 1 g Saturated Fat | 5 mg Cholesterol | 400 mg Sodium
49 g Total Carbohydrate | 8 g Dietary Fiber | 12 g Protein | 117 mg Calcium

corn pudding

Individual corn puddings are an elegant and unusual side dish, perfect for special occasions. Like a steamed pudding, their texture resembles that of a moist cake. Make a full recipe of the Country Corn Bread a day or two ahead. Save only what you need to make the puddings and enjoy the rest fresh from the oven, or simply buy corn muffins, as a short cut (see below for amount).

makes 4 servings

1 **Preheat the oven** to 375°F. Spray four 4-ounce custard cups or ramekins with nonstick spray and place in a roasting pan.

2 **Heat $1/4$ cup of the broth** in a saucepan, add the onion, bell pepper, jalapeño, and garlic. Cook, stirring often, until the vegetables begin to soften, about 7 minutes. Add the remaining $1/4$ cup broth and simmer, uncovered, until the mixture reduces by half, 5–10 minutes. Add the corn and bring to a boil.

3 **Transfer the corn mixture** to a medium bowl. Add the thyme, oregano, rosemary, salt, and pepper. Let stand until slightly cooled, then stir in the corn bread crumbs and egg whites.

4 **Pour the mixture** into the custard cups and place the roasting pan in the oven. Carefully fill the roasting pan with boiling water until it reaches two-thirds up the sides of the cups. Bake until a toothpick inserted in the middle of the puddings comes out clean, about 25 minutes.

$1/2$ cup low-sodium chicken broth

1 small onion, chopped

$1/2$ small red bell pepper, chopped

1 jalapeño pepper, seeded and minced (wear gloves to prevent irritation)

1 garlic clove, minced

$1/3$ cup fresh or thawed frozen corn kernels

$1/4$ teaspoon chopped fresh thyme

$1/4$ teaspoon chopped fresh oregano

$1/4$ teaspoon chopped fresh rosemary

$1/4$ teaspoon salt

$1/4$ teaspoon crushed black peppercorns

$1 1/2$ cups (5 ounces) crumbled Country Corn Bread (page 292)

2 egg whites

Per serving

119 Calories | 3 g Total Fat | 1 g Saturated Fat | 14 mg Cholesterol | 352 mg Sodium
23 g Total Carbohydrate | 2 g Dietary Fiber | 4 g Protein | 48 mg Calcium

2 POINTS per serving

stuffed cabbage rolls

Stuffed with citrus-scented brown rice, these rolls are delicious served on a bed of lentils with stewed tomatoes and chopped chives. Or serve them as is with a chopped potato. Dried fruits, such as currants, chopped dried apricots, and dried cranberries, may be added to the filling if you wish. The stuffed cabbage rolls may be prepared up to 1 day ahead, tightly wrapped, and refrigerated. Steam them to reheat before serving.

makes 4 servings

1 medium Savoy cabbage head (about 1¹/₂ pounds)

1 tablespoon vegetable oil

¹/₄ cup minced onion

1¹/₄ cups long-grain brown rice

2¹/₂ cups low-sodium vegetable broth

1 tablespoon grated orange zest

1 tablespoon chopped fresh thyme

¹/₄ teaspoon salt

Freshly ground pepper

1 **Fill a large saucepan** two-thirds full of water and bring to a boil. Fill a large bowl two-thirds full with ice water.

2 **Carefully separate the cabbage leaves,** discarding the tough ones close to the core. With tongs, working in batches, immerse the leaves in the boiling water until wilted, 15–30 seconds. Immediately transfer to the ice water to stop the cooking. Drain the cabbage. Reserve 8 large leaves; thinly slice the remaining cabbage.

3 **Preheat the oven** to 325°F. Heat a large ovenproof saucepan. Swirl in the oil, then add the onion. Sauté until translucent, 3–5 minutes. Add the rice and toss to coat. Add the sliced cabbage, the broth, orange zest, thyme, salt, and pepper; bring to a simmer. Cover and bake until the rice is tender and has absorbed all the liquid, about 40 minutes. Fluff with a fork.

4 **Divide the rice mixture** among the 8 reserved cabbage leaves. Fold in the sides of the leaves over the stuffing, then roll the leaves to enclose the stuffing. Steam until heated through, about 5 minutes.

6 _POINTS_ per serving

Per serving (2 rolls)

335 Calories | 6 g Total Fat | 1 g Saturated Fat | 0 mg Cholesterol | 434 mg Sodium
63 g Total Carbohydrate | 8 g Dietary Fiber | 10 g Protein | 2 mg Calcium

stuffed cabbage rolls

saffron potatoes

Vivid yellow saffron potatoes flecked with fresh green herbs are a flavorful and beautiful complement to poached fish.

makes 4 servings

2 cups low-sodium chicken broth

¹/₈ teaspoon saffron threads

1 pound boiling potatoes

1¹/₂ teaspoons chopped fresh parsley

¹/₂ teaspoon chopped fresh thyme

1 **Heat the broth** in a medium saucepan. Remove from the heat and crumble in the saffron threads. Cover and set aside to steep.

2 **Peel the potatoes** and cut into 1-inch cubes.

3 **Return the saffron broth** to the heat. Add the potatoes and bring to a boil. Reduce the heat and simmer, covered, until the potatoes are tender, 15–20 minutes. Drain the potatoes and toss with the parsley and thyme.

Chef's Tip

Saffron, the stigma of a particular type of crocus flower, is the world's most expensive spice. Each flower yields only 3 stigmas, which must be handpicked and dried. There are over 14,000 stigmas in each ounce of saffron. A little goes a long way, though, so it's worth the price. Choose saffron threads rather than powdered saffron, which loses its flavor quickly. Store saffron in an airtight container in a cool, dry, dark place.

2 POINTS per serving

Per serving

92 Calories | 1 g Total Fat | 0 g Saturated Fat | 0 mg Cholesterol | 38 mg Sodium
18 g Total Carbohydrate | 2 g Dietary Fiber | 4 g Protein | 14 mg Calcium

sweet potato cakes

Russet potato, chives, and dill balance the flavor of sweet potato in these creamy cakes. To save on cleanup, cook both types of potato in the same pan—but keep an eye on them, because sweet potatoes tend to cook faster than russets.

makes 4 servings

1 medium ($^1/_2$-pound) russet potato, peeled and quartered

1 medium ($^1/_2$-pound) sweet potato, peeled and quartered

$^2/_3$ cup fresh bread crumbs

$^1/_4$ cup fat-free milk

$1^1/_2$ tablespoons mayonnaise

1 tablespoon chopped fresh chives

1 tablespoon chopped fresh dill

$^1/_2$ teaspoon crushed black peppercorns

1 Preheat the oven to 250°F. Combine the russet potato and sweet potato and enough water to cover in a large saucepan. Bring to a boil; reduce the heat and simmer, covered, until the sweet potato is tender, about 15 minutes. Using tongs, transfer the sweet potato to a nonstick baking sheet and continue to simmer the russet potato until tender, 5–10 minutes more. Drain the potato and place on the baking sheet. Place the potatoes in the oven to steam-dry, about 5 minutes. Remove from the oven and increase the oven temperature to 475°F.

2 Pass the hot potatoes through a food mill or ricer set over a large bowl. Let stand until slightly cooled. Stir in the bread crumbs, milk, mayonnaise, chives, dill, and pepper. Form into 8 small cakes, about $^1/_2$-inch thick. Spray a nonstick baking sheet with nonstick spray and arrange the cakes on the baking sheet.

3 Bake 8 minutes; turn and bake until lightly browned on both sides, 4 minutes more.

Chef's Tips

To make fresh bread crumbs, remove the crusts from fresh or day-old white bread. Pulse the bread in a food processor to form small crumbs.

To get a perfectly smooth texture in these cakes, puree the potatoes using a food mill or a ricer (a special kitchen tool resembling a giant garlic press, used to evenly mash root vegetables). If you have neither tool, you can use a potato masher, but the texture of the cakes will not be as creamy. Avoid using a food processor to puree potatoes; the sharp blade of the processor can cause the starch granules in the potatoes to rupture, resulting in a gluey texture.

Per serving (2 cakes)

167 Calories | 3 g Total Fat | 1 g Saturated Fat | 2 mg Cholesterol | 110 mg Sodium 32 g Total Carbohydrate | 2 g Dietary Fiber | 4 g Protein | 43 mg Calcium

3 POINTS per serving

rösti potatoes with celeriac

Rösti (pronounced ROOSH-tee), a Swiss potato specialty, are crisp golden potato pancakes. In this variation, celeriac gives the rösti an unusual twist. Rösti may be prepared as individual cakes, as in this recipe, but it is also traditional to prepare large cakes and slice them into wedges. Rösti are especially complementary to roast pork.

makes 4 servings

1 medium (1/2-pound) russet potato, peeled

1 small (1/2-pound) celeriac, peeled

1 1/2 teaspoons Dijon mustard

2 tablespoons flour

1/4 teaspoon crushed black peppercorns

2 teaspoons olive oil

1 **Preheat the oven** to 475°F. Grate the potato and celeriac and combine with the mustard, flour, and pepper in a bowl. Divide the mixture into 8 even mounds.

2 **Heat 1 teaspoon** of the oil in a nonstick skillet. Transfer 4 of the mounds to the skillet and press with a spatula to form 4 patties, about 1/2-inch thick. Cook the rösti until golden brown, about 1 1/2 minutes per side. Repeat with the remaining oil and potato mixture to make a total of 8 rösti.

3 **Transfer the rösti** to a nonstick baking sheet, bake until heated through, about 5 minutes. Serve at once.

Chef's Tip

Celeriac, also known as celery root or celery knob, tastes like a cross between celery and parsley. It combines particularly well with potatoes. Choose firm celeriac with a minimum of knobs. Peel it with a paring knife, cutting away the knobs and tough skin to reach the tender white flesh beneath.

2 *POINTS* per serving

Per serving (2 patties)
100 Calories | 3 g Total Fat | 0 g Saturated Fat | 0 mg Cholesterol | 36 mg Sodium
11 g Total Carbohydrate | 2 g Dietary Fiber | 2 g Protein | 18 mg Calcium

potato pancakes with spicy tomato relish

Canned tomatoes and prepared horseradish make the relish a snap to prepare. Try this dish the day after you've served mashed potatoes for dinner; make extra to use in the pancakes, and this recipe will come together in minutes. Serve these pancakes as a side dish to beef or with a tossed green salad for lunch or a light supper.

makes 4 servings

$1/4$ cup drained canned diced tomatoes

$1/2$ teaspoon prepared horseradish

Pinch chopped fresh thyme

1 large ($3/4$-pound) russet potato, peeled and quartered

$2/3$ cup minced scallions

$1/3$ cup grated Parmesan cheese

$1/4$ cup plain nonfat yogurt

1 egg white

Pinch freshly ground pepper

1 **To prepare the relish,** combine the tomatoes, horseradish, and thyme in a bowl; cover and refrigerate.

2 **Preheat the oven** to 250°F. Combine the potato and enough water to cover in a saucepan. Bring the water to a boil; reduce the heat and simmer, covered, until tender, about 20 minutes. Drain the potato and arrange on a nonstick baking sheet. Place the potato in the oven to steam-dry, about 5 minutes. Remove from the oven and increase the oven temperature to 475°F.

3 **Place the potato** in a bowl and coarsely mash with a fork. Let stand until slightly cooled. Stir in the scallions, Parmesan cheese, yogurt, egg white, and pepper. Form into 8 small patties, about $1/2$-inch thick. Arrange the patties on a baking sheet lined with foil.

4 **Bake the patties 8 minutes;** turn and bake until lightly browned on both sides, about 4 minutes more. Top each pancake with the tomato relish.

Per serving (2 pancakes with 1 tablespoon relish)

137 Calories | 2 g Total Fat | 2 g Saturated Fat | 5 mg Cholesterol | 163 mg Sodium
23 g Total Carbohydrate | 2 g Dietary Fiber | 7 g Protein | 140 mg Calcium

3 *POINTS* per serving

potato gratin

Gruyère is the cheese classically used in a potato gratin. This cow's milk cheese, produced in both Switzerland and France, has a nutty, rich flavor and melts beautifully. It is well worth finding the real thing.

makes 4 servings

3/4-pound russet potatoes, peeled and cut into 1/4-inch slices

1 1/2 cups fat-free milk

1 garlic clove, minced

1/4 teaspoon salt

Freshly ground pepper

1 teaspoon cornstarch, dissolved in 2 teaspoons water

1/4 cup grated Gruyère cheese

3 tablespoons fresh bread crumbs

1/4 cup grated Parmesan cheese

1 **Preheat the oven** to 350°F. Spray an 8 × 8-inch baking dish with nonstick spray. Combine the potato, milk, garlic, salt, and pepper in a saucepan. Bring the mixture to a boil; reduce the heat, and keep at a gentle simmer for 6–7 minutes. The potatoes will still offer a slight resistance when pierced with a fork.

2 **Stir in the cornstarch mixture** and simmer until thickened, about 1 minute. Remove the pan from the heat and stir in the Gruyère cheese. Transfer the mixture to the baking dish. Combine the bread crumbs and Parmesan cheese in a small bowl; sprinkle over the mixture. Bake until the gratin is golden brown, about 45 minutes. Remove the gratin from the oven and let stand 10 minutes before serving.

Chef's Tip

To make fresh bread crumbs, remove the crusts from fresh or day-old white bread. Pulse the bread in a food processor to form small crumbs.

Per serving

4 *POINTS* per serving

166 Calories | 5 g Total Fat | 3 g Saturated Fat | 16 mg Cholesterol | 350 mg Sodium
20 g Total Carbohydrate | 1 g Dietary Fiber | 2 g Protein | 295 mg Calcium

broccoli-potato puree

This recipe is a great way to get kids to eat broccoli. Jazz it up by sprinkling grated Parmesan or shredded cheddar cheese on top.

makes 4 servings

1 Combine the water, potatoes, garlic, and salt in a large saucepan and bring to a boil. Reduce the heat and simmer, covered, until the potatoes are almost tender, about 10 minutes. Add the broccoli and cook until it is just tender, about 5 minutes more.

2 Drain the vegetables and puree; serve at once.

1 cup water

4 small all-purpose potatoes, peeled and cubed

3 garlic cloves, peeled

1/2 teaspoon salt

2 cups chopped broccoli florets and stems

Chef's Tip

To get a perfectly smooth texture, puree the potatoes and broccoli using a food mill or a ricer (a special kitchen tool resembling a giant garlic press, used to evenly mash root vegetables). If you have neither tool, you can use a potato masher, but the texture will not be as creamy. Avoid using a food processor to puree potatoes; the sharp blade of the processor can cause the starch granules in the potatoes to rupture, resulting in a gluey texture.

Per serving

103 Calories | 0 g Total Fat | 0 g Saturated Fat | 0 mg Cholesterol | 307 mg Sodium
23 g Total Carbohydrate | 3 g Dietary Fiber | 3 g Protein | 32 mg Calcium

1 *POINT* per serving

potato puree with roasted eggplant and garlic

Roasting changes the character of eggplant and garlic immensely, giving them a sweet, mellow flavor. A touch of heavy cream, along with olive oil, gives the puree richness and full flavor, but you may substitute whole or fat-free milk for the cream if you wish.

makes 4 servings

1 small (12- to 14-ounce) eggplant

2 garlic cloves, unpeeled

2 large russet potatoes (about 1 1/2 pounds), peeled and quartered

1 1/2 tablespoons fat-free milk

1 1/2 tablespoons heavy cream

2 teaspoons extra-virgin olive oil

1/4 teaspoon salt

1 **Preheat the oven** to 400°F. Spray a baking sheet with nonstick spray. Slice the eggplant in half lengthwise and score the flesh. Wrap the garlic in foil. Place the garlic and eggplant on the baking sheet and roast until very soft, about 30 minutes for the garlic and 45 minutes for the eggplant. Peel and mash the garlic in a medium bowl. Scoop out the eggplant and combine with the garlic. Reduce the oven temperature to 250°F.

2 **Combine the potatoes** and enough cold water to cover in a saucepan. Bring the water to a boil; reduce the heat and simmer, covered, until the potatoes are tender, about 20 minutes. Drain the potatoes and arrange on a nonstick baking sheet. Place the potatoes in the oven to steam-dry, about 5 minutes. Pass the hot potatoes through a food mill or ricer set over a large bowl. Stir in the roasted eggplant and garlic.

3 **Bring the milk,** cream, and oil to a simmer in a saucepan. Beat the hot milk mixture into the potato mixture. Season with the salt and serve at once.

Chef's Tip

To get a perfectly smooth texture, puree the potatoes using a food mill or a ricer (a special kitchen tool resembling a giant garlic press, used to evenly mash root vegetables). If you have neither tool, you can use a potato masher, but the texture of the cakes will not be as creamy. Avoid using a food processor to puree potatoes; the sharp blade of the processor can cause the starch granules in the potatoes to rupture, resulting in a gluey texture.

---

3 *POINTS* per serving

Per serving
177 Calories | 3 g Total Fat | 1 g Saturated Fat | 2 mg Cholesterol | 159 mg Sodium
32 g Total Carbohydrate | 6 g Dietary Fiber | 5 g Protein | 35 mg Calcium

moo shu vegetables

Sweet and spicy crisp vegetables wrapped in thin pancakes make a healthy and easy alternative to ordering in. Moo shu pancakes are available in Asian groceries and well-stocked supermarkets, but if you can't find the pancakes, flour tortillas can be substituted. Cut the vegetables ahead of time and store in the refrigerator until stir-fry time. Almost as fast as the wok is heated, the moo shu will be ready. For more information on cutting the vegetables into julienne, see page 67.

1 **Preheat the oven** to 250°F.

2 **Heat a nonstick wok** or skillet over high heat until a drop of water skitters. Pour in the oil and swirl to coat the pan. Add the garlic and ginger and stir-fry until fragrant, about 30 seconds. Add the bell peppers, celery, carrot, cabbage, and fennel. Stir-fry until tender, about 5 minutes. Stir in the hoisin sauce and soy sauce; remove the pan from the heat.

3 **Place the pancakes** on a baking sheet, cover with a damp towel, and warm in the oven until soft, 4 minutes.

4 **To serve,** divide the vegetables among the pancakes; fold the ends of the pancakes inward and roll around the vegetables.

makes 4 servings

1 1/2 tablespoons Asian (dark) sesame oil

1 garlic clove, minced

1 1/2 teaspoons minced peeled fresh ginger

3 small red bell peppers, julienned

1 medium celery stalk, julienned

1 medium carrot, peeled and julienned

1 cup shredded napa cabbage

1/2 cup julienned fennel

2 tablespoons hoisin sauce

1 1/2 tablespoons reduced-sodium soy sauce

8 moo shu pancakes

Chef's Tip

Hoisin sauce is a sweet, thick, reddish-brown sauce used widely in Chinese cooking, most often as a condiment or glaze for roast or grilled meats and poultry. Occasionally referred to as Chinese barbecue sauce, it is made from fermented soybean pate, sugar, garlic, chile, and spices, usually Chinese five-spice or star anise. Hoisin sauce is readily available in the Asian ingredients section of most supermarkets, or in Asian grocery stores. Keep opened hoisin in the refrigerator almost indefinitely (if the hoisin is canned, transfer it to a sterilized glass jar with a tight-fitting lid).

Per serving

140 Calories | 6 g Total Fat | 1 g Saturated Fat | 0 mg Cholesterol | 460 mg Sodium
20 g Total Carbohydrate | 3 g Dietary Fiber | 3 g Protein | 41 mg Calcium

3 POINTS per serving

harvest stew with fresh herb dumplings

Here is a modern vegetarian twist on the classic chicken and dumplings. Grated apple and pear nectar meld to create a light and fruity sauce for a mélange of sturdy vegetables and fluffy steamed dumplings.

makes 6 servings

STEW

1 cup pear nectar

1 cup low-sodium vegetable broth

1 tablespoon Dijon mustard

3 teaspoons chopped fresh thyme

1 teaspoon salt

Freshly ground pepper

1 small (1-pound) butternut squash, peeled and cut into 1-inch chunks

3 small turnips, peeled and quartered

2 carrots, peeled and sliced

2 zucchini, sliced

1 medium onion, chopped

$1/2$ tart apple, cored, peeled, and grated

6 garlic cloves, chopped

DUMPLINGS

1 cup all-purpose flour

2 teaspoons baking powder

$1/2$ cup low-fat buttermilk

2 tablespoons unsalted butter, melted

1 tablespoon chopped scallions

1 **To prepare the stew,** whisk together the pear nectar, broth, mustard, 2 teaspoons of the thyme, $1/2$ teaspoon of the salt, and the pepper in a large saucepan. Add the squash, turnips, carrots, zucchini, onion, apple, and garlic. Bring the mixture to a boil; reduce the heat and simmer, covered, until the vegetables are just tender, about 15 minutes.

2 **Meanwhile, to prepare the dumplings,** combine the flour, baking powder, and the remaining $1/2$ teaspoon salt in a large bowl. Combine the buttermilk and butter in another bowl. Add the buttermilk mixture to the flour mixture and stir just until the mixture forms a soft dough. Stir in the scallions and the remaining 1 teaspoon thyme.

3 **Drop the dough** by 6 heaping tablespoons onto the simmering stew. Simmer the stew, uncovered, for 10 minutes, then cover and cook until the dumplings are firm, about 10 minutes more.

Chef's Tip

To peel the squash, cut in half crosswise, separating the narrow top part of the squash from the round bottom part. This step makes it easier to handle the squash. Remove the seeds. Use a very sharp, sturdy vegetable peeler or a sharp knife to cut the skin away from the squash.

4 POINTS per serving

Per serving (about $1 1/2$ cups stew and 1 dumpling)
225 Calories | 5 g Total Fat | 3 g Saturated Fat | 12 mg Cholesterol | 762 mg Sodium
42 g Total Carbohydrate | 5 g Dietary Fiber | 6 g Protein | 120 mg Calcium

harvest stew with fresh herb dumplings

vegetable stew

Packed with colorful vegetables, this hearty and warming stew is full of slightly sweet and spicy flavors. Serve the stew over a bed of couscous or rice.

makes 4 servings

1 tablespoon olive oil

1 large onion, chopped

1 medium leek, cleaned and sliced

2 garlic cloves, minced

2¹/₂ teaspoons curry powder

1 teaspoon minced peeled fresh ginger

1 cup cubed peeled butternut squash

¹/₂ cup sliced zucchini (¹/₂-inch thick)

3 cups low-sodium vegetable broth

1¹/₂ cups cubed peeled eggplant

2 carrots, peeled and chopped

1 celery stalk, chopped

¹/₃ cup currants

3 tablespoons canned tomato puree

¹/₃ cup canned chickpeas, rinsed

¹/₃ cup cooked fava or lima beans

2 teaspoons fresh lemon juice

¹/₄ teaspoon salt

1¹/₂ teaspoons grated lemon zest

1 **Heat the oil** in a large pot, then add the onion, leek, and garlic. Sauté until the onion is translucent, 3–5 minutes. Add the curry powder and ginger; sauté until fragrant. Stir in the squash and zucchini. Add enough of the broth to cover the vegetables; simmer 10 minutes. Add the remaining broth, the eggplant, carrots, celery, currants, and tomato puree. Simmer, partially covered, until the vegetables are tender, 20–25 minutes.

2 **Stir the chickpeas** and fava beans into the simmering vegetables; add the lemon juice and salt. Cover and cook until heated through, 3–5 minutes. Divide the stew among 4 bowls and sprinkle with the lemon zest.

Chef's Tips

Leeks often pick up sand between their layers as they grow. To clean a leek, trim the dark green tops (reserve the tops for flavoring soups or stews) and the roots, leaving the root end intact to hold the layers together. Slice the leek lengthwise, fan open the layers, and rinse thoroughly under running water.

To peel the squash, cut the top and bottom off the squash, then cut in half crosswise, separating the narrow top part of the squash from the round bottom part. This step makes it easier to handle the squash. Remove the seeds. Use a very sharp, sturdy vegetable peeler or a sharp knife to cut the skin away from the squash.

4 *POINTS* per serving

Per serving

236 Calories | 6 g Total Fat | 1 g Saturated Fat | 4 mg Cholesterol | 384 mg Sodium
38 g Total Carbohydrate | 8 g Dietary Fiber | 9 g Protein | 103 mg Calcium

chapter 14

fruits

tropical fruit salsa

This savory fruit salsa makes an excellent side dish for grilled chicken, fish, or shellfish. Canned or bottled fruit may be used in this recipe, but fresh ripe fruit is preferable for the best flavor and quality.

makes 4 servings

1 tablespoon chopped fresh cilantro

1/2 tablespoon fresh lime juice

1/2 tablespoon white wine vinegar

1 teaspoon minced jalapeño pepper (wear gloves to prevent irritation)

1/2 teaspoon extra-virgin olive oil

1/8 teaspoon salt

Freshly ground pepper

1/2 medium mango, cut into small cubes (about 3/4 cup)

1/4 small papaya, cut into small cubes (about 1/2 cup)

1/3 cup chopped red onion

1/4 cup fresh pineapple cubes

1/2 small red bell pepper, chopped

Stir together the cilantro, lime juice, vinegar, jalapeño, oil, salt, and pepper in a bowl. Add the mango, papaya, onion, pineapple, and bell pepper; toss to combine. Let stand about 1 hour at room temperature to blend the flavors. If not serving immediately, cover and refrigerate up to 1 day. Return to room temperature before serving.

Chef's Tip

This salsa can be turned from savory to sweet simply by changing a few ingredients: Substitute mint for the cilantro, strawberries for the red pepper, honey for the olive oil, and leave out the vinegar, salt, and pepper. Serve over vanilla frozen yogurt for dessert, or serve at brunch with muffins, pancakes, or French toast— or as a filling for crêpes.

1 *POINT* per serving

Per serving

42 Calories | 1 g Total Fat | 0 g Saturated Fat | 0 mg Cholesterol | 110 mg Sodium
9 g Total Carbohydrate | 2 g Dietary Fiber | 1 g Protein | 15 mg Calcium

cubing fresh pineapple

Slice away the pineapple top with a large knife. For stability, cut off the base of the pineapple. Use your knife to pare off the skin starting at the top and cutting downward. Turn the pineapple and continue until all skin is removed. Make sure that your cuts are deep enough to remove the "eyes" but not so deep that a great deal of edible flesh is removed.

To make neat dice or cubes, slice the pineapple evenly at the desired thickness until you reach the core on the first side. Turn the pineapple, and make slices from the opposite side, as well as from both ends, until you reach the core.

Stack the long slices, aligning the edges, and make parallel cuts of the same thickness through the stack. Turn the pile of pineapple sticks and cut crosswise at even intervals to make cubes.

mango chutney

Mango chutney is delicious with grilled fish or meat. It can also be stirred into chicken salad or used as a spread on a chicken or turkey sandwich. Make the chutney ahead, cool to room temperature, and refrigerate in an airtight container, for up to 2 days.

makes 4 servings

1 medium mango, cut into small cubes (about 1^1/$_2$ cups)

^{1}/$_3$ cup chopped onion

^{1}/$_4$ cup raisins

^{1}/$_4$ cup orange juice (2 tablespoons if using a very ripe mango)

2 tablespoons packed dark brown sugar

2 tablespoons chopped walnuts

1 tablespoon cider vinegar

2 teaspoons minced jalapeño pepper (wear gloves to prevent irritation)

2 teaspoons fresh lemon juice

1 teaspoon minced peeled fresh ginger

^{1}/$_2$ teaspoon minced garlic

^{1}/$_2$ teaspoon grated lemon zest

^{1}/$_8$ teaspoon ground mace

Pinch ground cloves

Stir together all the ingredients in a large saucepan. Bring the mixture to a boil; reduce the heat and simmer, stirring occasionally, until the mango is soft, about 10 minutes. Let cool before serving.

2 *POINTS* per serving

Per serving

123 Calories | 3 g Total Fat | 0 g Saturated Fat | 0 mg Cholesterol | 9 mg Sodium
26 g Total Carbohydrate | 2 g Dietary Fiber | 2 g Protein | 24 mg Calcium

working with mangoes

A mango has a large flat seed in the center of the flesh. Cutting as closely as possible to the seed on one of the wider sides, cut the flesh away from the seed. Follow the natural curve of the seed as you cut.

Use the tip of a paring knife to score the flesh in a crosshatch pattern, cutting just to, but not through, the skin.

Hold the mango half with both hands with thumbs on the top edges of the flat side. Place fingertips on rounded bottom and push so the mango turns "inside-out," to look like a hedge-hog. You can slice the cubes away from the skin now, or present the fruit as is on a fruit plate.

green papaya salsa

Green papaya, the unripe version of the sweet-tart fruit, can be prepared like a vegetable, as it is in this warm condiment. Green papayas, available from Asian groceries and some supermarkets, should not be completely green and hard. If you can't find green papaya, select papaya that is slightly underripe. Try the salsa as a piquant topping for grilled seafood.

makes 6 servings

2 cups finely chopped peeled green papaya

1 medium tomato, peeled, seeded, and finely chopped

1 small sweet onion, finely chopped

$1/2$ jalapeño pepper, seeded and minced (wear gloves to prevent irritation)

2 tablespoons orange juice

2 teaspoons fresh lime juice

$1^1/2$ tablespoons chopped cilantro

1 tablespoon chopped mint

$1/2$ teaspoon salt

Combine the papaya, tomato, onion, jalapeño, and orange and lime juices in a large skillet. Heat gently just until warmed through. Remove from the heat and stir in the cilantro, mint, and salt. Serve warm or at room temperature.

Chef's Tip

To peel the tomato, bring a large pot of water to a boil. Have ready a bowl of ice water. Cut a shallow "X" into the bottom of the tomato. Submerge in boiling water for 10–15 seconds. Plunge into ice water, then remove immediately, and peel the tomato with a paring knife, starting at the "X." If the tomato does not peel easily, return it to the boiling water briefly, shock it in the ice water again, and peel. Cut the tomato in half horizontally and remove the seeds, then chop.

0 POINTS per serving

Per serving (about $1/3$ cup)
37 Calories | 0 g Total Fat | 0 g Saturated Fat | 0 mg Cholesterol | 183 mg Sodium
9 g Total Carbohydrate | 2 g Dietary Fiber | 1 g Protein | 21 mg Calcium

blackberries with citrus sauce

The blackberry, also known as a bramble, is available fresh from spring through late summer. Select berries that are deep purple, plump, and without hulls. If the hull is intact, the berry is probably immature and tart. Use fresh berries immediately, or store them in the refrigerator in a single layer on a baking sheet for 1–2 days.

makes 4 servings

1 **To prepare the citrus sauce,** combine the orange juice, sugar, lemon juice, lime juice, cornstarch, orange, lemon, and lime zest, and the water in a small saucepan; stir until the cornstarch is dissolved. Cook stirring constantly, until thickened, about 3 minutes. Remove from the heat.

2 **Divide the blackberries** into 4 bowls; serve, topped with the warm sauce.

3 tablespoons fresh orange juice

2 tablespoons granulated sugar

2 tablespoons fresh lemon juice

1 tablespoon fresh lime juice

1 1/2 teaspoons cornstarch

1/2 teaspoon grated orange zest

1/2 teaspoon grated lemon zest

1/2 teaspoon grated lime zest

1/3 cup cold water

3 cups blackberries, rinsed

Chef's Tip

If you're lucky, you may be able to find some of the delicious relatives of the blackberry at your farmers' market, such as the large, shiny-black, sweet Marion berry or the burgundy-red, slightly tart loganberry. All will work beautifully in this recipe. If fresh berries are unavailable, frozen will work in a pinch.

Per serving

92 Calories | 0 g Total Fat | 0 g Saturated Fat | 0 mg Cholesterol | 0 mg Sodium
23 g Total Carbohydrate | 6 g Dietary Fiber | 1 g Protein | 38 mg Calcium

1 *POINT* per serving

gingered pears

Ginger, a spice typically used in Asian recipes, imparts a delightful spiciness to sweet pears. This recipe uses both crystallized ginger and ginger marmalade. You can find both in specialty food shops.

makes 4 servings

4 small pears, peeled, halved, and cored

1 tablespoon minced crystallized ginger

1 tablespoon ginger marmalade

2 tablespoons water

1 **On the rounded,** skin side of each pear half, cut a small, flat section so the pear will not tip or turn when filled. Arrange the pears in a 1-quart, shallow, microwavable dish.

2 **Fill the center of each pear** with an equal amount of ginger and marmalade. Sprinkle the pears with the water and cover the dish with wax paper. Microwave the pears on High for 3 minutes, then baste with the pan juices. Continue to microwave on High until the pears are tender, about 1 minute more. Drizzle with the pan juices and serve at once.

Chef's Tip

When cooking with pears, select fruit that is still quite firm; soft fruit will fall apart during cooking. Some varieties of pears are very large, but the Seckel pear variety is small and will cook well. The firm-fleshed Anjou pear also cooks nicely.

Per serving

2 *POINTS* per serving

121 Calories | 1 g Total Fat | 0 g Saturated Fat | 0 mg Cholesterol | 3 mg Sodium 31 g Total Carbohydrate | 4 g Dietary Fiber | 1 g Protein | 20 mg Calcium

poached pears in warm cider sauce

This elegant and healthy dessert has three pear elements: pear chips, poached pears in spiced cider sauce, and Pear Sorbet. Don't be deterred; each part of the recipe is easy to prepare and everything can be made ahead. At serving time, simply assemble the elements. If pear wine is unavailable, substitute any white or blush wine with ample fruit and floral characteristics, such as Riesling, Gewürztraminer, or white Zinfandel.

makes 6 servings

8 Bartlett pears

3 cups sugar

2 cups pear wine

$1^1/_2$ cups water

1 vanilla bean, halved lengthwise

2 cups apple or pear cider

1 cinnamon stick

Pinch ground nutmeg

1 teaspoon arrowroot

$1^3/_4$ cups Pear Sorbet (page 326)

1 **To prepare the pear chips,** preheat the oven to 200°F. Line a baking sheet with parchment paper and lightly spray with nonstick spray. Slice two of the pears (with peel and core intact) very thinly, using a mandoline or slicing knife. Arrange the pear slices on the baking sheet and bake until dry and crisp, about 3 hours. Cool and store the pear chips in an airtight container up to 5 days.

2 **To prepare the poached pears,** combine the sugar, wine, water, and vanilla bean in a medium saucepan; bring to a simmer. Core and peel the remaining six pears. Add the pears to the simmering liquid and cook, covered, until tender, about 30 minutes. Remove the pan from the heat and let stand until cool. Store the pears in the poaching liquid until needed, refrigerating if not using immediately. (Leftover poaching liquid can be used again to poach more pears, or it can be frozen into a sorbet.)

3 **To prepare the spiced cider sauce,** combine the cider, cinnamon stick, and nutmeg in a medium saucepan. Bring to a boil, reduce the heat, and simmer until the cider is reduced to $1^1/_2$ cups, about 15 minutes. Discard the cinnamon stick. Dissolve the arrowroot in 1 teaspoon of cool water and stir into the simmering cider. Stir until thickened, about 1 minute.

4 **To serve,** remove the pears from the poaching liquid and place each in a wide bowl or soup plate. Cover with warm cider sauce, then add a small scoop of Pear Sorbet and three pear chips. Serve at once.

Per serving

389 Calories | 1 g Total Fat | 0 g Saturated Fat | 0 mg Cholesterol | 1 mg Sodium
83 g Total Carbohydrate | 4 g Dietary Fiber | 1 g Protein | 37 mg Calcium

7 POINTS per serving

broiled pineapple with coconut

The rich tropical flavors of rum, pineapple, and coconut come together in this simple and satisfying dessert. Canned pineapple makes this recipe a breeze to prepare, but if time allows, consider using fresh. Fresh pineapple, trimmed and sliced into rings, is available in the produce section of most supermarkets.

makes 4 servings

2 tablespoons dark rum

2 teaspoons packed dark brown sugar

$1/2$ cup pineapple juice from canned pineapples

8 canned pineapple slices (no sugar added)

2 tablespoons + 2 teaspoons shredded coconut

1 **Preheat the broiler.** Line a 1-quart shallow baking dish with foil. Combine the rum, brown sugar, and pineapple juice in a small bowl; stir until the sugar is dissolved.

2 **Arrange the pineapple slices** in a single layer in the baking dish; drizzle evenly with the rum mixture. Broil the pineapple 5 inches from the heat until the slices are lightly browned, 5–8 minutes. Sprinkle with the coconut and continue broiling until the coconut is lightly browned, 3–4 minutes more.

3 **Drizzle the pineapple slices** with the pan juices and serve at once.

---

2 *POINTS* per serving

Per serving
104 Calories | 1 g Total Fat | 1 g Saturated Fat | 0 mg Cholesterol | 12 mg Sodium
22 g Total Carbohydrate | 1 g Dietary Fiber | 1 g Protein | 18 mg Calcium

baked figs

Here, figs and almond paste are baked in an easy to assemble "beggar's purse" made with phyllo. This is a great dessert to try when fresh figs are available, late spring through summer. Once baked, dust the purses with confectioners' sugar and serve with fresh raspberries. Peeled and cored pear slices can be used if figs are not available.

makes 6 servings

6 ripe medium figs

2 tablespoons almond paste

6 (12 × 17-inch) sheets phyllo dough, room temperature

1 tablespoon unsalted butter, melted

2 tablespoons confectioners' sugar

1 **Preheat the oven** to 300°F. Lightly spray a baking sheet with nonstick spray. Remove the stems from the figs and cut an "X" into the top third of each fig.

2 **Roll the almond paste** into six balls. Press one ball onto the bottom of each fig.

3 **Cut each phyllo sheet** into quarters. Stack four quarters on top of each other, staggering the corners. Brush the top sheet with the melted butter and place a fig in the center of the stack. Wrap the sheets around the fig, twisting the top shut to make a beggar's purse. Brush the outside with melted butter. Repeat with the remaining figs and phyllo.

4 **Bake until the figs are soft** and the phyllo is golden brown, about 30 minutes. Serve warm, dusted with the confectioners' sugar.

Per serving

85 Calories | 4 g Total Fat | 2 g Saturated Fat | 5 mg Cholesterol | 2 mg Sodium
14 g Total Carbohydrate | 2 g Dietary Fiber | 1 g Protein | 26 mg Calcium

2 POINTS per serving

winter fruit compote

This recipe can be doubled and stored in the refrigerator; serve it warm with oatmeal or French toast for a special breakfast, or with bread pudding for dessert. Select a variety of favorite dried fruits: dried cherries, blueberries, currants, cranberries, apricots, dates, figs, raisins, and prunes all work well in this compote.

makes 4 servings

1 cup mixed dried fruits

1/4 cup white port wine or white grape juice, warm

1/2 cup apple cider

1 (3-inch) cinnamon stick

1 teaspoon arrowroot

1/4 teaspoon grated lemon zest

1/8 teaspoon freshly grated nutmeg

1 **Coarsely chop the larger fruits** (for example, the apricots, prunes, apples), leaving the smaller fruits (for example, the raisins, currants, cherries) whole. Soak the dried fruit in the wine until it begins to plump, about 30 minutes. Drain the fruit, reserving 1 tablespoon of the wine.

2 **Bring the cider** and cinnamon stick to a boil in a small saucepan. Dissolve the arrowroot in the reserved wine. Add to the cider and simmer until thickened, about 2 minutes.

3 **Stir in the soaked fruit,** the lemon zest, and nutmeg. Bring to a boil; reduce the heat and simmer, uncovered, 1 minute. Remove from the heat, discard the cinnamon stick, and serve warm. If making ahead, let cool, cover, and refrigerate for up to 2 days. Reheat before serving.

2 _POINTS_ per serving

Per serving
133 Calories | 0 g Total Fat | 0 g Saturated Fat | 0 mg Cholesterol | 5 mg Sodium
27 g Total Carbohydrate | 2 g Dietary Fiber | 1 g Protein | 18 mg Calcium

winter fruit compote, with french toast

tropical fruit parfait with honey vanilla yogurt

This beautiful fruit parfait is simple to make, yet looks very elegant. Start this recipe early or a day ahead of serving, because the yogurt cheese needs to drain for at least five hours. The ingredients can be organized ahead of time, but wait to assemble the parfaits until just before serving time.

makes 4 servings

1 vanilla bean

2 cups yogurt cheese

1/4 cup honey

1 medium banana, cut into small cubes (about 2/3 cup)

1/3 medium mango, cut into small cubes (about 1/2 cup)

1/4 small papaya, cut into small cubes (about 1/2 cup)

1/4 cup chopped dried apricot halves

1/2 cup low-fat granola

1 **Place four 10-ounce parfait** or wine glasses in the refrigerator to chill, at least 1 hour ahead.

2 **Split the vanilla bean** and scrape the seeds in one bowl (see Chef's Tips below). Stir in the yogurt cheese and honey; cover and refrigerate until needed. Combine the banana, mango, papaya, and apricots in another bowl; cover and refrigerate until needed.

3 **To assemble the parfaits,** fill each chilled glass with equal amounts of the mixed fruit, alternate with a layer of the yogurt mixture, then another layer of fruit, and finish with the yogurt mixture. Top the parfaits with the granola and serve at once.

Chef's Tips

To make the yogurt cheese, spoon 1 quart plain nonfat yogurt into a strainer lined with a coffee filter or cheesecloth and place over a bowl. Cover and refrigerate at least 5 hours or overnight. Discard the liquid in the bowl.

Real vanilla beans are necessary for this recipe. They are expensive, but worth it. The seeds from the beans give the yogurt true vanilla flavor and a speckled look that announces the presence of real vanilla. If vanilla extract were used instead, the alcohol it contains would be apparent in the yogurt. Quality vanilla beans should be pliable and smell strongly of vanilla, indicating freshness. To remove the seeds from the beans, split the beans lengthwise with a paring knife. Use the knife to gently scrape the sticky seeds out of the bean.

6 *POINTS* per serving

Per serving
317 Calories | 5 g Total Fat | 3 g Saturated Fat | 15 mg Cholesterol | 204 mg Sodium
57 g Total Carbohydrate | 3 g Dietary Fiber | 14 g Protein | 463 mg Calcium

mandarin frappé

Frappé refers to a mixture of fruit juice or liqueur poured over crushed ice. Any orangelike citrus fruit juice, such as tangelo, tangerine, or Valencia orange, may be substituted in this refreshing drink. Use a blender to crush the ice in small batches.

makes 2 servings

1 **Fill a cocktail shaker cup** with crushed ice, add the orange juice and lime juice; stir or shake to chill completely.

2 **Fill 2 tall glasses** with crushed ice. Strain the chilled juice into the ice-filled glasses.

3 **Garnish each frappé** with a lime slice and serve at once.

3 cups crushed ice, or as needed

1 1/2 cups fresh mandarin orange juice

2 1/2 tablespoons fresh lime juice

2 lime slices

Per serving

91 Calories | 1 g Total Fat | 0 g Saturated Fat | 0 mg Cholesterol | 2 mg Sodium
22 g Total Carbohydrate | 1 g Dietary Fiber | 1 g Protein | 25 mg Calcium

2 *POINTS* per serving

---

tropical smoothie

This smoothie is always a hit; it is refreshing and high in vitamin C. Try it for a quick, on-the-go breakfast.

makes 4 servings

Combine the pineapple juice, frozen strawberries, and the banana in a blender. Puree until very smooth. Divide the smoothie into 4 tall cocktail glasses and garnish each with a fresh strawberry (if using).

1 1/2 cups unsweetened pineapple juice, chilled

8 frozen strawberries

1 banana, sliced

4 fresh strawberries, hulled (optional)

Per serving

91 Calories | 0 g Total Fat | 0 g Saturated Fat | 0 mg Cholesterol | 2 mg Sodium
23 g Total Carbohydrate | 2 g Dietary Fiber | 1 g Protein | 23 mg Calcium

1 *POINT* per serving

cantaloupe cocktail

Cantaloupes are a sweet and juicy source of vitamins A and C. Select cantaloupes that are fragrant, heavy for their size, and have well-raised netting.

makes 4 servings

$^1/_2$ medium cantaloupe, peeled and chopped (about 2$^1/_2$ cups)

1$^1/_4$ cups fresh orange juice

2 tablespoons fresh lime juice

2 tablespoons honey

$^1/_4$ teaspoon vanilla extract

6 ice cubes

4 lime slices

1 **Place four pilsner** or wine glasses in the freezer to frost, at least 1 hour ahead.

2 **Combine the cantaloupe,** orange juice, lime juice, honey, vanilla, and ice cubes in a blender; puree until very smooth.

3 **Divide the cantaloupe mixture** into the frosted glasses and garnish with the lime slices. Serve at once.

2 POINTS per serving

Per serving

107 Calories | 1 g Total Fat | 0 g Saturated Fat | 0 mg Cholesterol | 10 mg Sodium
27 g Total Carbohydrate | 2 g Dietary Fiber | 1 g Protein | 24 mg Calcium

chapter 15

breads

spiced whole-wheat muffins

These chewy, easy-to-make muffins are packed with toasty, whole-grain flavor, and the sweetness of raisins.

makes 12 servings

1 cup raisins

1 cup warm water

1 cup all-purpose flour

1 cup whole-wheat flour

2$\frac{1}{2}$ teaspoons baking powder

2 teaspoons cinnamon

$\frac{3}{4}$ teaspoon ground mace

$\frac{1}{4}$ teaspoon ground cloves

$\frac{1}{3}$ cup sugar

$\frac{1}{3}$ cup plain nonfat yogurt

1 egg

2$\frac{1}{2}$ tablespoons vegetable oil

1 **Combine the raisins** with the warm water in a bowl; soak 20 minutes. Drain the raisins, reserving $\frac{3}{4}$ cup of the liquid.

2 **Preheat the oven** to 375°F. Spray a 12-cup muffin pan with nonstick spray or line with foil or paper liners.

3 **Combine the all-purpose flour,** whole-wheat flour, baking powder, cinnamon, mace, and cloves in one bowl. Combine the reserved raisin liquid, the sugar, yogurt, egg, and oil in a bowl. Add the raisin liquid mixture to the flour mixture; stir just until blended. Stir in the plumped raisins.

4 **Spoon the batter** into the cups, filling each about two-thirds full. Bake until the surface of the muffins are golden brown and spring back when lightly pressed, or until a toothpick inserted in a muffin comes out clean, about 15 minutes. Cool in the pan on a rack 5 minutes; remove from the pan and cool completely on the rack. Store in an airtight container for up to 3 days.

3 *POINTS* per serving

Per serving

163 Calories | 4 g Total Fat | 1 g Saturated Fat | 18 mg Cholesterol | 90 mg Sodium
31 g Total Carbohydrate | 2 g Dietary Fiber | 3 g Protein | 32 mg Calcium

maple-pear oatmeal muffins

Select Bosc, Bartlett, or Anjou varieties for this recipe, and make sure the pear is firm but ripe. These sweet muffins will keep, stored in an airtight container at room temperature for up to 3 days.

1 Preheat the oven to 400°F. Spray a 12-cup muffin tin with non-stick spray or line with foil or paper liners.

2 Combine the flour, baking soda, baking powder, cinnamon, and salt in one bowl. Combine the pecans and 2 tablespoons of the oats in another bowl. Combine the remaining oats, the pear, buttermilk, brown sugar, syrup, oil, and egg in a bowl; let stand 5 minutes. Add the oat-pear mixture to the flour mixture; stir just until blended.

3 Spoon the batter into the cups, filling each about two-thirds full. Sprinkle with the pecan-oat mixture. Bake until a toothpick inserted in a muffin comes out clean, 18 to 20 minutes. Cool in the pan on a rack 5 minutes; remove from the pan and cool completely on the rack.

makes 12 servings

1 3/4 cups all-purpose flour

1 teaspoon baking soda

1 teaspoon baking powder

1 teaspoon cinnamon

1/2 teaspoon salt

2 tablespoons finely chopped pecans

1 1/2 cups quick-cooking rolled oats

1 large pear, cored, peeled, and chopped

1 cup fat-free buttermilk

1/2 cup packed dark brown sugar

1/3 cup pure maple syrup

2 tablespoons vegetable oil

1 egg

Per serving

220 Calories | 5 g Total Fat | 1 g Saturated Fat | 18 mg Cholesterol | 256 mg Sodium
40 g Total Carbohydrate | 2 g Dietary Fiber | 5 g Protein | 60 mg Calcium

4 *POINTS* per serving

oat bran and dried fruit muffins

Dried fruit adds sweetness and a chewy texture to these moist, golden-brown muffins. Be creative in choosing dried-fruit combinations, such as blueberries and mangoes, apricots and raspberries, or prunes and cherries.

makes 12 servings

1 1/4 cups dried fruit, coarsely chopped

1 cup old-fashioned rolled oats

3/4 cup oat bran

1/2 cup + 1 tablespoon all-purpose flour

1 medium banana, mashed

3 tablespoons packed light brown sugar

5 teaspoons baking powder

1 teaspoon cinnamon

1 cup fat-free milk

1/4 cup fresh orange juice

2 egg whites

2 tablespoons vegetable oil

2 teaspoons grated orange zest

1 **Preheat the oven** to 400°F. Spray a 12-cup muffin pan with nonstick spray or line with foil or paper liners.

2 **Combine the dried fruit,** rolled oats, oat bran, flour, banana, brown sugar, baking powder, and cinnamon in a food processor. Pulse until the mixture is just blended, then transfer to a bowl.

3 **Combine the milk,** orange juice, egg whites, oil, and orange zest in another bowl. Add the milk mixture to the dried fruit mixture; stir just until blended.

4 **Spoon the batter** into the cups, filling each about two-thirds full. Bake until the surface of the muffins are golden brown and spring back when lightly pressed, or until a toothpick inserted in a muffin comes out clean, about 15 minutes. Remove from the pan and cool on a rack 10 minutes before serving. Store in an airtight container at room temperature for up to 3 days.

3 POINTS per serving

Per serving

168 Calories | 4 g Total Fat | 1 g Saturated Fat | 0 mg Cholesterol | 187 mg Sodium
31 g Total Carbohydrate | 3 g Dietary Fiber | 5 g Protein | 78 mg Calcium

oat bran and dried fruit muffins; and orange, cranberry, and apricot muffins (page 290)

orange, cranberry, and apricot muffins

For a fresh twist on the morning muffin, juice any variety of orange on hand—navel, temple, or Valencia—to flavor the batter. Use a thick-handled wooden spoon to stir this stiff and sticky batter. These easy muffins can be stored in an airtight container at room temperature for 3 days.

makes 12 servings

1 cup all-purpose flour

3/4 cup whole-wheat flour

1/4 cup wheat germ

2 teaspoons baking powder

1/2 teaspoon baking soda

1/4 teaspoon salt

4 tablespoons (1/2 stick) unsalted butter or margarine, cut into small cubes

1/2 cup sugar

2/3 cup orange juice

1 egg

1 cup sweetened dried cranberries

1 cup chopped dried apricot halves

1. **Preheat the oven** to 350°F. Spray a 12-cup muffin tin with nonstick spray or line with foil or paper liners.

2. **Combine the all-purpose flour,** whole-wheat flour, wheat germ, baking powder, baking soda, and salt in a bowl. With a fork or your fingers, combine the butter with the dry ingredients until the mixture is crumbly. Stir in the sugar.

3. **Combine the orange juice** and egg in another bowl. Add the juice mixture to the flour mixture; stir just until blended. The dough will be very stiff. Stir in the cranberries and apricots.

4. **Spoon the batter** into the cups, filling each about three-quarters full. Bake until the surface of the muffins are golden brown, or until a toothpick inserted in a muffin comes out clean, about 20 to 25 minutes. Cool in the pan on a rack 5 minutes; remove from the pan and cool completely on the rack.

Chef's Tip

For a more intense orange flavor, add 2 teaspoons grated orange zest to the dough when folding in the cranberries and apricots.

4 POINTS per serving

Per serving
211 Calories | 5 g Total Fat | 3 g Saturated Fat | 29 mg Cholesterol | 216 mg Sodium
39 g Total Carbohydrate | 3 g Dietary Fiber | 4 g Protein | 27 mg Calcium

peppery popovers

Popovers puff and have a spectacular rise in the oven, as the moisture in the batter heats and turns into steam. Take care not to open the oven door and let the steam escape while the popovers are baking.

makes 8 servings

1 **Preheat the oven** to 450°F. Spray an 8-cup popover pan or muffin tin with nonstick spray.

2 **With an electric mixer** at medium speed, beat the eggs until frothy. Beat in the milk, then the flour, salt, and pepper.

3 **Spoon 1/4 cup batter** into each cup. Bake 15 minutes; reduce the oven temperature to 400°F and bake until browned, about 12 minutes longer. Serve at once.

2 eggs

1 cup fat-free milk

1 cup all-purpose flour

1/2 teaspoon salt

Freshly ground pepper

Chef's Tip

Use popover pans or single-weight muffin fins. Don't use insulated tins; they won't get hot enough to generate sufficient steam to make the popovers rise.

Per serving

86 Calories | 1 g Total Fat | 0 g Saturated Fat | 54 mg Cholesterol | 177 mg Sodium
14 g Total Carbohydrate | 0 g Dietary Fiber | 4 g Protein | 46 mg Calcium

2 *POINTS* per serving

country corn bread

Buttermilk lightens the texture of this corn bread and adds a rich and tangy flavor. Bake it in a pan—or, Southern style, in a cast-iron skillet. For variety, try adding chili powder, chopped scallion, chopped bell peppers, minced jalapeño pepper, corn kernels, or cayenne to the batter.

makes 6 servings

3/4 cup + 1 tablespoon yellow cornmeal

2/3 cup all-purpose flour

1 tablespoon baking powder

2 teaspoons sugar

1/4 teaspoon salt

2/3 cup fat-free buttermilk

1 egg

1 egg white

1 **Preheat the oven** to 375°F. Spray an 8 × 8-inch baking dish or an 8-inch ovenproof skillet with nonstick spray.

2 **Combine the cornmeal,** flour, baking powder, sugar, and salt in a large bowl. Combine the buttermilk, egg, and egg white in another bowl. Add the buttermilk mixture to the cornmeal mixture; stir just until blended.

3 **Using a rubber spatula,** transfer the batter into the baking dish or skillet and spread evenly. Bake until golden brown and a toothpick inserted in the center comes out clean, about 15 minutes. Cool for 5 minutes on a rack; serve warm.

Chef's Tip

To create a country-style pot pie, place a favorite stew in an ovenproof dish and spread the corn bread batter on top. Bake in a 375°F oven until the stew is bubbling, the crust is golden brown, and a toothpick inserted in the center of the corn bread comes out clean.

3 *POINTS* per serving

Per serving
147 Calories | 2 g Total Fat | 1 g Saturated Fat | 36 mg Cholesterol | 343 mg Sodium
27 g Total Carbohydrate | 2 g Dietary Fiber | 5 g Protein | 74 mg Calcium

potato-yogurt bread

Pureed potato and yogurt keep this golden, slightly sour bread moist and dense. To get the best texture, use a baking potato (for example, Idaho or russet), which is high in starch and low in moisture. Use a food mill or ricer to get the smoothest puree—but not a food processor, which will make the potato gluey in texture. Avoid using waxy potatoes with less starch and more moisture, such as red bliss or Yukon gold.

makes 16 servings

1 (about 9-ounce) baking potato, peeled and quartered

1 cup plain low-fat yogurt

1/4 cup warm (105°–115°F) water

2 1/4 teaspoons honey

2 envelopes active dry yeast (1/2 ounce)

2 teaspoons fat-free dry milk

4 cups + 2 tablespoons bread flour

1/2 cup whole-wheat flour

2 teaspoons salt

1 **Place the potato** and enough water to cover in a saucepan; bring to a boil. Reduce the heat and simmer, covered, until the potato is tender, about 15 minutes. Drain and return the potato to the pan. Place over low heat and let steam-dry about 5 minutes, shaking the pan occasionally. Puree the hot potato using a ricer or food mill, and let cool to room temperature.

2 **Combine the yogurt,** water, honey, yeast, and dry milk in a large bowl. Stir in the potato, bread flour, whole-wheat flour, and salt. Knead by hand or in a mixer fitted with a dough hook at medium speed until a smooth, elastic dough develops, about 5 minutes. Add more bread flour, one tablespoon at a time, if the dough is too wet.

3 **Spray a large bowl** with nonstick spray; put the dough in the bowl. Cover loosely with plastic wrap and let the dough rise in a warm spot until it doubles in size and holds an impression for a few seconds when pressed with a finger, about 1 hour.

4 **Turn out the dough** on a lightly floured counter. Deflate the dough by kneading it briefly. Shape the dough into a loaf, cover with plastic wrap, and let it rise 30 minutes in a warm spot.

5 **Preheat the oven** to 350°F. Place the loaf on a baking sheet, make a few shallow slashes across the top, and bake until the crust is golden brown and the loaf sounds hollow when tapped on the bottom, about 45 minutes. Cool completely on a rack before serving.

Per serving

162 Calories | 1 g Total Fat | 0 g Saturated Fat | 1 mg Cholesterol | 304 mg Sodium
32 g Total Carbohydrate | 2 g Dietary Fiber | 6 g Protein | 39 mg Calcium

3 *POINTS* per serving

black pepper biscuits

Perfect with chowder or stew, these tender biscuits are quick and easy to prepare. Use freshly ground pepper for the best flavor.

makes 14 servings

2¼ cups all-purpose flour

1 tablespoon + 2 teaspoons baking powder

1 tablespoon sugar

2 teaspoons coarsely ground pepper

¼ teaspoon salt

¼ cup cold unsalted butter, cut into small cubes

1 cup + 2 tablespoons fat-free buttermilk

1 **Preheat the oven** to 375°F. Spray a nonstick baking sheet with nonstick spray.

2 **Combine the flour,** baking powder, sugar, pepper, and salt in a large bowl. With a fork, cut the butter into the flour mixture until crumbly.

3 **Make a well in the flour mixture,** pour in 1 cup of the buttermilk, and gently stir until just blended. Do not overmix. Turn out the dough on a lightly floured counter and roll to a ¹/₂-inch thickness. Cut the dough with a 2¹/₄-inch round biscuit cutter, gathering the scraps and re-rolling as necessary.

4 **Arrange the biscuits** on the baking sheet and brush the tops with the remaining 2 tablespoons buttermilk. Bake until golden brown, 12 to 15 minutes. Cool slightly on a rack. Serve warm. Store any leftover biscuits in an airtight container for up to 2 days.

2 *POINTS* per serving

Per serving

117 Calories | 4 g Total Fat | 2 g Saturated Fat | 10 mg Cholesterol | 236 mg Sodium
18 g Total Carbohydrate | 1 g Dietary Fiber | 3 g Protein | 51 mg Calcium

herb-cracker crust

This crispy Herb-Cracker Crust is ideal for covering pot pies, such as Chicken and Shrimp Pot Pie (page 171). Simply roll out the dough and cut to fit the bowls or dish in which you plan to serve the pot pie. Bake the crusts while the pot pie filling simmers and place them on the hot pie filling as soon as they come out of the oven. Or, make the crusts ahead and wrap airtight for 1 day or freeze for up to 2 weeks. Thaw and re-crisp in a 300°F oven for 5 minutes before topping the pot pies.

makes 4 servings

1 cup all-purpose flour

3/4 teaspoon sugar

1/4 teaspoon salt

1/8 teaspoon baking powder

1 tablespoon cold unsalted butter, cut into small cubes

1/3 cup + 2 tablespoons chilled fat-free buttermilk

1 tablespoon + 1 teaspoon chopped fresh basil

1 tablespoon + 1 teaspoon chopped fresh parsley

2 teaspoons chopped fresh tarragon

1 **Combine the flour,** sugar, salt, and baking powder in a medium bowl. With a fork, cut the butter into the flour mixture until it forms a mealy mixture. Add the buttermilk, basil, parsley, and tarragon; knead to form a stiff dough. Wrap in plastic wrap and let the dough rest in the refrigerator 20 minutes.

2 **Preheat the oven** to 400°F. Spray 2 nonstick baking sheets with nonstick spray.

3 **Working on a lightly floured counter** with a heavy rolling pin, roll the dough into a large thin circle, about 1/8-inch thick. Cut into four 6-inch circles (or other shape, depending on desired use), gathering the scraps and re-rolling as necessary. (If cutting 6-inch circles, you should get three from the first rolling of dough and one more from the scraps.)

4 **Bake until the crust** is golden brown on the bottom, about 10 minutes; turn and continue baking until crispy, about 5 minutes more.

Per serving

155 Calories | 4 g Total Fat | 2 g Saturated Fat | 9 mg Cholesterol | 219 mg Sodium
26 g Total Carbohydrate | 1 g Dietary Fiber | 4 g Protein | 43 mg Calcium

3 *POINTS* per serving

chickpea flatbread with variations

Like sourdough bread, this flatbread is leavened with a sour starter, made by allowing a thin yeast batter to ferment until it becomes sour and foamy. It takes a bit of time for the starter and the dough to develop properly, but the actual hands-on work is not involved and the unique, mildly nutty flavor of the bread is worth the wait. Serve it with grilled kebabs, soup, or salad.

makes 12 servings

2 cups warm (105°–115°F) water

1 tablespoon + 1 teaspoon honey

1 envelope active dry yeast ($^{1}/_{4}$ ounce)

$2^{1}/_{2}$ cups bread flour

$1^{1}/_{3}$ cups chickpea flour

$1^{1}/_{3}$ cups semolina flour

2 tablespoons chopped chives

$^{3}/_{4}$ teaspoon salt

$^{3}/_{4}$ cup cornmeal, or as needed

1 **To prepare the sour starter,** combine $^{1}/_{2}$ cup of the warm water with the honey in a small bowl. Stir in the yeast and enough bread flour to make a thin batter. Cover the batter with plastic wrap, place in a warm area, and let stand until it becomes frothy and increases in bulk, 1 hour.

2 **Combine the remaining** $1^{1}/_{2}$ cups warm water and the remaining bread flour, the chickpea flour, semolina flour, chives, salt, and the sour starter. Knead by hand or in a mixer fitted with a dough hook at medium speed until a smooth, elastic dough develops, about 8 to 10 minutes. Add more bread flour, 1 tablespoon at a time, if the dough is too wet.

3 **Spray a large bowl** with nonstick spray; put the dough in the bowl. Cover loosely with plastic wrap and let the dough rise in a warm spot until it doubles in size and holds an impression for a few seconds when pressed with a finger, about 1 hour.

4 **Turn out the dough** on a lightly floured counter. Deflate the dough by kneading it briefly. Divide the dough into 12 equal pieces and shape each into a ball. Cover the dough balls with plastic wrap and let them rise 1 hour in a warm spot.

5 **Preheat the oven** to 500°F. Line two baking sheets with parchment paper, spray with nonstick spray, and sprinkle with a handful of the cornmeal. Flatten 6 of the dough balls into $7^{1}/_{2}$-inch circles and place on the baking sheets. Bake until golden brown, 6 to 7 minutes. Cool completely on a rack. Repeat with the remaining dough balls, using baking sheets prepared with new parchment paper, nonstick spray, and cornmeal. Store the flatbreads in an airtight container for up to 2 days.

5 *POINTS* per serving

Per serving

260 Calories | 1 g Total Fat | 0 g Saturated Fat | 0 mg Cholesterol | 158 mg Sodium
55 g Total Carbohydrate | 3 g Dietary Fiber | 7 g Protein | 21 mg Calcium

variations

Grilled Flatbread: Spray a grill rack with nonstick spray; prepare the grill. Grill the dough 5 inches from the heat until the flatbread puffs, blisters, and cooks thoroughly, 2 to 3 minutes on the first side and 1 minute on the second. Alternatively, broil the dough 5 inches from the heat, for the same amount of time.

Sesame Chickpea Flatbread: Add 1 tablespoon toasted white sesame seeds and 1 tablespoon black sesame seeds before kneading the dough.

Chef's Tips

This flatbread uses a combination of chickpea flour, semolina flour, and bread flour. Chickpea flour is also known as besan or gram flour. It is a common ingredient in East Indian cooking and is available from Indian or Asian markets, and health-food stores. Semolina flour is a coarsely ground durum wheat flour often used to make pasta. It can be purchased from Italian specialty markets, and health-food stores.

Black sesame seeds, more fragrant and flavorful than the white kind, release a wonderful aroma as they are toasted. Find them in Asian grocery stores.

To toast the sesame seeds, place them in a dry skillet, over medium-low heat. Cook, shaking the pan and stirring constantly, until the black sesame seeds are fragrant and the white sesame seeds begin to brown lightly, 1 to 2 minutes. Watch them carefully; sesame seeds can burn quickly. Transfer the seeds to a plate to cool.

grilled naan with eggplant puree

Naan is an East Indian flat bread traditionally baked in a *tandoor*, a wood-fired brick-and-clay oven. Here, a grill is used to replace the high heat of the tandoor. A nonstick skillet or cast-iron pan set over medium-high heat may also be used to cook the naan, but it will lack a smoky, grilled flavor. Serve naan and eggplant puree as an appetizer or side dish to Indian-style foods.

makes 4 servings

³/₄ cup semolina flour

¹/₂ teaspoon baking powder

¹/₂ teaspoon salt

3 tablespoons nonfat yogurt

1 tablespoon olive oil

1 egg white

¹/₂ small eggplant, split lengthwise

¹/₄ cup minced onion

¹/₂ teaspoon minced jalapeño

1 **To prepare the naan,** sift the flour, baking powder and ¹/₄ teaspoon of the salt into the bowl of an electric mixer fitted with a dough hook. Add 2 tablespoons of the yogurt, the oil, and egg white. Mix at medium speed, adding a little warm water if necessary to make a soft pliable dough. Continue to knead the dough at medium speed for 3 minutes, scraping down the sides of the mixer bowl as needed.

2 **Spray a large bowl** with nonstick spray; put the dough in the bowl. Cover loosely with plastic wrap and set aside in a warm spot for about 3 hours.

3 **Meanwhile, to prepare the eggplant puree,** preheat the oven to 350°F. Spray the cut sides of the eggplant with nonstick cooking spray. Place on a baking sheet cut side up and roast in the oven until soft and browned, 25 to 30 minutes. When cool enough to handle, remove the skin, place the eggplant in a bowl and mash the pulp thoroughly. Add the onion, jalapeño, the remaining 1 tablespoon yogurt, and remaining ¹/₄ teaspoon salt; blend thoroughly. Set aside.

4 **Spray the grill rack** with nonstick spray; prepare the grill. Deflate the naan dough, knead briefly, and divide it into 4 equal pieces. Pull each piece of dough into a 6-inch-long teardrop shape. Grill the dough 5 inches from the heat, until browned and slightly puffy, about 2 minutes per side. Serve the eggplant puree with the warm bread.

Chef's Tip

Semolina flour is a coarsely ground durum wheat flour often used to make pasta. It can be purchased from Italian specialty markets and health-food stores.

1 *POINT* per serving

Per serving

65 Calories | 4 g Total Fat | 1 g Saturated Fat | 0 mg Cholesterol | 380 mg Sodium
7 g Total Carbohydrate | 2 g Dietary Fiber | 2 g Protein | 62 mg Calcium

chapter 16

desserts

sponge cake

Sponge is a light cake that relies on egg whites to lighten and raise the batter. This basic sponge cake is egg yolk-free and contains only a minimum amount of fat to make it tender. Sponge cakes can be flavored with citrus zest or ground nuts. Once a sponge cake has been baked, it can be soaked with flavored simple syrup and layered, or rolled jelly roll–style around fruit or other fillings. Serve the cake with fresh fruit and a scoop of sorbet or frozen yogurt.

makes 16 servings

2/3 cup cake flour

1/4 cup cornstarch

1/4 teaspoon salt

8 egg whites

1 cup confectioners' sugar, sifted

1/2 teaspoon cream of tartar

1 tablespoon unsalted butter, melted

1 1/2 teaspoons vanilla extract

1/4 cup ground walnuts or hazelnuts (optional)

1 tablespoon grated citrus zest (optional)

1 teaspoon almond extract (optional)

1 **Preheat the oven** to 325°F. Spray a 10-inch cake pan or an 11 × 17-inch jelly-roll pan with nonstick spray, dust with flour, and line with parchment paper.

2 **Combine the cake flour,** cornstarch, and salt in a medium bowl; sift three times.

3 **With an electric mixer** on medium speed, beat the egg whites in a large bowl until thick and foamy. Gradually sprinkle in the sugar and cream of tartar; continue beating until the egg whites form medium peaks, 3–5 minutes.

4 **Add the flour mixture** in 3 additions, gently folding each addition into the egg whites until well combined. Fold in the butter, vanilla. If using, fold in the walnuts, citrus zest, and almond extract. Pour the batter into the pan. Bake until a toothpick inserted in the center comes out clean and the cake begins to pull away from the sides of the pan, about 25 minutes for a jelly roll and 35 minutes for a round cake. Cool the cake in the pan on a rack for 10 minutes; remove from the pan and cool completely on the rack.

variation

Chocolate Sponge Cake: Replace 1/4 cup of the cake flour with 1/4 cup unsweetened Dutch cocoa powder, plus 1/2 teaspoon instant espresso powder.

1 *POINT* per serving

Per serving
65 Calories | 1 g Total Fat | 0 g Saturated Fat | 2 mg Cholesterol | 72 mg Sodium 11 g Total Carbohydrate | 0 g Dietary Fiber | 2 g Protein | 2 mg Calcium

Chef's Tips

Simple syrup is easy to make: Combine $1/2$ cup water with $1/2$ cup sugar in a saucepan, and bring just to a boil. Remove the syrup from the heat and let stand until cool. Simple syrup can be flavored with dissolved espresso powder, rum, or any type of liqueur, such as Kirsch or Triple Sec.

Sponge cake keeps well in the freezer. To freeze, allow the cake to cool to room temperature, cover it with plastic wrap, and freeze for up to 1 month.

Allow the egg whites to come to room temperature. Make sure the bowl and beaters are squeaky clean and dry, and that the egg whites are free of any yolk. Start slowly and, when the whites become quite foamy, increase the speed of the mixer and beat to the desired peak stage.

Egg whites will take on eight times their volume when whipped with a balloon whisk in a copper bowl, but perfect fluffy whites are possible with an electric beater and a metal bowl. Egg whites can be beaten to soft, medium, and stiff peaks. After the soft-peak stage, sugar is usually added gradually while beating to help stabilize the egg whites.

- Soft peak: When the beater is pulled up through the egg whites, a droopy, rounded peak will form. At this stage, the surface of the whites looks moist and glossy.

- Medium peak: When the beater is pulled up through the egg whites a rounded but fairly stable peak will form. At this stage, the surface of the whites looks moist and glossy.

- Stiff peak: When the beater is lifted out of the egg whites, they will stand up in stiff, stable peaks. It is crucial to stop beating while the surface is still moist and glossy. Over-beaten egg whites may still resemble those at the stiff-peak stage, but their surface will look dry and they will have lost their elasticity. If the whites are beaten further, the egg protein will gather into globs and the moisture will weep out.

To fold egg whites, use a rubber spatula; cut down to the bottom of the bowl, lift and turn the whites over, turn the bowl and repeat.

chocolate angel food cake

Slices of angel food cake can be grilled briefly and topped with fresh berries or a toasted marshmallow for a truly unique dessert.

makes 12 servings

1^1/$_3$ cups cake flour

^{1}/$_2$ cup unsweetened Dutch cocoa powder

1 teaspoon baking powder

12 egg whites

1^2/$_3$ cups confectioners' sugar, sifted; + (optional) more for dusting the cake

1 teaspoon cream of tartar

2 tablespoons unsalted butter, melted

2 teaspoons vanilla extract

1 **Preheat the oven** to 325°F. Lightly spray a 10-inch tube pan with nonstick spray.

2 **Combine the cake flour,** cocoa, and baking powder in a medium bowl; sift twice.

3 **With an electric mixer** on medium speed, beat the egg whites in a large bowl until thick and foamy. Gradually sprinkle in the sugar and cream of tartar; continue beating until the egg whites form medium peaks, about 3–5 minutes.

4 **Add the flour mixture** in 3 additions, gently folding each addition into the egg whites until well combined. Fold in the butter and vanilla.

5 **Pour the batter** into the pan. Bake until a toothpick inserted in the center comes out clean and the cake begins to pull away from the sides of the pan, about 30 minutes. Allow the cake to cool completely on a rack before removing it from the pan. Dust the top of the cake with confectioners' sugar (if using).

Chef's Tip

For tips on beating egg whites, see page 301.

3 *POINTS* per serving

Per serving (one 2-inch slice)
141 Calories | 2 g Total Fat | 1 g Saturated Fat | 6 mg Cholesterol | 95 mg Sodium
25 g Total Carbohydrate | 0 g Dietary Fiber | 5 g Protein | 23 mg Calcium

chocolate cake

The full flavor of this light chocolate cake is enhanced with espresso; butter-milk gives it a tangy and rich quality. Serve the cake with raspberries, or for something even richer, a scoop of coffee-flavored frozen yogurt. This cake also makes a great base for a trifle or tiramisù. To freeze the cake, let cool to room temperature, wrap tightly, and store in the freezer for up to 1 month.

makes 8 servings

1 cup all-purpose flour

2 tablespoons unsweetened Dutch cocoa powder; + (optional) more for dusting the cake

1/4 teaspoon baking soda

1/4 teaspoon baking powder

1/4 teaspoon salt

1/3 cup fat-free buttermilk

1 teaspoon vanilla extract

1/2 teaspoon instant espresso powder

1 1/2 cups sugar

1/3 cup unsalted butter, softened

1 egg

2 egg whites

1 **Preheat the oven** to 350°F. Lightly spray a 10-inch tube pan with nonstick cooking spray. (If using a fluted tube pan, dust lightly with flour after spraying.)

2 **Sift together the flour,** cocoa, baking soda, baking powder, and salt in a medium bowl.

3 **Combine the buttermilk,** vanilla, and espresso powder in a small bowl; set aside.

4 **With an electric mixer** on medium speed, beat the sugar and but-ter in a large bowl until light and fluffy. Add the egg and continue beating until well incorporated. Add the flour mixture in 2 addi-tions, alternating with the buttermilk mixture, mixing until each addition is fully incorporated. Beat until the batter is smooth.

5 **With an electric mixer** on medium speed—make sure to clean the beaters—beat the egg whites in a large bowl until they form soft peaks, 2–3 minutes. Using a whisk, gently mix one-third of the whites into the batter to lighten it. With a rubber spatula, gently fold in the remaining whites. Pour the batter into the pan. Bake until a toothpick inserted in the center of the cake comes out clean, about 40 minutes. Cool the cake in the pan on a rack 10 minutes; remove from the pan and cool completely on the rack. Dust the top of the cake with cocoa (if using).

Chef's Tip

For tips on beating egg whites, see page 301.

Per serving

286 Calories | 9 g Total Fat | 5 g Saturated Fat | 49 mg Cholesterol | 222 mg Sodium
49 g Total Carbohydrate | 1 g Dietary Fiber | 3 g Protein | 25 mg Calcium

6 *POINTS* per serving

carrot cake

Pineapple keeps this spiced carrot cake moist and delicious. For a pretty presentation, cover the baked cake with a paper doily before dusting it with confectioners' sugar. After dusting, carefully lift away the doily, leaving the sugared design intact.

makes 16 servings

3/4 cup all-purpose flour

2/3 cup whole-wheat flour

1 teaspoon baking soda

1 teaspoon baking powder

1 teaspoon cinnamon

1 cup + 2 tablespoons sugar

1/2 cup vegetable oil

2 eggs

4 medium carrots, peeled and grated (2 cups)

1 cup drained canned crushed pineapple or pineapple tidbits (no sugar added)

1/2 cup raisins

2 egg whites

1/4 cup confectioners' sugar

1 **Preheat the oven** to 350°F. Line a 9-inch cake pan with parchment paper, lightly spray with nonstick spray, and dust with flour.

2 **Sift together the all-purpose flour,** whole-wheat flour, baking soda, baking powder, and cinnamon in a bowl.

3 **Beat the sugar,** oil, and whole eggs until smooth in another bowl. Add the flour mixture and stir until just combined. Stir in the carrots, pineapple, and raisins.

4 **With an electric mixer** on medium speed, beat the egg whites in a large bowl until they form medium peaks, 3–5 minutes. Using a whisk, gently stir one-third of the whites into the batter to lighten it. With a rubber spatula gently fold in the remaining whites. Pour the batter into the pan and bake until a toothpick inserted in the center of the cake comes out clean, about 45 minutes.

5 **Cool in the pan** on a rack for 10 minutes; remove the cake from the pan and cool completely on the rack. Dust the top of the cake with the confectioners' sugar.

4 *POINTS* per serving

Per serving
198 Calories | 8 g Total Fat | 1 g Saturated Fat | 27 mg Cholesterol | 124 mg Sodium
31 g Total Carbohydrate | 2 g Dietary Fiber | 3 g Protein | 20 mg Calcium

carrot cake

fudge brownies

These tall, cakey brownies, lightened with whipped egg whites, have a wonderful fudge flavor. Serve with tall glasses of cold low-fat milk.

makes 16 servings

1¼ cups all-purpose flour

½ cup unsweetened Dutch cocoa powder

¼ teaspoon baking powder

¼ teaspoon salt

3 tablespoons unsalted butter

1¼ cups sugar

1 egg, beaten

½ teaspoon vanilla extract

⅓ cup water

2 egg whites

1 **Preheat the oven** to 350°F. Lightly spray an 8 × 8-inch baking pan with nonstick spray.

2 **Sift together the flour,** cocoa, baking powder, and salt in a bowl.

3 **Melt the butter** in a saucepan, remove the pan from the heat, and stir in the sugar. Add the whole egg and vanilla; beat 1 minute. Stir in the flour mixture and the water.

4 **With an electric mixer** on medium speed, beat the egg whites in a large bowl until they form soft peaks, about 4 minutes. With a whisk, gently mix one-third of the whites into the batter to lighten it, then gently fold in the remaining whites.

5 **Scrape the batter** into the baking pan. Bake until a toothpick inserted in the center comes out clean, about 25 minutes. Cool in the pan on a rack for 15–20 minutes before cutting. Store the brownies in an airtight container for up to one week.

3 *POINTS* per serving

Per serving (1 brownie)
125 Calories | 3 g Total Fat | 2 g Saturated Fat | 20 mg Cholesterol | 59 mg Sodium
24 g Total Carbohydrate | 0 g Dietary Fiber | 2 g Protein | 15 mg Calcium

polenta soufflé

This unusual dessert soufflé begins with a polenta base to which fruit is added. Stiffly beaten egg whites are folded into the base to make a light and fluffy concoction. Use naturally soft, ripe, full-flavored fruits, such as berries, mangoes, and peaches, to flavor the soufflé batter. This is delicious served with Berry Coulis (page 325). In the autumn and winter, try using applesauce or unsweetened pumpkin puree instead of fresh fruit in the soufflés.

makes 6 servings

1 **Bring the milk** and orange zest to a boil in a small saucepan, remove from the heat and let steep 30 minutes. Remove the zest and pour the milk into a large saucepan.

2 **Bring the milk** to a simmer. Reserve 3 tablespoons of the sugar and set aside. Add the remaining sugar to the milk, stirring to dissolve. Slowly sprinkle in the cornmeal, whisking constantly. Add the fruit puree and chopped fruit.

3 **Bring the polenta** to a boil, reduce the heat and simmer, whisking constantly, until the mixture pulls away from the sides of the pan, about 20 minutes. Pour into a large bowl, cover loosely with plastic wrap, and let stand until cool, 20–30 minutes.

4 **Preheat the oven** to 400°F. Brush six 4-ounce mini-soufflé dishes with the softened butter, then dust each with 1 teaspoon of the reserved sugar. Refrigerate until ready to use. Reserve the remaining sugar.

5 **With an electric mixer** on medium speed, beat the egg whites in a large bowl until soft peaks form, 2–3 minutes. Sprinkle in the remaining sugar; continue beating until stiff peaks form, about 4 minutes. Stir the polenta just to loosen it, then, with a whisk, gently mix in about one-third of the egg whites to lighten the polenta mixture. Add the remaining egg whites. With a rubber spatula, gently fold the egg whites until incorporated.

1 1/2 cups fat-free milk

1 tablespoon grated orange zest

1/3 cup sugar

1/3 cup yellow cornmeal

1/3 cup fruit puree or juice

2 tablespoons finely chopped fresh fruit

2 tablespoons unsalted butter, softened

4 egg whites

2 tablespoons confectioners' sugar

continues on page 308

Per serving

120 Calories | 0 g Total Fat | 0 g Saturated Fat | 1 mg Cholesterol | 70 mg Sodium
24 g Total Carbohydrate | 1 g Dietary Fiber | 5 g Protein | 78 mg Calcium

2 POINTS per serving

continued from page 307

6 **Spoon the batter** into the soufflé dishes, filling each about three-quarters full. Arrange the dishes in a roasting pan. Place the pan in the oven, then carefully fill the roasting pan with hot water until it reaches two-thirds up the sides of the soufflé dishes. Bake until golden brown and puffed, about 25 minutes. Carefully remove the soufflés from the water bath, dust with the confectioners' sugar, and serve at once.

variation

Chocolate Polenta Soufflé: Add $1/4$ cup espresso or strong coffee to the milk after infusing with the orange zest in Step 1. Add $1/3$ cup unsweetened cocoa powder and $1/2$ teaspoon cinnamon to the simmering milk and coffee, along with the cornmeal in Step 2. Replace the fruit puree or juice with 1 ounce grated or chopped semi-sweet baking chocolate. Dust the finished soufflé with confectioners' sugar and serve with coffee-flavored frozen sorbet or yogurt.

Chef's Tip

For tips on beating egg whites, see page 301.

folding ingredients into egg whites

Beat to form stiff peaks, moving the beaters around the bowl evenly.

To test the peaks, turn off the beater, and lift it out of the egg whites: they will stand up in stiff, stable peaks.

Gently whisk 1/3 of the whites into the other ingredients, here the polenta, to lighten it and make it possible to fold in the remaining whites. Add the remaining 2/3 egg whites to the polenta mixture. Using a rubber spatula, cut down to the bottom of the bowl, lift and turn the whites over. Turn the bowl and repeat until just incorporated.

rice pudding

This rice pudding, which makes a simple and comforting dessert for cold-weather months, takes on a pleasant tang from the yogurt and a creamy texture from the ricotta. As a variation to cinnamon, try drizzling the pudding with Berry Coulis (page 325) and top with fresh berries.

makes 4 servings

1^1/$_2$ cups water

^{1}/$_2$ cup long-grain white rice

^{1}/$_2$ cup golden raisins

3 tablespoons sugar

1 teaspoon fresh lemon juice

Pinch freshly grated or ground nutmeg

Pinch cinnamon + (optional) more for sprinkling the pudding

Pinch salt

^{1}/$_2$ cup part-skim ricotta cheese, pureed

2 tablespoons fat-free milk

2 tablespoons plain nonfat yogurt

1 teaspoon vanilla extract

1 **Combine the water,** rice, raisins, sugar, lemon juice, nutmeg, cinnamon, and salt in a medium saucepan. Cover and simmer until the rice is tender and has absorbed the liquid, about 18 minutes.

2 **Scrape the rice** into a bowl, cover loosely with plastic wrap, and let stand until cool, about 15 minutes.

3 **Once the rice is cool,** fold in the ricotta, milk, yogurt, and vanilla. Spoon the rice pudding into 4 bowls or dessert glasses and refrigerate until chilled, about 1 hour. If not using immediately, cover the puddings individually and refrigerate for up to one day.

5 *POINTS* per serving

Per serving

238 Calories | 3 g Total Fat | 2 g Saturated Fat | 10 mg Cholesterol | 127 mg Sodium
46 g Total Carbohydrate | 2 g Dietary Fiber | 6 g Protein | 124 mg Calcium

chocolate yogurt mousse

Start this recipe early or a day ahead of serving; the yogurt will need to drain for at least five hours. Keep an instant-read thermometer on hand when whisking the egg whites into a meringue for the mousse. Spoon the mousse into champagne or parfait glasses, and serve with Almond Tuiles (page 314).

makes 6 servings

1½ ounces semi-sweet dark baking chocolate

½ cup + 1 tablespoon yogurt cheese

¼ cup unsweetened Dutch cocoa powder, sifted twice

4 egg whites

⅓ cup sugar

1 **Place the chocolate** in a microwavable bowl and microwave on High for 30-second intervals, stirring after each interval, until melted. (Alternatively, melt in a double boiler.) Stir a few spoonfuls of the yogurt cheese into the warm chocolate just to cool it slightly, then stir the chocolate mixture into the remaining yogurt cheese.

2 **Fill a large saucepan** two-thirds full of water and bring to a simmer. Place the bowl of yogurt mixture over the hot water, then fold in the cocoa, stirring gently, until glossy (this step loosens the mixture and makes it easier to fold in the meringue). Remove bowl from saucepan; set aside and keep warm.

3 **To prepare the meringue,** combine the egg whites and sugar in a clean stainless-steel bowl. Place the bowl over the saucepan of simmering water and gently whisk until the egg whites are foamy and reach 135°F on an instant-read thermometer. Remove the bowl from the heat and, with an electric mixer on medium speed, beat the egg whites until medium peaks form, 3–5 minutes.

4 **Fold the meringue** into the yogurt mixture and spoon the mousse into champagne or parfait glasses. Chill until firm, about 4 hours.

Chef's Tip

To make yogurt cheese, spoon 1 cup plus 2 tablespoons plain nonfat yogurt into a strainer lined with a coffee filter or cheesecloth and place over a bowl. Cover and refrigerate at least 5 hours or overnight. Discard the liquid in the bowl.

Per serving

118 Calories | 3 g Total Fat | 2 g Saturated Fat | 2 mg Cholesterol | 79 mg Sodium
19 g Total Carbohydrate | 1 g Dietary Fiber | 6 g Protein | 108 mg Calcium

2 *POINTS* per serving

chocolate fudge cookies

These fudge cookies are chewy and moist because of the applesauce and prune and chestnut purees. The cookies do not change shape at all during baking, so be sure to shape them nicely before putting them in the oven. Chestnut puree can be purchased at well-stocked groceries and gourmet markets.

makes 10 servings

1/3 cup dried pitted prunes or prune puree (lekvar)

1/3 cup applesauce

1/3 cup chestnut puree

2 tablespoons sugar

2 tablespoons Dutch cocoa powder

1 tablespoon water

1 tablespoon dark rum

1/4 cup chopped dark chocolate or semi-sweet chocolate chips

1/2 cup all-purpose flour

1 teaspoon baking powder

Confectioners' sugar or cocoa powder, for dusting the cookies (optional)

1 **Preheat the oven** to 350°F. Line a baking sheet with parchment paper. If using whole prunes, puree in a mini food processor. Combine the prune puree with the applesauce and chestnut puree in a large bowl.

2 **Combine the sugar,** cocoa, water, and rum in a small saucepan. Heat, stirring as needed, until the sugar dissolves, about 2 minutes.

3 **Place the chocolate** in a microwavable bowl and microwave on High for 10-second intervals, stirring after each interval, until melted. (Alternatively, melt in a double boiler.)

4 **Add the cocoa mixture** and melted chocolate to the prune mixture; stir until smooth. Sift together the flour and baking powder in a small bowl, and stir into the chocolate-prune mixture until just combined.

5 **Drop the dough** by teaspoons onto the baking sheet to make a total of 20 cookies. Spread the dough slightly, using the back of a small spoon. Bake until dry to the touch, about 10 minutes. Cool on the baking sheet for 10 minutes, then transfer the cookies to a rack to cool completely. Dust with the confectioners' sugar or cocoa powder (if using). Store in an airtight container for up to 4 days.

---

2 *POINTS* per serving

Per serving (2 cookies)

91 Calories | 2 g Total Fat | 1 g Saturated Fat | 0 mg Cholesterol | 43 mg Sodium
19 g Total Carbohydrate | 1 g Dietary Fiber | 1 g Protein | 18 mg Calcium

fudge brownies (page 306), and chocolate fudge cookies

almond tuiles

French for "tiles," tuiles are so called because, when molded into their classic arc shape, they resemble a type of roof tile used throughout the Mediterranean. These thin, crisp, and fragile cookies can be cut and molded into variety of shapes. The classic French tuile is made with crushed almonds, but the batter can also be flavored with other nuts, citrus, or vanilla. An offset spatula has a long, narrow, rounded blade that angles away from the handle, easing work with batters.

makes 12 servings

$2/3$ cup almond paste

$1 2/3$ cups confectioners' sugar

$1/3$ cup bread flour

3 egg whites

$1 1/2$ tablespoons whole milk

1 **Combine the almond paste,** sugar, and flour in a food processor and pulse to a fine, granular consistency. With the machine running, add the egg whites and milk through the feed tube. Process until smooth. Pour the tuile batter into a bowl, cover, and refrigerate until thoroughly chilled, 6–8 hours.

2 **Preheat the oven** to 375°F. Spray a baking sheet liberally with nonstick spray or cover with a silicone baking mat. Working in batches, drop spoonfuls of batter onto the baking sheet or silicone mat, if using, with an offset spatula or the back of a spoon, spread out the batter very thinly.

3 **Bake until the batter** loses its glossy appearance and the edges look dry, 10–12 minutes. Remove the baking sheet from the oven. Shape the tuiles while still warm or, if making flat tuiles, allow them to cool and become stiff before removing them from the pan. Store the tuiles in an airtight them container for up to 3 days. The baked scraps can be ground into cookie crumbs and saved for another use.

Chef's Tips

Tuile batter can be very sticky. To prevent it from sticking to your baking sheet, either spray the sheet very well with nonstick spray, or use a silicone baking mat. These baking mats, also known by the trade name Silpat®, are a great fat-saving tool. When they are used to line a baking sheet, there is no need to grease the sheet further, yet baked items release effortlessly. Silicone baking mats can be purchased in well-stocked kitchenware stores or via mail-order through a baking equipment supplier.

To make the classic arc-shaped tuiles or edible cups for mousse, frozen yogurt, or sorbet, lift the still-hot tuiles from the baking sheet, and drape over a rolling pin or inverted bowl or glass. As the tuiles cool, they become stiff. Tuiles can only be molded while they are hot, so bake only as many as you can handle at a time.

3 *POINTS* per serving

Per serving (1 tuile)
130 Calories | 4 g Total Fat | 0 g Saturated Fat | 0 mg Cholesterol | 16 mg Sodium
23 g Total Carbohydrate | 1 g Dietary Fiber | 2 g Protein | 25 mg Calcium

almond-fudge truffles

Named after the costly truffle, here's a confection to be enjoyed. These truffles are rolled in cocoa powder to resemble freshly dug real truffles.

makes 24 servings

$1/2$ cup + 2 tablespoons unsweetened cocoa powder

1 cup sifted confectioners' sugar

$1/2$ cup light cream cheese, at room temperature

$1/2$ teaspoon almond extract

1 **Reserve 2 tablespoons** of the cocoa powder on a sheet of wax paper. Combine the remaining $1/2$ cup of cocoa powder, the confectioners' sugar, cream cheese, and almond extract in a food processor or in a bowl. Pulse until the mixture is smooth, or with an electric mixer on high-speed whip until the mixture is smooth.

2 **Drop the cream cheese mixture** by rounded teaspoons into the reserved cocoa powder, making 24 truffles, roll into balls and refrigerate until firm, 1–2 hours.

Chef's Tips

Refrigerate mixture (approximately 30 minutes) before rolling so it is less sticky.

Put truffles in foil candy cups for an elegant presentation or to fill a gift box.

Per serving

45 Calories | 1 g Total Fat | 1 g Saturated Fat | 2 mg Cholesterol | 27 mg Sodium
6 g Total Carbohydrate | 1 g Dietary Fiber | 1 g Protein | 10 mg Calcium

1 *POINT* per serving

apple cobbler

Fruit cobblers are simple to make and superb when the fruit is perfectly ripe. This is a dessert to please a crowd: It will be enjoyed by the youngest and by the most sophisticated palates. This recipe makes individual cobblers, but you can also bake a single cobbler in the same baking dish used to bake the apples in Step 1. Serve the warm cobbler with vanilla frozen yogurt.

makes 6 servings

3 Jonagold or other baking apples, peeled, cored, and cut into $^1/_2$-inch cubes (about 4 cups)

$^1/_4$ cup applesauce

$^1/_2$ cup fat-free milk

$^1/_2$ cup flour

$^1/_3$ cup sugar

1$^1/_2$ teaspoons baking powder

1 teaspoon vanilla extract

$^1/_4$ teaspoon cinnamon

$^1/_8$ teaspoon salt

1. **To prepare the apple filling,** preheat the oven to 375°F. Spray an 8 × 8-inch baking dish with nonstick spray. Arrange the apples in the baking dish; bake until tender, about 15 minutes. (Alternatively, arrange the apples in a microwavable dish; microwave on High for 3 minutes, until the apples are tender.) Let the apples cool, then stir in the applesauce.

2. **To assemble the cobblers,** reduce the oven temperature to 350°F. Spray six 4-ounce custard cups or ramekins with nonstick spray.

3. **Combine the milk,** flour, sugar, baking powder, vanilla, cinnamon, and salt in a bowl and whisk until smooth.

4. **Divide the apple mixture** into the cups and top each with the batter. Bake the cobblers until golden brown, about 20 minutes. (If making a single, large cobbler, simply pour the batter over the apples and bake for about 30 minutes.) Serve warm.

variation

Berry Cobbler: Replace the apple filling with 2–3 cups fresh blueberries, raspberries, or blackberries, combined with 1$^1/_2$ tablespoons honey or sugar, and a pinch of cinnamon or nutmeg.

1 *POINT* per serving

Per serving

93 Calories | 0 g Total Fat | 0 g Saturated Fat | 0 mg Cholesterol | 158 mg Sodium
21 g Total Carbohydrate | 2 g Dietary Fiber | 2 g Protein | 48 mg Calcium

apple strudel

This strudel is easy and quick to prepare because it is made with phyllo dough. For a flavorful touch, plump the raisins in brandy rather than water. Serve the warm strudel with caramel sauce or vanilla frozen yogurt. A serrated knife will make slicing the strudel easier.

makes 8 servings

¼ cup golden raisins

¼ cup warm water or brandy

6 (about 1¾ pounds) Granny Smith apples, cored, peeled, and sliced

¼ cup packed light brown sugar

2 teaspoons cinnamon

¼ teaspoon freshly grated nutmeg

3 (12 × 17-inch) sheets phyllo dough, room temperature

2 tablespoons unsalted butter, melted

1 **Combine the raisins** with the water in a small bowl and soak 20 minutes. Drain, discarding the liquid.

2 **Preheat the oven** to 350°F. Spread the apples on a baking sheet lined with parchment paper. Bake until the apples are tender, 30–45 minutes. Remove from the oven and let cool completely.

3 **Combine the apples** and the plumped raisins in a medium bowl. Add the brown sugar, cinnamon, and nutmeg; toss to combine.

4 **Stack the phyllo sheets** on a baking sheet lined with parchment paper. Brush the top sheet with 2 teaspoons of the melted butter. Arrange the apple filling in an even layer along one of the long sides of the dough. Roll the dough around the filling. Brush with the remaining melted butter and, with a sharp knife, lightly cut the top of the strudel diagonally to indicate 8 portions, being careful not to cut all the way through. (At this point, the strudel can be wrapped and frozen for up to one month before baking.)

5 **Bake the strudel** until golden brown, about 45 minutes. Let cool 10 minutes on a rack. Trim the ends just to remove the extra crust, then slice the strudel along the marks and serve warm.

Chef's Tip

Phyllo is a very thin, fragile dough. It can dry out quickly, so follow package directions on storage and handling carefully. You can usually find phyllo dough in the freezer section of your supermarket, but it must be fully thawed before using. Store unopened phyllo dough in the refrigerator for up to one month. Once the dough has been opened, use it within a few days.

Per serving (one 1½-inch slice)

148 Calories | 4 g Total Fat | 2 g Saturated Fat | 8 mg Cholesterol | 70 mg Sodium
30 g Total Carbohydrate | 3 g Dietary Fiber | 1 g Protein | 1 mg Calcium

3 *POINTS* per serving

berry napoleon

This elegant French dessert is usually made with puff pastry. In this version, Almond Tuiles are used to sandwich layers of fresh berries and creamy, honey-laced ricotta.

makes 6 servings

2/3 cup part-skim ricotta cheese

1 1/2 tablespoons honey

1/4 teaspoon vanilla extract

12 (4-inch round) Almond Tuiles (page 314)

1 tablespoon confectioners' sugar

1 pound blackberries and raspberries (about 3 1/4 cups)

3/4 cup Berry Coulis (page 325)

1 **To prepare the ricotta filling,** puree the ricotta, honey, and vanilla in a food processor.

2 **Dust the tuiles** with the confectioners' sugar.

3 **To assemble the Napoleons,** spoon 1 teaspoon of the ricotta filling onto the center of a plate. Top with 3 tablespoons of the berries, then with 1 tuile. Spoon 1 teaspoon of ricotta filling onto the tuile and spread it to the edges. Top with 3 more tablespoons of the berries, then with a tuile. Spoon the Berry Coulis around the Napoleon in six 1/2-teaspoon "pools." Repeat with the remaining ricotta filling, tuiles, and berries to make a total of 6 Napoleons. Serve at once.

7 *POINTS* per serving

Per serving

394 Calories | 10 g Total Fat | 2 g Saturated Fat | 9 mg Cholesterol | 66 mg Sodium
10 g Total Carbohydrate | 7 g Dietary Fiber | 9 g Protein | 154 mg Calcium

warm strawberries with frangelico, frozen yogurt, and shortcake

This twist on the classic strawberry shortcake features an ample helping of ruby port-sweetened strawberries, complemented by a sweet biscuitlike shortcake and hazelnut liqueur-flavored frozen yogurt. Prepare all the simple components ahead so you can assemble the desserts in a snap just before serving.

makes 6 servings

1 cup all-purpose flour

2 tablespoons sugar

2 teaspoons baking powder

2 tablespoons chilled unsalted butter, cut into pieces

1/4 cup fat-free milk

1/8 teaspoon grated orange zest

2 tablespoons whole milk

1/3 cup ruby port wine

4 cups quartered strawberries

1/3 cup seedless raspberry jam

1 pint vanilla frozen yogurt, softened

3 tablespoons Frangelico liqueur

1 **To prepare the shortcake,** preheat the oven to 375°F. Lightly spray a baking sheet with nonstick spray.

2 **Combine the flour,** sugar, and baking powder in a food processor; pulse to combine. Add the butter and pulse until it forms a mealy mixture. With the machine running, add the milk and orange zest through the feed tube. Pulse the mixture until it forms a dough.

3 **Turn out the dough** on a lightly floured counter and roll out to a 1/2-inch thickness. Use a 2-inch round biscuit cutter to cut the dough into 6 cakes, gathering the scraps and re-rolling as necessary.

4 **Arrange the shortcakes** on the baking sheet and brush the tops with the milk. Bake until the cakes are puffed and light golden brown on top, 15–20 minutes. Remove the shortcakes from the oven and keep warm.

5 **To prepare the strawberries,** heat the port over low heat in a saucepan, then add the strawberries and jam. Gently stir until warmed through.

6 **To prepare the frozen yogurt,** stir the Frangelico into the frozen yogurt until well combined; keep in the freezer until ready to use.

7 **To serve,** slice the warm shortcakes in half horizontally and place each on a plate, cut side up. Top with the warm strawberry mixture, then a small scoop of the frozen yogurt. Serve at once.

Chef's Tip

To soften frozen yogurt, place it in the refrigerator to thaw for 20 minutes.

Per serving

325 Calories | 8 g Total Fat | 5 g Saturated Fat | 13 mg Cholesterol | 227 mg Sodium
54 g Total Carbohydrate | 3 g Dietary Fiber | 5 g Protein | 122 mg Calcium

7 *POINTS* per serving

lemon tart

This beautiful lemon tart features a cookielike crust that is quick to prepare. The translucent lemon curd filling is light and sets with just a small amount of gelatin. Garnish the tart with lemon twists and sprigs of mint, or a mixture of half whipped cream, half vanilla nonfat yogurt.

makes 8 servings

CRUST

1 cup self-rising flour

1/4 teaspoon baking powder

1/3 cup sugar

1 egg

1/2 teaspoon grated lemon zest

1/4 teaspoon vanilla extract

1 tablespoon canola oil

LEMON CURD

3 tablespoons water

1 teaspoon unflavored gelatin

4 eggs

1 1/2 cups fresh lemon juice

1 1/2 cups sugar

1 1/2 tablespoons grated lemon zest

2 teaspoons vanilla extract

1 **To prepare the crust,** whisk together the flour and baking powder in a medium bowl. Whisk together the sugar, egg, lemon zest, and vanilla in a large bowl, until the sugar dissolves. Whisk in the oil. Sprinkle in the flour mixture and mix just until combined; the mixture should resemble a thick batter rather than a dough. Cover with plastic wrap and refrigerate at least 20 minutes.

2 **Preheat the oven** to 425°F. Spray a 9-inch tart pan with a removable bottom with nonstick spray. Flour your hands lightly and press the batter into the pan and up the sides. Prick the bottom with a fork. Spray a sheet of foil with nonstick spray and line the batter with the foil, with the sprayed side down. Top with pie weights or dried beans. Bake 8 minutes; remove the foil and pie weights. Continue baking the crust until golden brown, about 4 minutes more. Remove from the oven and cool completely on a rack.

3 **To prepare the lemon curd,** measure the water into a small microwavable bowl, sprinkle in the gelatin, and let stand until softened, at least 5 minutes. Beat the eggs until well combined.

4 **Combine the lemon juice,** sugar, and lemon zest in a small saucepan. Bring to a simmer, then remove from the heat. Whisk about 1/2 cup of the hot lemon mixture into the eggs to warm them, then pour the eggs into the remaining lemon mixture. Return the pan to the heat, and cook, whisking constantly, until the lemon curd starts to gently simmer and thicken. Remove from the heat.

5 **To assemble the tart,** microwave the gelatin on Medium for 10-second intervals, stirring after each interval, until melted. Strain the lemon curd through a fine-mesh sieve, then stir in the gelatin and vanilla. Let cool to room temperature, then pour the curd into the crust. Cover the tart with plastic wrap and chill for at least 4 hours or overnight.

6 POINTS per serving

Per serving

304 Calories | 5 g Total Fat | 1 g Saturated Fat | 133 mg Cholesterol | 252 mg Sodium 60 g Total Carbohydrate | 1 g Dietary Fiber | 6 g Protein | 76 mg Calcium

lemon tart

tarte tatin

This famous dessert is an upside-down tart prepared in a skillet. First, sugar is caramelized in the skillet, apples are added to cook briefly in the caramel, then the mixture is covered with pastry and baked. The skillet is inverted onto a serving plate and the hot caramel trickles down over the apples. Pears can be substituted for an excellent variation.

makes 12 servings

SWEET RICOTTA PASTRY

1³/₄ cups all-purpose flour

¹/₃ cup sugar

1¹/₂ teaspoons baking powder

Pinch salt

¹/₄ cup (¹/₂-stick) chilled unsalted butter, cut into small cubes

¹/₂ cup chilled part-skim ricotta cheese

¹/₃ cup chilled fat-free milk

1 chilled egg white

1¹/₂ teaspoons vanilla extract

FILLING

³/₄ cup sugar

1 tablespoon unsalted butter

6 Granny Smith apples, peeled, cored, and sliced (about 1³/₄ pounds)

1 **To prepare the Sweet Ricotta Pastry,** combine the flour, sugar, baking powder, and salt in a food processor; pulse briefly to evenly mix. Add the butter and pulse until the mixture is crumbly.

2 **Whisk together the ricotta,** milk, egg white, and vanilla in a medium bowl; add to the processor and pulse until a dough forms. Gather the dough into a ball, cover with plastic wrap, and refrigerate until firm, at least 1 hour. (The dough can be frozen for up to 2 weeks. Thaw overnight in the refrigerator.)

3 **Turn out the dough** on a lightly floured counter and roll out to a 12-inch circle. Slide the dough onto a baking sheet, cover with plastic wrap, and refrigerate.

4 **To assemble the Tarte Tatin,** preheat the oven to 350°F. Place the sugar in an ovenproof 12-inch nonstick skillet or sauté pan set over low heat. Cook until the sugar melts and turns to golden caramel, 5–10 minutes. Do not stir the sugar while it is caramelizing, but shake the skillet occasionally as necessary to redistribute the sugar. Carefully add the butter and apples; sauté until the apples are tender and coated with the caramelized sugar, and no moisture from the apples remains in the bottom of the skillet. Remove from the heat.

continues on page 324

5 *POINTS* **per serving**

Per serving

228 Calories | 6 g Total Fat | 4 g Saturated Fat | 16 mg Cholesterol | 139 mg Sodium
41 g Total Carbohydrate | 2 g Dietary Fiber | 0 g Protein | 34 mg Calcium

tarte tatin

continued from page 322

5 **Arrange the apple slices** in concentric circles in the pan. Remove the chilled dough from the refrigerator, make a few slits in the dough with a sharp knife, and carefully place the dough over the pan, covering the apples. Tuck the edges of the dough down into the pan around the apples, being careful not to burn yourself. Place the tart over high heat and cook until a caramel aroma rises from the pan. Finish cooking the tart in the oven until the crust is golden brown, about 20 minutes.

6 **Loosen the edges** of the crust from the pan with a small knife. Place a large serving plate over the pan. Using hot pads, invert the tart onto the plate. If an apple sticks to the pan, remove it and arrange it on the tart. Scrape any remaining caramel from the bottom of the pan onto the apples. Let cool 10 minutes; serve warm.

Chef's Tip

Prepare the Sweet Ricotta Pastry dough at least $1\frac{1}{2}$ hours in advance, so the dough has a chance to rest and is very chilled. Once the dough has been rolled out, place it on a baking sheet, cover it with plastic wrap, and refrigerate until ready to place it on the skillet.

berry coulis

This smooth, highly versatile dessert sauce bursts with berry flavor. Try it over vanilla frozen yogurt or rice pudding. The coulis may be stored in the refrigerator for 5–8 days or frozen for 2–3 months.

makes 6 servings

1 **Puree the all the ingredients** in a blender or food processor. Check the consistency and taste of the coulis, adding more wine for a smoother texture, and more honey for a sweeter taste.

2 **Strain the coulis** through a fine-mesh sieve to remove the seeds.

2 cups fresh or thawed frozen raspberries, strawberries, or other berries

$1/4$ cup honey

$1/4$ cup dry or sweet white wine

1 tablespoon kirschwasser (optional)

Chef's Tips

Kirschwasser, German for "cherry water," is a clear brandy distilled from cherry juice and pits. It may also be labeled "kirsch." When buying, avoid the sweetened cherry brandies sold under the same name.

If using frozen berries, choose Individually Quick Frozen (IQF) or low-sugar berries.

Per serving

71 Calories | 0 g Total Fat | 0 g Saturated Fat | 0 mg Cholesterol | 1 mg Sodium
18 g Total Carbohydrate | 3 g Dietary Fiber | 0 g Protein | 11 mg Calcium

1 *POINT* per serving

pear sorbet

This sorbet is a light and refreshing dairy-free frozen fruit dessert. The small amount of alcohol in the recipe keeps the mixture soft enough to scoop. If you cannot find pear wine, substitute any other fruity white wine or 3 tablespoons of Poire William, a pear-flavored brandy from Switzerland.

makes 4 servings

3 (about 1 pound) very ripe pears, peeled, cored, and sliced

1/2 cup water

2/3 cup sugar

1/3 cup pear wine or 3 tablespoons Poire William

1 vanilla bean, halved lengthwise

1 **Combine the pears,** water, sugar, wine, and vanilla bean in a saucepan. Bring the mixture to a boil; reduce the heat and simmer until the pears are very tender, about 10 minutes.

2 **Remove the vanilla bean halves,** scrape out the seeds, and add to the mixture. Puree the pears with the poaching liquid in a food processor or blender. Strain the pear puree through a fine-mesh sieve. Cover with plastic wrap and refrigerate until chilled, 2 hours or overnight.

3 **Freeze the chilled pear puree** in an ice cream machine, according to the manufacturer's directions.

Chef's Tips

If the sorbet melts partially or becomes very hard in the freezer, simply allow the entire batch to melt and re-freeze it in an ice cream machine to restore its soft, smooth texture.

Although there are many excellent pure vanilla extracts available, real vanilla beans are necessary for this recipe. They are expensive, but worth it. The seeds from the beans give the sorbet true vanilla flavor and a speckled look that announces the presence of real vanilla.

5 *POINTS* per serving

Per serving
259 Calories | 0 g Total Fat | 0 g Saturated Fat | 0 mg Cholesterol | 1 mg Sodium
58 g Total Carbohydrate | 2 g Dietary Fiber | 0 g Protein | 14 mg Calcium

index   Page references in *italics* refer to photographs.